THE PATENT GAME

PATENT BASICS AND STRATEGIES FOR INNOVATORS, ENTREPRENEURS, AND BUSINESS LEADERS

VANCE V. VANDRAKE, III, ESQ.

D1256869

patentgame.com

ISBN: 978-0-9991144-2-1

Editor — Kevin Michell
Legal Editor — Eric Robbins
Layout Editor, Book & Cover Design — Brianna Brailey

Published by Legal Technology Press, in the United States of America

Legal Technology Press
230 Findlay Street
Cincinnati, OH 45202

THANK YOU!

DANOKEEFFE
STEVENGOLDSTEIN
CHANELLE
BEKAH
ERICROBBINS
ESSANASE
KICKLEE
HAILEY
BRIDGETKOCHERSPERGER
RANMULLINS
ULMERANDBERNE
MARY
ALEXISDANKOVICH
MARKHOMER
PAPA
DAVELITTLE
BRIANNABRAILEY
HRISSINGH
MAXBERG
JEFFVAITEKUNAS
SHERYLRITTER
ALWALLANDER
DAVEKNOX
MIMI
KEVINMICHELLE
SCOTTKADISH

"ALL YOUR BASE ARE BELONG TO US."

— ZERO WING

"ALL OUR PATENTS ARE BELONG TO YOU."

— ELON MUSK

TABLE OF CONTENTS
PART 1: THE BASICS

TABLE OF CONTENTS
PART 2: PLAYING THE GAME
Patent Plinko® and Choosing the Right Patent Strategy

PART 1:
THE BASICS

CHAPTER 1:
THE GAME

"EITHER YOU PLAY THE GAME OR LET THE GAME PLAY YOU."

— J. COLE

Many people may have the impression that the patent process is administrative in nature and to some extent this is true, but even within governmental constraints there is the enormous potential for variation and creativity. The patent process can seem like a uniform set of bureaucratic procedures not unlike renewing your driver's license, selling a car, or buying a house. However, the reality couldn't be further from the truth: The patent game is dynamic and multidimensional and, for those with a high intellectual property intelligence quotient ("IP IQ", as I'll call it throughout this book), the rewards can be substantial. Playing the patent game well can lead to market dominance, higher business valuations, and financial success. Playing this game poorly can leave you, like the great inventor Nicolas Tesla at the end of his life, penniless and destitute. How well you play will materially impact your odds of winning this high-stakes game.

The patent game, like any other game, has its players, rules, board, pieces, power ups, timers, strategies, and tactics. Those with a high IP IQ have an advantage that allows them to dominate a technology sector, make a personal fortune, advance in their careers, and substantially increase the value of a business.

The ancient game Go, which is made up of a board with a 19×19 grid of lines, black stones, and white stones, can seem deceptively simple to an outsider. Despite having very basic game pieces and relatively simple rules, Go is considered one of the most complex games played because of the sheer magnitude of

possible moves (estimated to be at least 2×10^{170}, an amount that dwarfs the number of permutations in chess). Similarly, the patent game has a limited number of pieces with defined move sets, but the potential combinations in which these pieces can be moved in concert are numerous.

The first half of this book will introduce the basics of the patent game, who can play, what the global board looks like, the pieces that are available to players, and how those pieces can be moved. Once I've taken you through these basics, we'll play a version of patent Plinko® to help you determine which specific strategies are optimal for your invention or business. Each of the strategies I'll outline includes an introduction, typically with a game-related comparison, a step-by-step discussion of the strategy with graphics, pros and cons, and a practical real world example. Like any game, you need to learn the basics before you can move on to more sophisticated strategic considerations.

Not that long ago patent practitioners had to sell clients on the idea of protecting innovations with patents. That often proved challenging given the high costs involved with pursuing patent protection. These days the general public is savvy to the exclusionary benefits, seemingly overnight millionaires, and huge infringement judgements from patenting disruptive technology. Perhaps you have seen the high-stakes patent battles occurring between Samsung and Apple or Mark Cuban on *Shark Tank* grilling inventors about whether they have a patent in place for a new bathtub scrub.

It will seem daunting at first. When you first peel the plastic off a new board game, the players, rules, pieces, and strategies are completely foreign. It can feel like it's going to take a lot of time and work to learn the game for very little reward. Starting the patent process can feel overwhemling, like trying to learn a famously complex game like Go or chess for the first time. Despite how it might appear from an outsider or first-timer's view, the patent game is very approachable. And if you commit to learning the basics, your newfound skill will pay dividends.

Everyone knows that wonderful feeling when you finally get a handle on a great game. As you get more comfortable with the gameplay, your focus shifts from remembering the specific rules or individual pieces to developing a strategy to beat your friends and family. I see patent law as a vibrant and exciting board game and I hope you'll come to see it in this same light.

Malcolm Gladwell was spot-on with his argument that mastery of anything — despite what we might perceive as prodigious or savant-like talent — is the product of *a lot of time* and hard work. No doubt there are aspects of your life to which you have dedicated enough time to become a true expert. But mastering the nuances of patent law probably *isn't* where you've chosen to spend your time. For one reason or another, though, you've reached the point where knowing the basics of the patent game has become important. Maybe you've taken on a new role at your job, you are finally ready to pursue that million-dollar idea you've been thinking about, or you work in venture capital and want to make better investments. You should take an active role in how your intellectual property is developed, protected, and enforced, regardless of whether you're a startup CEO, the head of engineering for a Fortune 500 company, or a garage inventor. Possessing a high IP IQ will help you communicate effectively and intelligently with investors, customers, your corporate board, and your patent attorney.

My goal with this book is not to instantly turn you into the equivalent of a chess grandmaster. As with any game, the players in the patent game have different levels of experience and expertise that arise out of some combination of interest and necessity. If, like me, you develop a passion for the nuances of patent law, I would encourage you to read this book cover to cover. However, if your needs are more specific, there are concepts you need to understand, or you need to quickly identify a patent strategy for your business, I've formatted this book so that you can quickly and efficiently find the information you are looking for.

There are four primary intellectual property tools — patents, trademarks, copyrights, and trade secrets — that can be used to protect your business. Each has its own specific uses, term limits, functions, advantages, and limitations. This book focuses on patents while only occasionally touching on trade secrets when they are relevant to a patent-related strategy.

An exhaustive, textbook-like discussion of patent law can be a dense thicket of exceptions and nuance that can prove challenging even for the highly trained patent practitioner. This book focuses more on the general rules to arm you with enough information to sit at the board and play the patent game. Because no one understands your business and its needs better than you, the more clearly you can articulate your needs, resource constraints, and endgame in the context of a patent-related strategy, the more effectively you'll arrive at an optimized solution.

In my college days, I was always the guy with a chess or Scrabble® board ready to teach any willing participant how to play. I like to win as much as the next person, but I'm more passionate about teaching and making a seemingly complex game or subject accessible. Sometimes one good analogy or practical comparison is all it takes for you to understand a new and difficult concept. Whether or not you love board games, I'm hopeful that some of the connections and comparisons that I make in this book will resonate.

Professionally, I've been practicing patent law as both a patent agent and patent attorney for almost fifteen years and, in doing so, have helped add more than a billion dollars of value to businesses, large and small, looking to raise capital, secure an important customer, attack infringers, license technology, or to sell the company. As a partner in my law firm, Ulmer & Berne LLP, I've had the opportunity to work with incredible clients developing revolutionary technology. There is no greater reward than playing a positive role in the success of an innovator. Having co-founded three startups myself, I've always been passionate about helping entrepreneurs win the patent game when facing long odds and much larger competitors.

An incredible teacher or mentor can shape the direction of our lives by making an otherwise dull and difficult subject exciting. In my life, it was meeting Dr. Jeff Vaitekunas at Ethicon Endo-Surgery, a Johnson & Johnson Company, when I was a somewhat directionless 20-year-old. While I was passionate about science, games, and art, I had never found the perfect marriage of these seemingly disparate interests.

When I met Jeff—something my mother attributes to divine intervention—he had a doctorate in bio-medical engineering, was a drummer in a band, and rebuilt rusted-out motorcycles from the 1970s that he raced in parking lots on the weekends. Jeff was the coolest person I'd ever met. I decided that summer I was going to do whatever Jeff did for a living. It just so turned out that he was a patent agent at Ethicon. Jeff was able to take an esoteric discipline and make it both fun and meaningful and I wouldn't have picked this career if not for meeting him.

Just as great teachers can change our lives for the better, terrible teachers can make us despise something we might otherwise love. I've sat through innumerable presentations on patents and patent law over the years that, at best, made me want to take a nap and, at worst, made me look for the nearest fork to stick in my eye. Patent law can be a dreadfully boring subject, but it doesn't have to be. One of the lessons Jeff taught me was the value of paying it forward. Jeff had great mentors and, by teaching me, he meaningfully changed my life. My goal for you, the reader, is to pass this knowledge on to you and maybe inspire you to become as passionate about playing the patent game as I am.

CHAPTER 2:
COACHING, TRUST, AND ASYMMETRICAL TRANSACTIONS

"BE ON THE LOOKOUT FOR CLEVER HUCKSTERS WHO PREY ON INSECURITY AND IGNORANCE TO SELL PEOPLE WHAT THEY DON'T NEED AT PRICES THEY SHOULDN'T HAVE TO PAY."

— JAMES SUROWIECKI

Most people beginning to play the patent game will start by searching for a patent agent or patent attorney. This is your "coach" and it's important to have a good one. Bobby Fischer—arguably the best chess player of all time—had an outstanding coach in William Lombardy, who started working with Fischer when Bobby was just 11 years old and helped him through the World Chess Championships in 1972. When speaking about his role in Fischer's development, Lombardy said, "Since Bobby, when I first met him at age 11½, stated that he would be a world chess champion, I believed it was my job as his friend and confidant to do everything legitimately in my power to ensure the young player's dream would come true!" This should be the role of your patent agent or attorney: They should be your coach, business advisor, *and* cheerleader.

You might already have found a great attorney, in which case what you learn in this book will help you communicate with them more effectively. However, if you have not yet identified this trusted advisor, it's important to make the right choice. Your coach will play a critical role in your success when playing the patent game.

The title of Marshall Goldsmith's best-selling book, *What Got You Here Won't Get You There*, is pertinent advice. This book you're reading was born, at least partially, out of a frustration I've had for many years: You can't trust your patent attorney. I don't mean this in the sense that your patent attorney is out to get you or your patent agent is going to steal your ideas. Most patent professionals are ethical and highly intelligent people. In order to become a patent attorney one is required to have a technical degree, go to law school,

and pass *two* bar exams. But this education doesn't necessarily translate into business acumen. The skills that make many patent attorneys successful in engineering school and law school might have little or nothing to do with applying that book knowledge to real-world business applications.

Being a truly great patent attorney requires equal parts book smarts and street smarts. A good number of patent attorneys don't have the best communication skills or bedside manner — they're not exactly at the top of the list when it comes to cocktail party invitations. One could make a case that self-selecting into engineering programs and law school is a way to *compensate* for a lack of communication or business skills. These "engi-nerds", as I affectionately refer to my patent colleagues, may struggle to craft strategies that drive real value, are creative, or shrewdly play the game for your benefit when necessary or appropriate.

So how do you find a great coach? Educating yourself and increasing your IP IQ can help you better identify the *right* patent professional and to see them as your coach rather than the sole judge of how patents will play a role in your business.

There are excellent patent attorneys who brilliantly blend technical and legal knowledge with practical business acumen. But does that describe *your* patent attorney? How would you even know? This is where asymmetrical transactions come into play.

An asymmetrical transaction results when the knowledge between two or more people about a particular subject is lopsided. Picture a yokozuna, the highest rank attainable in sumo, going up against a hapless spectator who happens to wander into the ring. The more unbalanced the distribution of knowledge between two or more parties (where one party knows a great deal more than the other), the more asymmetrical the transaction will be. Most transactions are asymmetrical to some degree, but the magnitude and impact of this disparity varies depending upon what is being bought and what is being sold. Your patent attorney — the "seller" in this equation — likely knows more about patent law than you, the "buyer", at this stage. The knowledge gap in patent law between patent attorney and client can be particularly large. The high stakes of the patent game make your awareness of this disparity of vital importance. If you buy a lemon from a used car dealer, you might be out a few thousand bucks. But if your patent attorney sells you a lemon strategy, then you could be out millions. Despite being smart from a technical perspective, these attorneys may not be self-aware enough to know what they don't know, yet they'll be implicitly trusted by clients with a key value driver. What can you do to protect yourself?

Traditional vetting of patent attorneys only goes so far. Impressive school credentials, a strong background in technology, and practical, relevant work experience can be helpful, as can referrals, references, and impressive client lists. But all of this is circumstantial. An attorney who has worked exclusively with Fortune 500 companies for the last 30 years may appear to be a strong candidate, but do they understand the needs of your early stage technology company? Maybe they've been doing the same thing the same way for a long time without much concern for budget and, thus, won't have a mind for frugality. Similarly, a great startup attorney may not understand the dynamics inherent to working with a multinational corporation. Referrals to specific law firms can be even less trustworthy: "Go speak with X, Y, Z firm. They do great patent work" may not mean they can do great work for *you*. Experienced users of legal services know that quality, expertise, and the ability to communicate like a normal human being can vary widely, even within firms that have a great reputation.

Failed engagements between patent attorneys and clients are often exacerbated by the patent process, which can run as slow as molasses. Years could pass before you have an inkling that your chosen approach is sub-optimal, at which point it may be too late to take remedial action. The blame can't always be placed on the patent attorney when things go sideways—business owners, inventors, and business leaders sometimes do a poor job communicating objectives, resource constraints, and long-term business goals. Because of the asymmetries inherent in the process, it can be rather difficult for everyone to be in sync.

I've had the opportunity, on many occasions, to review the patent portfolios and strategies of companies working with other lawyers. While it's not professional to throw rocks at other attorneys or firms, it can be infuriating to see that these "strategies" are not a perfect fit for the client's business or, worse, are driving zero business value while draining critical resources. In certain cases, after hundreds of thousands of dollars (or more!) have been spent without any appreciable value creation, the client *still* has no idea that things have veered so dramatically off course. It may be impossible to fully resolve the asymmetrical transaction between a patent attorney and a neophyte client, but there has to be a better way. Right?

When inventors and business owners *actively* participate in the development of a patent strategy, even without a deep knowledge of patent law, the outcome will be dramatically improved. It's important to understand that this book is not a substitute for a great patent attorney — we all need a good coach in areas where we are not experts. However, increasing your IP IQ will help you choose better counsel and lead to improved strategy when playing the game. As an inventor or business leader, if you can suggest to your attorney that "strategies #4 and #6 are of particular interest because of X, Y, and Z," then you'll be well on your way. And even if you're not 100 percent right about the best strategy, you'll have started a conversation in which you are an active participant. If you aren't in the driver's seat then you'll at least be riding shotgun, which is certainly better than being left on the side of the road.

CHAPTER 3: YOUR RATING: INTELLECTUAL PROPERTY INTELLIGENCE QUOTIENT/IP IQ

"IF YOU CAN'T SPOT THE SUCKER IN THE FIRST HALF HOUR AT THE TABLE, THEN YOU ARE THE SUCKER."

— MATT DAMON IN ROUNDERS

Many games incorporate some sort of rating system to rank its players. This serves a number of useful purposes, such as informing a player about his or her abilities relative to others, showing a player's progress, and helping to facilitate fair matchups between competitors. In chess, the most common international rating system is the Elo system developed by Arpad Elo, who himself acknowledged that no rating system is perfect. He once compared the process of rating players to "the measurement of the position of a cork bobbing up and down on the surface of agitated water with a yard stick tied to a rope and which is swaying in the wind." In other words, rating systems are inherently imperfect. But even imperfect attempts at quantifying ability can have tremendous practical value in the real world.

Rating systems associated with any game tend to form a natural bell curve with the vast majority of players grouped together in the middle ranges. This bell curve is similar, in many respects, to those associated with the measurement of an individual's intelligence quotient. As illustrated below, most chess players fall into the 1300-1700 range with a much smaller number of true experts and novices at the extreme ends of the curve.

One unique aspect of chess as a game is that players with higher rankings will consistently beat players with lower ratings, even when the difference between their respective rankings appears nominal. For example, a player with a 1450 rating may very well beat a player with a 1400 rating in 10 out of 10 contests. Luck — which plays a more significant role in games where randomness is a factor — has little or no impact on chess matches. The better chess player will almost always win.

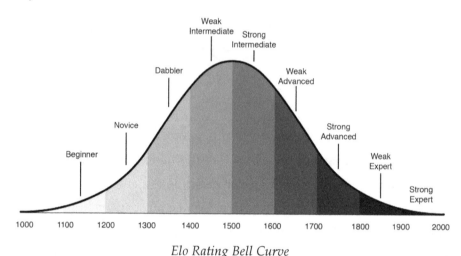

Elo Rating Bell Curve

What does this have to do with patent law? Your knowledge of general patent law, how the "pieces" move, and how those movements can be combined into a cohesive strategy defines your intellectual property intelligence quotient — your IP IQ. Where do you stack up on the IP IQ bell curve relative to your peers, colleagues, and competitors? It's safe to assume, since you are reading this book, that you likely belong in the beginner, novice, or dabbler categories. If that's the case, you have already demonstrated the good sense to "know what you don't know" and the desire to increase your knowledge. As *GI Joe: A Real American Hero* taught many of us while we were still in our Saturday morning pajamas, knowing is half the battle. By the end of this book, you'll have built up your IP IQ and moved yourself at least one standard deviation towards mastery.

Have you ever watched a competitive game of chess played between experts?

Probably not. And even if you play and enjoy chess, watching it as a spectator may not strike you as interesting. It's difficult to consider chess a spectator sport because the rationale behind the moves of an expert is impossible for a novice to divine through observation alone. An advanced player might make a move in anticipation of a competitor's actions, planning for an outcome likely to occur 12 moves in the future, that the novice player is simply unable to see. The outward and visible movements of the pieces will be obvious, but the underlying strategy and the deeper battle between the competitors will remain a mystery. The patent game, in many respects, is very similar.

There is no Elo rating or quantifiable scale for your IP IQ, but you may intuitively have a sense of where you rate compared to your peers. Are you the person in IP-related meetings who listens quietly with little to contribute, or do you confidently give thoughtful suggestions and insight? Or, perhaps, are you somewhere in between? It's prudent to be aware of your own skills and limitations — if there are deficiencies you recognize and can actively address, you'll improve more quickly. Like in any game, your skills can improve rapidly with a good coach, strong resource materials and, most importantly, practice.

A lot of inaccurate information about patent protection is passed off as trade wisdom, such as the usefulness of mailing yourself a letter to secure your invention, the purported inability to secure patents in certain fields like software, and the general lack of value that should be attributed to patents. Your ability to communicate effectively and, thus, to learn faster from true masters will increase as your IP IQ increases, leading you to be able to better differentiate fact from fiction. That way you won't embarrass yourself in business meetings by saying you plan to "patent your business name" or that you have a "provisional patent." Inaccurate statements such as these are like losing a chess game in four moves!

One of the ways that gamification makes sense in patent law is the prevalence of head-to-head matchups. Like chess, the better player in these duels almost always wins. Obvious battles occur during patent litigation, but these multimillion-dollar lawsuits are more akin to Bobby Fischer and Boris Spassky playing in the 1972 World Championships than a casual game over bourbon with your college buddy. In patent litigation, the game is being played at advanced levels by true experts with incredibly high stakes. Patent litigation is often a "bet the farm" proposition for a business and sometimes for all parties involved. The very best patent lawyers wage these battles against one another, but it can be hard to gather practical and useful information by merely following the outcomes of these lawsuits for the same reasons it's difficult for a novice to learn by watching experts play chess.

For the typical innovator or businessperson, the more common matchups in patent law occur on a smaller level with much less fanfare. I have worked with hundreds of technology startup companies dependent upon angel or venture capital funding for their very existence and long-term success. These investor groups, rightly, tend to be concerned about the soundness of the company's patent and intellectual property strategy. However, the level of patent due diligence that funding groups conduct varies *dramatically* as does the organizational IP IQ. The sophistication of these groups, when it comes to patent issues, is frequently lower than you might expect considering the amount of capital being invested. If you are the CEO of a startup company, the collective angel group may be the competitor in the patent game you need to dominate. I've found that startup CEOs with an IP IQ higher than the angel group, even if it's only by a small margin, will consistently win the matchup. The CEO may win by successfully convincing the angel group of the soundness of a startup's IP and, by extension, that the company is worth a substantial investment. Sophisticated startup founders are more likely to exit a company, become successful serial entrepreneurs, and buy a Lamborghini or two.

The reverse of this scenario is also true. If the IP IQ of the angel group is greater than that of the startup company, then that startup will have an *extremely* difficult time satisfying the investors. If the angel group can pose questions that the startup is unable to answer or, worse, that the founder doesn't understand, the company will lose credibility (and maybe the deal itself). A poorly-educated startup may be unable to correct negative assumptions and errors made by prospective investors evaluating the company's intellectual property. Early stage investment is a balance of risk versus reward, and if a startup doesn't understand the basics of intellectual property, the real or imagined risks of prospective investors can be difficult to mitigate.

There is an important distinction between the underlying substance of a company's IP portfolio and the way it is presented to third parties. Having a solid intellectual property position itself is valuable, but it's just as important for founders and businesspeople to accurately articulate the strengths of the portfolio and underlying strategy. In practice, I've found the ability to effectively present this information can make or break a deal despite the actual strengths and weaknesses that might be present.

The patent game is by no means limited to startups and venture capitalists. In the corporate world, internal departments are constantly vying for resources. These internal decisions often involve two parties sitting down at the board to play the patent game against one another. For example, a director of Research and Development may be facing off with the company's CEO or CFO to secure the resources needed to develop and protect a new innovation. A director of R&D with a high IP IQ that can clearly articulate the value of protecting a new innovation is more likely to get the allocation she is seeking. If the CEO has the upper hand in terms of IP IQ, the R&D director may be unable to give satisfactory answers that justify the expenditure of resources on development and patent protection. Many of these head-to-head matchups are subtle, and one or both parties may not even realize the game is afoot, but if you increase your IP IQ you'll tip the advantage in your favor.

As the value of patents and IP becomes more clearly understood in a given business, the ranks of those within the company with a higher IP IQ will frequently rise to the top. This is particularly true with technology companies: There are very few transactions, product releases, partnerships, and business decisions that *don't* involve patents and intellectual property. IP and patents are everywhere—if you are prepared, you will be able to capitalize when opportunities arise. Where are these "matches" happening internally within your business? These head-to-head matchups happen in board meetings, during departmental meetings, via email, and by the water cooler. Businesspeople with higher IP IQs are the ones most likely to be rewarded with promotions, greater resources, and the freedom to develop important new technology.

IP IQ, like chess ratings or actual IQ, can be an amorphous concept and difficult to quantify. However, having a specific rating is less important than knowing, generally, where you fall on the spectrum relative to your peers, boss, and competitors. Are you playing at a sufficiently high level given the competition you're likely to face? If not—or if you want to be ready for anything that might be thrown at you—then you're reading the right book.

CHAPTER 4:
DEFINING WINNING: VALUE IS IN THE EYE OF THE PATENT HOLDER

As with any game, you should play the patent game with the end in mind. If you don't know what you want, or why you want it, then it will prove impossible to devise an optimal strategy. The traditional benefit associated with patents — the ability to monopolize a given technology — is important, but it's by no means the only contributor to value. Before selecting a patent strategy, it's important to identify the factors that will further or constrain your business objectives.

While we take the fun in games for granted, the enjoyment in most cases comes from a battle of wills constructed around a limited resource. Games artificially impose scarcity on one or more elements whether it's money in Monopoly®, time in Boggle®, land in Risk®, sheep in Settlers of Catan®, or your dignity in Dungeons & Dragons® (just kidding about that last one...). Scarcity naturally leads to competition, and the player most effectively able to secure these limited resources to achieve his or her objectives will be the winner. One way to quantify this tension is with the Project Management Triangle, which may already be a familiar concept to you.

Colloquially, you may be familiar with the saying "you can only choose two: fast, cheap, or good". The basic tenets of this model are that the quality or success of a project is constrained by its cost, schedule, and scope. You can trade between constraints but changes in one will necessitate changes in the others to compensate. Said differently, you can choose at most *two* of broad scope, a speedy completion, or low cost, but you can't have all three simultaneously for any significant duration of time. If a project needs to be completed faster, for example, you may need to increase the budget or reduce the scope. Similarly, increasing the scope of a project may require an increase in budget or a longer timeline. Despite the pleading requests at three in the morning from broke start-up founders, there isn't a magic strategy that maximizes all three of these factors over the long haul.

Identifying critical resource constraints early in the patent game can help you more effectively optimize your patent strategy. In the second section of this book, I'll show you a version of the Plinko game from *The Price is Right* that can help guide your innovation or business towards an optimal patent strategy. The entry slot where you drop your patent equivalent of a Plinko chip will depend upon which of cost, scope, or timing is the most compelling consideration for your business.

There are no one-size-fits-all approaches in the patent game and a strategy that is optimal for one business could be a disaster for another. The best strategy for you is the one that matches your definition of success while realistically balancing resource constraints and other business considerations. Although you may have a general sense as to how a patent strategy can benefit your company, the next two chapters will help refine how you define value and, ultimately, success.

4a MONOPOLY®, COST, AND TIMING CONSIDERATIONS

"I THINK IT'S WRONG THAT ONLY ONE COMPANY MAKES THE GAME MONOPOLY."

– STEVEN WRIGHT

Patent rights are akin to a physical property right, like a property card in the game Monopoly®, that allows you to exclude or punish other players for encroaching on your territory. Issued utility patents in most countries give you a 20-year period of exclusivity during which you can exclude third parties from making, using, selling, or importing the invention. This exclusivity can be a key value driver for an early stage company by increasing the purchase price or business valuation when bringing on new investors.

Patent rights—including rights in *pending* applications—can be bought, sold, and traded just like Monopoly properties. Some of these patent properties, like Boardwalk and Park Place, have tremendous value, while others, like Baltic Avenue, have lesser value. However, just like in the game Monopoly, owning some of these lesser properties can be part of a winning strategy. Purchasing patent rights is common—which is referred to as an assignment of rights—and mutually beneficial trading also happens with regularity.

In Monopoly, when someone lands on your territory, they are required to pay you rent. There is a cost for using the property of another player. In the patent game equivalent, a company using your patented technology without your consent is an infringer that may be required to pay you a royalty, damages, or leave your space altogether. If a company uses your technology with consent this is called a license. The royalties and payments associated with a license can vary widely as can territory, length of term, and other restrictions associated with use of the patented technology.

In Monopoly, the owner of all of the same color properties on the board has the right to charge more rent, build houses, and eventually add a hotel to extract as much cash as possible from the other players. Early in the game, there's often a mad dash to acquire as many properties as possible. This is closely analogous to the collective rush for patent acquisition when a hot new technology is discovered. In both cases, players are often unable to immediately secure all of the properties needed to establish a complete monopoly, at least at first. Those who are able to secure an early monopoly and who possess the capital to build upon these properties become formidable adversaries. Other players might find themselves saying a little prayer before rolling the dice since landing on heavily developed monopolies can be expensive and, in some cases, result in bankruptcy.

In the patent game, large companies are particularly adept at securing these monopolies. And those landing on these territories without permission often pay dearly. As Bobby Fischer correctly said, "Tactics flow from a superior position." In some ways, the patent game is skewed heavily in favor of these larger companies with massive financial and legal resources. Imagine playing a game of Monopoly where your adversary has played thousands of times, has a detailed understanding of the rules, and has a hundred times the cash that you do.

If the patent game so heavily favors the experienced and well-capitalized, then how can a novice, cash-strapped player gain a foothold? A relatively small company might be able to secure a valuable property that a larger one needs to complete a monopoly. While there are only 28 total properties in the game Monopoly, the number of potential innovations to be patented is seemingly endless as new inventions are constantly being discovered. Smaller companies sometimes have the ability to move more quickly than larger established companies and this advantage can be used to secure new, valuable innovations as they emerge. Smaller companies may also be more willing to gamble on unproven or nascent technology fields to try and establish a patent position before attracting the interest of larger players. In Monopoly, the properties have set values, but in the patent game it can be difficult to predict the value of a patent for a given innovation. Companies pursuing patent protection often hope that these chosen property rights become self-sustaining profit centers or wind up becoming valuable to the company's overall strategy.

U.S. Patent 2,026,082

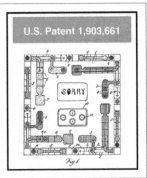
U.S. Patent 1,903,661

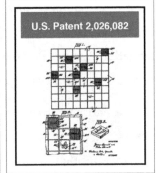
U.S. Patent 2,026,082

In the patent game, if a smaller player is successful in securing a property of interest to a major player, negotiations will typically ensue. The similarities between this stage of negotiation and how the game of Monopoly is played are numerous. Generally, each side will be aware of the other's cash position and assets, which can play heavily into these negotiations. Leverage plays a substantial role here. For example, a Monopoly player nearly out of cash might not be able to afford to land on a richer player's territory without going bankrupt. In patent-speak, this would mean a startup company might be unable to afford an infringement lawsuit. The larger company may use this proverbial stick to threaten litigation and strike a better deal. Conversely, the larger company might offer a carrot of sorts to the smaller company in the form of free "rent" for landing on its territory in exchange for its patents. In patent terms, this would be the larger company granting the smaller company a license in exchange for the transfer of ownership in the patent rights. It's also not uncommon for negotiations to involve multiple parties, cross-licenses, short term deals, and a fair amount of bullying.

We've all seen the situation where a Monopoly player on his last legs lands on a heavily developed monopoly and owes rent he's unable to pay. It's not uncommon for well-financed Fortune 500 companies to initiate patent litigation against a smaller company it knows can't afford to fight. One way out of this dilemma — in both the patent game and Monopoly — is for the player in dire straits to relinquish a valuable asset he possesses in exchange for the ability to keep playing. Litigation is sometimes the opening salvo in negotiations with smaller companies to secure valuable patent rights and, in some cases, to absorb the entire company.

Patents and patent applications can be swapped by the players, just the properties like in Monopoly. If one player holds a property that another needs to secure a better position, then a mutually beneficial trade might ensue. Two companies each holding patents valuable to the other might agree to a cross-license or other similar arrangement and, by doing so, materially improve their positions to the detriment of the other players. This can lead to *a lot* of frustration and anger (and occasional game piece throwing, if you've ever been in a Monopoly game where this sort of horse trading takes place) on the part of the disadvantaged players.

Patents are jurisdictional and there is no worldwide patent, so you should imagine a separate game of Monopoly being played in every country at the same time, often involving the same players. Each of these different games of Monopoly may have slightly different rules and property types, but the concept is basically the same.

Because of these nuances, companies hire various experts at the game—known as foreign patent counsel—who understand the particularities of playing these different versions of the game.

Of course, just because a company can secure a monopoly in a particular area doesn't mean it should spend the resources to do so. In Monopoly, the purple properties of Mediterranean and Baltic Avenues are inexpensive, but may not offer enough potential value to justify ownership or development. Players in the patent game need to carefully evaluate the substantive increase in value they can hope to achieve by pursuing a monopoly in a given area. Filing and prosecuting patent applications—which are actions analogous to building houses and hotels on a given property—can quickly get expensive. These builds can also pull resources from other important areas. As such, business owners and innovators need to carefully consider some key factors before moving forward.

FIVE KEY QUESTIONS BEFORE YOU BUILD

Question #1

How novel is the idea? If the technology is groundbreaking, this will *generally* increase the likelihood that you can secure broad, valuable patent protection. If the invention is a "me too" product—a small improvement over existing technology or a sub-optimal version of an existing product—then that territory might not be available for ownership. To determine just how novel, disruptive, and substantively valuable your invention is, research, including patent searchers should be strongly considered.

A staggering number of issued patents are never commercialized. Don't fall into the trap of believing that because "you've never seen anything like X, Y, Z on Amazon," it must, therefore, be patentable. And remember, a publication or patent from anywhere in the world can be used to defeat your ability to secure a patent.

Question #2

How protectable is subject matter, generally, in your technology sector? There are several fields, such as software business method patents and medical diagnostics, where even a major breakthrough can be difficult to patent because of eligibility issues. High-level litigation—sometimes occurring in the U.S. Supreme Court—has occasionally resulted in the courts ruling that wide swaths of certain fields are difficult to patent. This can be contrasted with mechanical devices, electrical devices, and pharmaceuticals, which may be more easily protected with utility patents. Consult with your patent attorney to ensure your technology and primary field of interest allow for the feasible issuance of a patent. Investing heavily in a monopoly in a difficult field can be like trying to build the foundation for your Monopoly hotels on a swamp—you'll just be throwing money at something that may never hold up.

Question #3

Can you secure broad and enforceable utility and/or design patents? Not all issued patents are created equal and there are major differences in the scope of protection that each patent grants its owner. In densely competitive fields like medical device manufacturing, it can be challenging to carve out valuable territory with so many different players jammed into the same space. You should ask yourself if your field is dense like Manhattan, where securing any property at all is difficult and expensive, or more akin to the Louisiana Purchase, where you can acquire huge swaths of property for a pittance. Property in Manhattan may be worth the premium, but if you are going to pay $1,000 per square foot you'll want to know that before committing.

Question #4

Will your strategy result in broad international protection? The importance of protection in foreign markets should be carefully evaluated. Foreign protection can get very expensive, but if you don't secure protection in these jurisdictions it's perfectly legal for your competitors to make, use, sell, and import the technology in those unprotected regions. If the primary market for your business is the United States, for example, then international protection *may* be a costly waste of resources. However, if your technology has a chance at broad global appeal, then you should consider which countries might ultimately be worth pursuing and to what extent you are willing to invest in that protection.

Question #5

How difficult is it to enforce patents in the countries of primary interest? If your primary markets are in countries with less-developed patent systems, then even a breakthrough technology in a traditionally patentable field may have significantly lower value. China and India have a reputation as being difficult countries in which to enforce patents. But it should be noted that as these economies have grown, so has a correspondingly greater respect for intellectual property rights. Because patents in most countries last for 20 years, you'll need to play the long game when determining where enforcement may be viable in the future.

Research the current environment for protection and enforcement in every jurisdiction of interest — or ask your patent attorney to do so — as there can be tremendous variation from country to country. Patents in some areas may be practically impossible to enforce for political reasons and in other countries, including the United States, enforcement is notoriously very expensive. The willingness of a given country to help the patentee protect its patented invention and the availability of channels to assert patent rights directly impacts patent value. In established jurisdictions such as the U.S. and Europe, a well-defined set of laws makes the process relatively predictable. In less-developed countries, a patentee may have difficulty holding an infringer accountable. Why pay to own Park Place and Boardwalk if you can't collect when someone lands on them?

4b POKER AND EXTERNALLY FOCUSED VALUE CONSIDERATIONS

"NINETY PERCENT OF THE HANDS AREN'T SHOWN IN A POKER GAME."

– DOYLE BRUNSON

In *The Glass Castle*, author Jeanette Walls wrote, "Whoever coined the phrase 'a man's got to play the hand that was dealt him' was most certainly a piss-poor bluffer." A company's brand can be as important as substantive business drivers. Sometimes the brand's public image matches reality, but not always and it more commonly exaggerates some positive elements. In poker, the perception that a player gives the others sitting at the table plays a role in his or her ultimate success or failure. This applies neatly to the patent game.

Only a relatively small percentage of hands are ever revealed in poker. The winner of most hands never has to reveal his or her cards because, if played correctly, the other players fold based on low perceived odds of winning, the large size of the pot, or intimidation from the players at the table with more chips. Similarly, just 3 percent of all patent litigations actually proceed to trial before a jury. The legal fees for patent litigation, if it goes the distance, can easily reach $2 million or more for each side, which is a heavy bet even for the largest of companies. This is particularly true when you consider that even if you are victorious you are unlikely to recover those hefty legal fees.

The risk associated with aggressively pursuing litigation is increased by the case ultimately being decided by a jury, which can be a dicey proposition when the lawsuit involves complex technology. *A lot* can go wrong with so many unpredictable factors. Trusting a jury with the future of your company can be daunting and, for this reason, settlements are quite common. Settlement between the parties is encouraged in part by the expensive "ante" of legal fees as well as the uncertainty of how the cards will fall during jury deliberations.

Poker skill certainly requires calculating probabilities, knowing how to play the odds, and making the right bets. However, the skill of giving your opponent the right perception of your hand can be just as important. What your opponent thinks you have can be more important than the cards you are actually holding. In both poker and the patent game, there are numerous factors that can be controlled and exploited to improve how your hand is perceived. One such factor is deterrence, a concept which I'll use often throughout this book. Deterrence is your ability to convince opponents that you have a strong hand, whether justified or not, and force them to fold. If you can win the game without having to show your cards, you'll save money, end disputes more quickly, and establish a precedence that you shouldn't be trifled with. The deterrent value of a given strategy is generally a combination of the substantive strength of the portfolio and the perception of strength. In war games, the number of nukes a rival has is important, but so is the perceived willingness of that opponent to use those weapons. It can be dangerous to bluff too often or to regularly overstate your position, but being cognizant of the impression you are giving others with respect to your patent portfolio can be valuable.

Different patent strategies will vary the perception they intend to give would-be competitors or third parties. Some strategies are backed by a robust arsenal of patents, whereas others seek to maximize the deterrent value of a more modest portfolio. North Korea's limited arsenal, but long-standing willingness to threaten anyone and everyone with a nuclear attack, has gotten them a seat at the global table. I'm not suggesting that you emulate North Korea when playing the patent game, but the perception you cultivate among those you're playing against can differ greatly from your actual capabilities and resources. Even with the weaker hand, a good poker player with a large stack of chips will often push around a player with a smaller stack. In the patent game, large companies can be formidable opponents because they may posture, even with seemingly weak patents, in an effort to push out the weaker hands. The believable threat that these companies are willing and able to draw a smaller party into lengthy and expensive litigation is a powerful deterrent. Even when the smaller company has a good hand, it will often fold or settle with the larger company out of fear and a lack of resources. At times, the patent game can feel like an adult version of a typical middle school playground: There is always somebody that wants to take your lunch money.

A subtler deterrent is the use of "patent pending" or "patented" on marketing materials, your website, and the product itself. This public notification that a patent has been filed can have a chilling effect on would-be competitors and puts them in a difficult situation: Will you get a broad patent? Will you sue them if a patent eventually issues? This anxiety can be compounded by the fact that most patent applications do not publish until 18 months after filing, meaning there is a very long blackout period during which competitors know that your technology is patent pending, but have no idea what, exactly, is covered by your patent application.

I have been in numerous situations where a client has identified a technology or product line it would like to legally copy if possible, but the competitor's technology is marked patent pending. In some cases, after a thorough search, I've been unable to find an underlying patent application supporting this patent pending notice. That might be perfectly reasonable because of the 18-month blackout period for most new applications, but there are plenty of times when I would suspect that the company never filed a patent application and is using the patent pending designation improperly. For risk averse companies—which many of my clients are—the inability to determine the scope of an unpublished application or to confirm that an application has actually been filed is enough for them to move on to something else. Just like a poker player that gets someone to fold by betting aggressively, sometimes the best deterrent is one that forces your competitors to bow out before the game even starts.

Remember: Don't be "that guy". Never use the patent pending designation unless you've gone through the trouble of filing a patent application. Don't go around marking everything as patent pending simply because no one can easily hold you accountable. But, once you do file a confidential patent application, use that designation as a deterrent to leave your competitors guessing.

While an application's pending status can intimidate competitors, your published application is an even more powerful deterrent. Once published – generally 18 months after the filing date – the entire contents of your application will be available as prior art against subsequently filed third party patent applications. Prior art is patent jargon for any evidence that an invention has previously been described, shown, or made. Your published application can block the patents of your competitors because it is now publicly accessible and available as prior art. Published applications are searchable in patent databases and are available for competitors and the public at large to view. This underscores the importance of a robust, well-written patent application – a weak application may embolden your competition, while a strong one might indicate that broad or disruptive patent protection is imminent. If you're at the poker table, get dealt two aces, and show everyone what you have, the rest of the table will almost certainly fold. But if you did the same thing with the weakest hand – a seven and a two of different suits – the reaction would be quite the opposite. What you choose to show publicly should be thoughtfully considered and in line with your overall patent strategy.

Published patent applications look a great deal like an issued patent in many respects and it's common to confuse the two if you haven't built up your IP IQ. You won't make this mistake after you've read this book, but one potential benefit of a published application is that a competitor with a low IP IQ might believe you have an issued patent when you don't. It's not your fault, then, if they fold.

Being patented is generally better than being patent pending in terms of actual and perceived deterrence. Having an issued patent of any type—even a design patent—gives you the legal right to describe your technology or design as patented. If you've spent the time and effort to secure an issued patent, don't miss the opportunity to put your competition on notice. Those with a low IP IQ may be unaware that there are different types of patents and that the scope of patents can vary dramatically—something you can use to your advantage. I've frequently been warned by inexperienced clients that a competitor has a terrifying patent on a given technology, only to find out that the patent in question is actually quite narrow in what it protects. Even a narrow utility or design patent can have a powerful deterrent effect. If you tell another player you have an ace they might assume you have a great hand even though the rest of your hand might be garbage. An issued patent in the patent game can be valuable, like an ace in poker, but the actual value will depend largely on the context of the game and how the rest of the hand is played.

A robust portfolio of patents and applications, both domestic and foreign, can create a powerful image of strength. Think of this: The United States currently has a stockpile of more than 4,000 nuclear weapons including 1,411 nuclear warheads deployed on various missiles and bombs. Don't tread on me, indeed. In patent terms, the cost and infrastructure to secure a portfolio of intimidating size and scope can imply you value intellectual property to the point that you are willing to invest heavily in its protection. This perception of strength can be further increased by a proven level of enforcement. The willingness to file lawsuits and take them the distance—to nuke your enemies, in a manner of speaking—will make competitors think twice about poking the bear by encroaching on your territory.

Scaring your opponents is a worthwhile consideration, but a perception of strength can also attract important allies. I will openly admit that I am terrible at dodgeball, which fortunately is not a skill required in my current profession. In middle school, as teams were starting to form, I would inevitably be one of the last kids picked. It usually came down to me and the undersized, nerdy kid who'd skipped a few grades. Why was I picked last? Although no one had seen me play dodgeball before, I probably *seemed* like I would be terrible based on physical characteristics and that I was terrible at most sports. They weren't wrong.

Being perceived negatively can be enough to prevent you from joining the winning team. Maybe when Trivial Pursuit® teams are assembling, you're the smart person everyone insists join their team. This may be because of your success in other games, the job you have, the fact you wear glasses, or really anything. How accurate are these assumptions? We've all seen the scrappy kid (not me) dominating at dodgeball and the doctor (or lawyer, for that matter…) who is dead weight on the trivia team. We constantly size up our competitors and potential allies during gameplay, assessing their strengths and weaknesses.

In team-oriented games — which the patent game very much is — it's helpful to be seen in a positive light. As a mirror image of deterrence, being seen as successful, a good teammate, and a valuable ally can manufacture tremendous value for your business. How will customers, competitors, partners, and potential acquisition partners view your business based on the way you project the strength of your portfolio? For some, such as entrepreneurs or independent inventors, it can be vital to cultivate this image of strength, skill, and sophistication. Reflect on the value of creating a positive patent perception and the role this might play in the success of your business. Most businesses and innovators are, in some fashion or another, courting teammates. Desirable teammates might vary depending on the size of your company, technology, or field of business in the same way the best dodgeball teammate isn't necessarily the best Trivial Pursuit partner. Identifying who you are trying to impress is an important step early in the process.

THE PERCEIVED VALUE TO YOUR CUSTOMERS

If you have a business-to-consumer company, you need to attract, court, and sell your widgets to as many customers as possible. Being patent pending or patented can help these customers better understand that your product truly is innovative and an improvement over other available options. Whether you're hawking dental floss or private jets, many of your potential customers are motivated to buy the newest, most innovative product. Establishing that you are patent pending or patented suggests that you are the original and not some cheap rip-off. In the consumer's mind, patents suggest the technology is exclusive to your company and that efforts to find the product elsewhere for a cheaper price would be futile. You might even be able to charge a premium for your technology because it's so innovative.

For business-to-business (B-to-B) companies, your customers are likely to be impressed by innovation. B-to-B sales tend to come with high price tags — cultivating the impression of innovation and exclusivity can be important to help justify higher prices and to land sales. Differentiation is key in the competitive world of B-to-B, as buyers often ask for proposals from several different vendors before committing. Being perceived as the most innovative company can set you apart. As a side benefit, it may also raise questions about whether your competitors are infringing upon your intellectual property.

THE PERCEIVED VALUE TO INVESTORS

A company seeking angel or venture capital needs to impress prospective investors. For many investors, it's important there is *something* proprietary about the businesses in which they choose to invest. If you don't have anything proprietary and you admit as much to your investors, it can be challenging to demonstrate how you can dominate your market without getting trampled by competitors. Investors generally aren't afraid to walk away from companies with no intellectual property because the investment appears too risky. For better or worse, some investors equate innovation with having some form of intellectual property. If you are running a startup in the midst of raising capital, you'll need to effectively articulate your IP position, even if it's not central to your business model. At a minimum, it can help answer that pesky question asked by many investors: "If you don't have any IP, then why can't [insert rich 800-lb. gorilla of a company] just come and steal your idea?" And in the era of the television show *Shark Tank*, it's more common than ever for a company seeking investment to be asked at least a few basic questions about its IP and patent position. Do yourself a favor: Check this box and move on.

PERCEIVED VALUE TO PARTNERS

It's hard to win a game of Trivial Pursuit by yourself — the combined knowledge of several people will almost always trump what a single person knows. However, people will want you on their team if you have a reputation for being successful. In the patent game, having a robust portfolio, a series of wins in litigation, or a number of lucrative licensing contracts makes you more attractive to partner with.

For smaller companies, it can be valuable to have a niche specialty for which you are known. A restaurant in my neighborhood has a weekly trivia contest with a "name that tune" round that is the bane of my existence. My trivia team was repeatedly crushed by a team with a guy who seemed to know the title and artist of every song ever made. After inquiring about his secret, this audiophile revealed that he had been a wedding DJ for years and was forced to learn song titles and artists to accommodate requests from guests. He wasn't particularly good at the rest of the questions, but we really wanted to poach him for our team because of his unique skill set. Smaller companies can make themselves valuable to larger companies in much the same way by demonstrating expertise in a narrow, but valuable space.

Companies frequently need to lean on the resources and expertise of other companies to be successful. However, businesses only want to go through the trouble of teaming up with others when the relationship is mutually beneficial. Being perceived as innovative can go a long way in making you attractive to prospective partners.

PERCEIVED EXIT VALUE

When you are trying to sell your company, your intellectual property portfolio and patent strategy can play a major role in defining the purchase price. Your business may be trying to justify a high purchase price—which may be well deserved—but perhaps the quantifiable metrics like sales and EBITDA don't justify this number. An early stage company's revenue and profits can lag well behind a reasonable valuation and the seller and the buyer might recognize that measurable metrics alone are not sufficient to justify an agreed-upon price. But to what can the difference in valuation be attributed? Intellectual property can be used to boost the purchase price to an acceptable amount by attributing value to this intangible asset. Without intellectual property or a patent strategy, it can be more challenging for you to negotiate a high sale price.

If you don't have your own factory, a stockpile of widgets, or significant acreage, how are you going to convince a multinational company to buy you at unicorn prices? If a technology company has few physical assets, and the founders don't plan to stay with the company long after acquisition, then what exactly is being bought and sold? What's left is usually some collection of intellectual property that includes patents, patent applications, trademarks, copyrights, know-how, software code, and trade secrets. Being able to articulate your intellectual property position can also dissuade the potential acquirer from passing on your offer and developing a competing technology themselves. Without a strong patent portfolio, customers and partners can become your fiercest adversaries. These "frenemies" of the business world need to be kept in check.

Businesses may vary in how important the value of perception is and the impact this perception has on fundraising, product success, and the ability to sell the business at a justifiable purchase price. However, for almost all businesses, that value is not zero.

CHAPTER 5:
WHY YOU NEED TO START PLAYING **NOW**

"WE DIDN'T LOSE THE GAME; WE JUST RAN OUT OF TIME."

– VINCE LOMBARDI

All kinds of games feature timers of some sort that force players to play by the rules and to do so *quickly*. The patent game similarly requires its players to adhere to strict timing requirements. Miss one of these deadlines and you might be out of the game completely. Patent law is chock full of imposed timers that can trip up players, even experienced ones. Of all the timing considerations in the patent game, arguably the most important is when you decide to sit down at the board and play.

I've heard a lot of excuses for not getting an early start, but you need to be aware that delaying the patent process can have severe consequences. The United States, as of 2013, changed the rules on the back of the patent game box and joined the rest of the world as a "first-to-file" country. As an inventor, you used to be able to document an early date of invention in a design notebook or a self-addressed and dated envelope containing a description of the invention. Even if you filed your patent application after someone else, you could still win if your date of invention pre-dated theirs. But, under the new system, those tactics are irrelevant. The now-obsolete first-to-invent system was thought to be more entrepreneur-friendly because it can, understandably, take time for inventors to find a patent attorney, draft a patent application, and to get the application on file. Fortune 500 companies often have an army of patent attorneys on staff just down the hall from the inventor who can quickly and efficiently prepare and file new patent applications. The old system was thought to give the little guys a chance to compete. With this new normal, it's basically a race to the patent office and the first applicant to file wins. If you are low on resources like cash and time, you are going to need to do your best to get your patent application on file quickly.

Every day that passes between intending to file and actually beginning the process is crucial. One of the excuses I frequently hear for not starting the patent process is that the invention is not yet perfect. Now, more than ever, there is tremendous risk in waiting to file a patent application until your invention is perfected. You should consider filing your patent application as soon as you have a workable solution and then file additional applications as you improve the invention. Inventors never stop inventing and you will inevitably come up with improved versions of your technology after your first patent application has been filed. Fortunately, as you will read in later sections, there are ways to capture iterative improvements with subsequent filings while still securing the earliest possible filing date.

There can be a strong temptation to publicly explore the value of your innovation before starting the patent process. Here be dragons, as the saying goes. Disclosing an invention before filing a patent application can have serious repercussions, including the loss of your rights to secure a patent both in the U.S. and abroad. In the United States, once an invention is made public, sold, or offered for sale, a one-year clock starts ticking during which you *must* file a patent application or you are forever barred from doing so. Most foreign countries have an even more draconian system called "absolute novelty." Under this standard, a public disclosure even *one day* before the filing of a patent application can destroy any and all patent rights. Do not pass GO and do not collect $200.

Yes, there are times when filing a patent application is premature, such as before a workable solution has been developed. But you should work closely with your patent attorney or agent early in the process so you can move quickly when you are ready to file. Maintain a healthy dialogue with your patent game coach and work together on determining the best time to plant the flag for your newly developed innovation. I have seen priority disputes between two filed applications directed to the same subject matter come down to a matter of mere *days*. It's a bad beat and a bitter pill to swallow. Always keep in mind that if you are working on a valuable invention, chances are that someone, somewhere in the world, is frantically working on the same thing. And the winner will take all.

CHAPTER 6:
THE BOARD: RISK® AND THE BATTLEFIELD

> **"THE BATTLEFIELD IS A SCENE OF CONSTANT CHAOS. THE WINNER WILL BE THE ONE WHO CONTROLS THAT CHAOS, BOTH HIS OWN AND THE ENEMIES'."**
>
> – NAPOLEON BONAPARTE

We've defined the game in general, so now let's define the board on which we'll be playing. There have been innumerable clichés used to describe intellectual property in concrete terms. Various textbooks will analogize intellectual rights to fences, walls, or other physical structures to help make these concepts appear less abstract. Securing intellectual property rights can be messier and much more challenging than the metaphor of putting up a fence might suggest.

As a self-proclaimed board game nerd, I find it helpful and interesting to imagine a Risk® board when considering the arena in which the patent game takes place. A standard Risk game board uses a map very familiar to most of us that has six continents further separated into 42 territories.

Not all of the Risk territories are created equal. Not every region is necessarily worth fighting for or expending resources such as time, money, or small plastic men to protect, so maybe hold off on pursuing expensive patent protection in the Republic of Moldova. While it can be exciting when something new is developed, it's imperative that you have a sense as to how valuable a prospective territory is before committing your resources. Focusing on a worthless territory can deplete resources and make more valuable areas subject to attack.

People who lose consistently when playing Risk often don't have a strategy going into the game. As Benjamin Franklin purportedly once said, "If you fail to plan, you are planning to fail." This is entirely applicable when it comes to the patent game.

A player earns bonus points in Risk for holding an entire continent, meaning they hold all of the territories within a particular continent until their next turn. For example, holding all four territories of South America is worth three bonus plastic men on every turn. The amount of bonus soldiers you receive varies by continent, but holding any continent provides an enormous competitive advantage over players who are choosing territories at random. Your patent strategy should be no different. One-off projects may have some value, but this is nothing compared to having a well-thought-out strategy that aims to dominate or monopolize a specific technology area. This is the business equivalent of holding a continent in Risk: You may have plans for global domination, but it's generally prudent to first establish a solid foundation before aggressively pushing into surrounding territories.

Problems can arise when you focus on the wrong territory. In Risk, Asia can appear very attractive because the holder of this giant landmass receives a whopping seven bonus soldiers. However, as any experienced Risk player will tell you, holding Asia early in the game is nearly impossible. Other competitors are constantly skirmishing on the edges of the continent, making test encroachments, and picking off poorly defended countries to weaken the monopoly. If you want Asia, you need *a lot* of resources and you need to be realistic about how to effectively use them.

Beware the equivalent of Asia in the patent game. Patent litigation can seem lucrative in light of highly publicized $1 billion infringement judgements, as can trillion-dollar markets like the music or travel industries. But can you target and hold that much territory? Amazon, which is now gobbling up metaphorical continents by making massive moves like acquiring Whole Foods, started out by selling books. Having vision is important to long term success, but patents are far more expensive than small plastic soldiers. It's important to be thoughtful about what's worth fighting for.

CHAPTER 7:
THE PLAYERS:
INVENTORS AND OWNERS

"CONTROL YOUR OWN DESTINY, OR SOMEONE ELSE WILL."

– JACK WELCH

Who, exactly, is sitting down at the board and controlling the pieces in the patent game? The players at the table are typically either the inventors or owners of the patentable technology. That seems simple enough, but determining inventorship can be challenging, even though it's often an afterthought. Not everyone gets to play this game and you can't be an inventor just because you want to, are the boss, or funded the innovation. Fortunately, there are general guidelines that can help you ascertain which individuals should and should not sit down with you at the board.

It's important to remember patent applications are *not* academic journal publications—authorship and inventorship do not necessarily overlap. Within academic institutions, it can be tempting and even commonplace to add a mentor, professor, or respected colleague as a co-author of a paper. Patent applications, however, are not the forum to express gratitude to an excellent teacher, your mother, or your graduate students. Similarly, within large companies, there can be political pressure to add a manager, division head, or CEO that, although they sign your checks, were not involved in developing the claimed innovation. These difficult inventorship decisions can be politically and interpersonally uncomfortable, but you need to make sure the rules are being followed in order to keep the game on track.

Improper inclusion of an individual as an inventor is referred to as a misjoinder, while exclusion of an individual that should have been listed is termed a non-joinder. Brushing aside the jargon, the key is to be careful not to add the wrong people or leave out actual inventors. Both misjoinder and non-joinder can have serious consequences, particularly if you *knowingly* added a non-inventor or *intentionally* left off someone that should have been listed. "I'm a good person, I'd never be tempted to do this," you say. I don't doubt you're right, but you might be surprised by how often this issue arises. One scenario I've seen on a number of occasions occurs when your buddy, who happens to work for a local technology company, has been helping you with your invention on weekends in your garage. Your friend has assumed his company would never care about what he does on his own time, but after collaborating with you for months he finally takes a look at his employment agreement. Like many such agreements — and you should check yours now if you have one — his states that *any* of his inventions, even those developed on his own time, away from work, and unrelated to his day job, are the property of his employer. All your work has been put in jeopardy. Merely leaving that person off the application as an inventor is not a viable option unless you work carefully with your attorney to determine if there's a way to do so properly. Although some unintentional errors in inventorship can be resolved with little consequence, many inventorship-related errors can have a lasting impact on the value and/or enforceability of your patent portfolio.

The legal definition of inventorship, for patent purposes, is any individual that makes a *material* contribution to *at least one* claim. Claims, which are described in more detail in Chapter 11, are numbered and concise descriptions of subject matter to be patented. Claims tend to be challenging for the layman to read and even more so to draft. But I view patent claims as a sort of nerd poetry, and that's probably an apt description.

Patent claims commonly represent only a subset of the disclosure contained in the entire patent application. A robust patent application may contain over 100 pages of disclosure, 20 or more individual figures, and many distinct versions or variations of the invention. However, a fraction of this disclosure may be covered by the claims. If an individual contributes to the disclosure of a patent application, but his or her contribution was not claimed—a relatively common occurrence—they should *not* be listed as an inventor. So not only can inventorship be difficult to determine at the outset, it can be a moving target as the claims in an application are amended, added, and cancelled.

Errors in inventorship can also be made when the definition of a "material contribution" to a patent claim is misunderstood. A material contribution should be meaningful and inventive, which disqualifies individuals that merely carried out testing and experimentation under the direction of the true inventor. In *Pinky and the Brain*, Brain is the only inventor in most of the diabolical schemes despite Pinky's constant involvement. The involvement of assistants, lab techs, graduate students, contract manufacturers, and the like should be scrutinized for whether their contributions rise to the level of legal inventorship. If your minions make relatively small decisions during the testing or experimentation process and these contributions do not materially impact the patent claims, then your minions must remain in the shadows where they belong. The temptation to include key employees, your kids, students, or anyone else contributing in a minor capacity can be as compelling as the temptation to add your boss as an inventor. There are better ways to reward these people for their loyalty, assistance, and support.

Before filing a patent application, it's good practice to require every prospective inventor to identify at least one specific patent claim to which they made a material contribution. This is their ticket into the patent game. Once the inventors have indicated the claims to which they contributed, you can work with your patent attorney to further refine the list before filing. Relying upon your attorney or agent to make the final determination can, in some circumstances, help mitigate any interpersonal fallout you might experience from including or excluding certain individuals. Blame the lawyers, it's fine—as a group we're used to everyone hating us.

A unique challenge can occur when trying to determine who should be listed as an inventor on a provisional patent application because this application type does not require any claims. We'll delve more into this common issue in Chapter 10 dedicated to provisional patent applications, but you can either take an expansive view of inventorship and include many individuals, or try to focus on including inventors whose contributions are likely to be claimed in a subsequent utility patent application.

As I briefly mentioned, inventorship may change when claims are amended, new claims are added, and claims are cancelled, even during the prosecution of an application before the United States Patent and Trademark Office (USPTO). If claims directed to an inventor's contribution are cancelled then the inventorship for the application may need to be revised. Similarly, if new claims are added, there may be individuals who were not previously listed that should now be added as inventors.

I'm frequently asked how many inventors are listed in a "typical" patent application. There really isn't a typical application, nor is there a right or wrong answer to this question. It's common to see between one and six inventors listed, particularly for an application with no more than 20 total claims. However, any number of inventors is theoretically possible if each made a material contribution to at least one claim. For example, U.S. Patent 9,081,501 for a "multi-petascale highly efficient parallel supercomputer" assigned to IBM, lists *61* inventors!

And there are, of course, no limits on the number of patents that can be applied for by a single inventor. As of June 30, 2016, Guinness World Records credits Shunpei Yamazaki of Japan as the most prolific inventor of all time with 11,353 issued patents. Thomas Edison, who looks like a slacker by comparison, has a measly 1,063 patents.

(12) **United States Patent**
Asaad et al.

(10) Patent No.: **US 9,081,501 B2**
(45) Date of Patent: ***Jul. 14, 2015**

(54) **MULTI-PETASCALE HIGHLY EFFICIENT PARALLEL SUPERCOMPUTER**

(75) Inventors: **Sameh Asaad**, Yorktown Heights, NY (US); **Ralph E. Bellofatto**, Yorktown Heights, NY (US); **Michael A. Blocksome**, Rochester, MN (US); **Matthias A. Blumrich**, Yorktown Heights, NY (US); **Peter Boyle**, Yorktown Heights, NY (US); **Jose R. Brunheroto**, Yorktown Heights, NY (US); **Dong Chen**, Yorktown Heights, NY (US); **Chen-Yong Cher**, Yorktown Heights, NY (US); **George L. Chiu**, Yorktown Heights, NY (US); **Norman Christ**, Yorktown Heights, NY (US); **Paul W. Coteus**, Yorktown Heights, NY (US); **Kristan D. Davis**, Rochester, MN (US); **Gabor J. Dozsa**, Yorktown Heights, NY (US); **Alexandre E. Eichenberger**, Yorktown Heights, NY (US); **Noel A. Eisley**, Yorktown Heights, NY (US); **Matthew R. Ellavsky**, Rochester, MN (US); **Kahn C. Evans**, Rochester, MN (US); **Bruce M. Fleischer**, Yorktown Heights, NY (US); **Thomas W. Fox**, Yorktown Heights, NY (US); **Alan Gara**, Yorktown Heights, NY (US); **Mark E. Giampapa**, Yorktown Heights, NY (US); **Thomas M. Gooding**, Rochester, MN (US); **Michael K. Gschwind**, Yorktown Heights, NY (US); **John A. Gunnels**, Yorktown Heights, NY (US); **Shawn A. Hall**, Yorktown Heights, NY (US); **Rudolf A. Haring**, Yorktown Heights, NY (US); **Philip Heidelberger**, Yorktown Heights, NY (US); **Todd A. Inglett**, Rochester, MN (US); **Brant L. Knudson**, Rochester, MN (US); **Gerard V. Kopcsay**, Yorktown Heights, NY (US); **Sameer Kumar**, Yorktown Heights, NY (US); **Amith R. Mamidala**, Yorktown Heights, NY (US); **James A. Marcella**, Rochester, MN (US); **Mark G. Megerian**, Rochester, MN (US); **Douglas R. Miller**, Rochester, MN (US); **Samuel J. Miller**, Rochester, MN (US); **Adam J. Muff**, Rochester, MN (US); **Michael B. Mundy**, Rochester, MN (US); **John K. O'Brien**, Yorktown Heights, NY (US); **Kathryn M. O'Brien**, Yorktown Heights, NY (US); **Martin Ohmacht**, Yorktown Heights, NY (US); **Jeffrey J. Parker**, Rochester, MN (US); **Ruth J. Poole**, Rochester, MN (US); **Joseph D. Ratterman**, Rochester, MN (US); **Valentina Salapura**, Yorktown Heights, NY (US); **David L. Satterfield**, Tewksbury, MA (US); **Robert M. Senger**, Yorktown Heights, NY (US); **Brian Smith**, Rochester, MN (US); **Burkhard Steinmacher-Burow**, Boeblingen (DE); **William M. Stockdell**, Rochester, MN (US); **Craig B. Stunkel**, Yorktown Heights, NY (US); **Krishnan Sugavanam**, Yorktown Heights, NY (US); **Yutaka Sugawara**, Yorktown Heights, NY (US); **Todd E. Takken**, Yorktown Heights, NY (US); **Barry M. Trager**, Yorktown Heights, NY (US); **James L. Van Oosten**, Rochester, MN (US); **Charles D. Wait**, Rochester, MN (US); **Robert E. Walkup**, Yorktown Heights, NY (US); **Alfred T. Watson**, Rochester, MN (US); **Robert W. Wisniewski**, Yorktown Heights, NY (US); **Peng Wu**, Yorktown Heights, NY (US)

(73) Assignee: **INTERNATIONAL BUSINESS MACHINES CORPORATION**, Armonk, NY (US)

(*) Notice: Subject to any disclaimer, the term of this patent is extended or adjusted under 35 U.S.C. 154(b) by 1083 days.

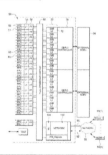

Although inventorship is important, the real player in the patent game is usually the owner of the patent application or patent. Inventorship and ownership do not necessarily correlate. In the United States, individual inventors must be listed on patent applications and issued patents, but this does not mean the inventor has *any* rights to the patent application. In most cases, the inventor works for a company to which he or she is obligated to assign, or transfer ownership of, the technology as a condition of employment. In effect, these inventors hand over their game pieces to the company and must be content to sit on the sidelines and watch. Once the technology has been assigned, these inventors can't make any patent-related decisions and often don't reap any of the rewards.

During my time at Ethicon Endo-Surgery I received an "Innovation Award" and a small cash prize for my inventive contribution to a radio-frequency medical device patent. We've all heard stories about employees inventing billion-dollar products for their companies and receiving only a token one-dollar check and a plaque. While this might seem unfair, it makes perfect sense when you consider one thing: If large companies were required to negotiate with employees every time an invention was created, the situation would quickly become untenable. Most companies require employees to agree to an Inventions Agreement or Assignment Agreement stating that anything developed by the employee, with varying degrees of scope, is owned by the employer. If you work for a company—especially a technology company—it's quite possible you've already relinquished your game piece. If you have a great idea and you aren't sure whether it's you or your company that owns the technology, make sure you control your game piece before sitting down at the board to play.

Although patent applications filed on behalf of a corporate entity make up the bulk of new filings, it's not uncommon to see patent applications and issued patents listing only the inventors as applicants. Of course, it's not required that your rights be assigned to a corporate entity—not every invention happens in some company's infrastructure. This approach can seem appealing to garage inventors and entrepreneurs, but there are potentially serious consequences to be aware of. When more than one inventor is an applicant and there is no obligation to assign the application to a single entity, **each inventor owns a 100 percent undivided interest in the patent application and any resultant patent.** Practically, this means each inventor can monetize the patent portfolio without accounting to any other inventors, which can dilute the exclusionary rights afforded by the patent process. Imagine that you and another player decide to share a monopoly on Park Place and Boardwalk but you each have the power to collect rent and to do deals without consulting with or sharing payments with the other player. Monopoly is already a great way to lose friends, so just imagine how ugly the game would get under *these* conditions. Do you really want someone renting out your property without your knowledge and without sharing in the proceeds? In most cases, inventors are generally better off assigning their rights to an entity controlled and governed by the inventors so that a united front can be presented for licensing and acquisition purposes. This arrangement is less likely to result in your co-inventor flipping over the board and refusing to ever play with you again.

CHAPTER 8:
THE BACK OF THE BOX: FOUNDATIONS FOR THE GAME

"YOU HAVE TO LEARN THE RULES OF THE GAME. AND THEN YOU HAVE TO PLAY BETTER THAN ANYONE ELSE."

– ALBERT EINSTEIN

I frequently reference the "back of the box" in my legal practice, the place where you'd find the rules printed for old-school board games. Fighting with your Grandma Judy about how to score Rack-O®? You go to the back of the box for the answers. These are the rules by which the game is played and without them the board and pieces have no meaning. The artificial constraints of these rules and how the players are forced to operate and compete within them create both opportunities to be exploited and landmines to avoid. Without rules you end up with something like Calvinball, the imaginary outdoor sport from *Calvin & Hobbes* — the final score is an incomprehensible Q to 12 and there are no real winners, only anarchy.

The patent game — like all other games save Calvinball — has a back of the box, in a manner of speaking. You'll need a basic understanding of the fundamental rules, what they mean, and how they work before trying to effectively move your pieces around the board. So let's start with the basics and work our way toward the more complex elements.

A patent is a set of exclusive rights granted by a government to an inventor for a limited period of time in exchange for the disclosure of an invention. It's a monopoly, but not one that lasts forever and there are important tradeoffs. Let's unpack that statement because *every* word in this definition has significant meaning.

EXCLUSIVE RIGHTS

A patent grants you an exclusive right—a monopoly—to exclude others from making, using, selling, offering for sale, or importing your patented invention into your protected territory. Returning to our Monopoly analogy, once you've claimed a territory in the board game, you are entitled to rent if a player lands on that square. In the patent game, if a third party infringes on your rights—meaning they make, use, sell, offer for sale, or import your invention—you could be entitled to financial damages or an injunction to stop the infringing behavior altogether (the equivalent of kicking them out of your territory). Monetary damages are the most common form of relief for infringement, particularly in the United States, where damages can exceed $1 billion. Patent infringement is not a criminal offense, so no one needs to use a "get out of jail free" card, even in cases of blatant, willful infringement. But monetary damages can be significant on their own and if willful infringement is shown, the damages are *tripled* (this is called trebled damages). Although patents can be expensive to acquire, the value of a monopoly on a valuable or disruptive technology is almost limitless. Park Place and Boardwalk are pricey, but if you can buy and develop them, you'll probably win the game.

GRANTED BY THE GOVERNMENT

Exclusive rights granted by the government mean that a patent is essentially a contract between the government of each territory and the patent applicant. Because patents are jurisdictional, *each* country's government from Albania to Zimbabwe needs to separately grant your patent rights to secure a monopoly in its territory. There is no such thing as a worldwide patent. Patent laws can also vary considerably between countries, but there are many treaties in place to help make international prosecution more efficient.

The countries you choose for protection can have a profound effect on the value of your global patent portfolio. Competitors can legally make, use, sell, import, and offer for sale your invention in any countries you haven't protected, so it's important to make sure key manufacturing and sales jurisdictions are identified and pursued to maximize protection. Conversely, some territories may have no real business value and will ultimately become nothing more than a massive drain on your resources. It can be tempting to pursue protection in a lot of different countries for fear that your technology will be copied, but it's cost prohibitive to protect your invention with a patent in *every* country in the world. Even if your pockets are deep, you need to make judicious choices, as multiple foreign filings and prosecution of related infringements can become astronomically expensive.

Many—perhaps most—inventors improperly believe that as part of a patent contract with the government you are entitled to practice (that is to say, to make, use, sell, or import) your own invention. Don't fall into this trap. I've heard this error made by very experienced business professionals, but it's false even if it does seem counterintuitive. Remember, a patent is a *negative* right only. You can exclude others from making, using, selling, and importing your patented invention, but you can't necessarily produce make, use, sell, or import your invention without potentially infringing upon someone else's patent.

Yes, there are times when you can't build and sell the product for which you just secured an expensive U.S. issued patent. How does this make any sense? It sometimes happens that a dominant patent exists on an underlying component of your newly developed technology, one that can prevent you from actually building and selling your product without infringing that dominant patent. Your patent may still be 100 percent valid and properly issued, but practicing your technology could result in a legitimate infringement claim brought by the dominant patent holder. The most common scenario where this occurs is with improvement patents over an existing technology, where the newly patented improvement incorporates key elements of the underlying technology. The improvement may be patentably distinct, but if *building* the improved technology uses protected elements from a patent for the underlying technology this is still infringement.

Imagine that you were the inventor and patent holder for Jenga®, the block stacking game marketed by Hasbro®. For the unfamiliar, players in Jenga take turns removing one block at a time from a tower constructed of 54 blocks. Each block removed must be placed on top of the existing tower, creating a progressively taller and more unstable structure. As a fun side note, the name Jenga is derived from "kujenga," a Swahili word which means "to build." The patent drawing here is one of the key figures from your Jenga patent.

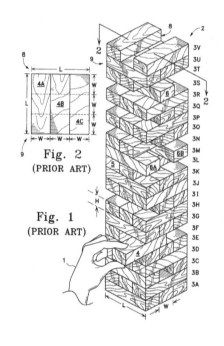

Fig. 2
(PRIOR ART)

Fig. 1
(PRIOR ART)

Your neighbor, after repeatedly losing to you, decides that the reason for his losses is that the table on which you are playing isn't flat. He surmises that this is an inherent problem with your Jenga game and, to fix this perceived problem, he devises a new system that includes a rotating turntable and a bubble level to ensure an even playing field. After meeting up with a local patent attorney, your neighbor gets his *own* patent on his variation of Jenga shown below. Needless to say, someone is not going to be getting a Christmas card this year.

Let's assume that both your patented system and your neighbor's version use 54 stackable blocks and that your issued patent claims cover *any* game that includes 54 stackable blocks used in a tower game. Your neighbor, despite also using 54

United States Patent [19]

Grebler et al.

[11] **Patent Number:** **5,611,544**

[45] **Date of Patent:** **Mar. 18, 1997**

[54] **STACKING BRICK TOWER GAME**

[75] Inventors: **Robert K. Grebler**, Santa Monica; **Paul Eveloff**, San Anselmo; **James E. Sheftel**, Santa Monica, all of Calif.

[73] Assignee: **Pokonobe Associates**, Larkspur, Calif.

[21] Appl. No.: **562,671**

[22] Filed: **Nov. 27, 1995**

[51] Int. Cl.⁶ A63F 9/00
[52] U.S. Cl. **273/447**; 273/450
[58] Field of Search 273/447, 448, 273/450; 446/85, 117, 118

[56] **References Cited**

U.S. PATENT DOCUMENTS

3,712,616	1/1973	Goldfarb et al.	273/447
3,899,169	8/1975	Rhodes et al.	273/450
4,522,393	6/1985	Dunn	273/450 X
4,902,010	2/1990	Davis et al.	273/450

FOREIGN PATENT DOCUMENTS

190876	8/1986	European Pat. Off.	273/447
2185691	7/1987	United Kingdom	273/447

OTHER PUBLICATIONS

Creative Playthings catalog, 1969–1970 p. 23 "Toppler".

Primary Examiner—Paul E. Shapiro
Attorney, Agent, or Firm—Robbins, Berliner, & Carson, LLP

[57] **ABSTRACT**

A game is played by building a tower of bricks in multiple levels, and players alternately removing a brick from one level and adding it to the top of the tower to build new levels, until collapse of the tower occurs. Bricks of a variety of different types are provided with each type having different physical characteristics, such as shape, size, surface configuration and/or coefficient of friction. At least two adjacent layers of the initial tower are formed from bricks of different types.

19 Claims, 11 Drawing Sheets

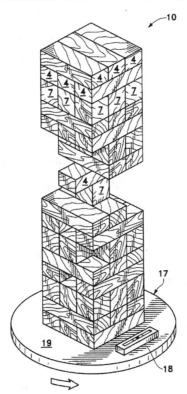

blocks in his tower game, was still able to secure an issued patent on his variation because the addition of a turntable and bubble level were found to be novel and non-obvious in view of your prior patent. Your neighbor's patent, however, is narrower and claims a system having 54 stackable blocks used in a tower game, but the claims also require a turntable and a bubble level. Can your jerk neighbor start selling his game in competition with yours? The answer is no. For your neighbor to build and sell his version of Jenga, he would need to use the elements from your patent that are protected; namely, the 54 stackable blocks used in a tower game. The addition of the turntable and bubble level might be novel and patentable, but patentability does not excuse his infringement of your broad dominant patent.

The lesson of this is simple — don't conflate the issuance of a patent with what is referred to as freedom-to-operate or non-infringement. Many business leaders or investors assume that they can pursue commercialization risk-free when a patent has been issued on a key piece of technology. This is not always the case. A complete freedom-to-operate or non-infringement review and analysis should be conducted before coming to such a conclusion.

LIMITED PERIOD OF TIME

The patent party can't last forever. The exclusive monopoly for a patent is not unlimited. As part of the patent contract, the patentee is only entitled to exclusive patent rights for a limited period of time. At some point, you'll have to forfeit those expensive hotels you built on Boardwalk and Park Place. The term of a patent is generally 20 years from the *filing date* of the non-provisional, PCT, or national stage application in almost every country in the world (we'll delve into those types of applications a little later in the book). Design patents, which are directed to non-functional and ornamental features, last for 15 years from *issuance* in the United States and this timing varies considerably in other countries.

I'm frequently asked whether it's permissible to refile a patent application directed to an expired patent, whether that expired patent was your own or one of your competitors. Similarly, I am regularly asked if, when approaching the end of the patent's term, there are mechanisms by which the patentee can extend the term of its patent beyond the original period of exclusivity.

The answer to both of these inquiries is "no". When the patent term runs out, the patent—including all of the disclosure in the patent—is dedicated to the public and can be freely practiced by anyone. This should not be confused with a patentee clawing back patent term because of USPTO or other government delays, something we'll discuss later in Chapter 18 dedicated to patent term adjustment and patent term extension. It's a common misconception that wealthy pharmaceutical companies are somehow manipulating the patent system to extend the terms of key patents. In reality, these companies are usually getting patents on new formulations, delivery mechanisms, or other improvements and variations of the original, now-expired technology. These new versions or delivery mechanisms, which can look very similar to the originally patented technology, can sometimes give the appearance that these companies are illegitimately extending patent term on blockbuster drugs, for example.

DISCLOSURE OF THE INVENTION

There's no such thing as a free lunch. An inventor's contribution to the patent contract is the *complete* disclosure of his or her invention. Most governments are generally opposed to monopolies, which is why antitrust laws abound. Therefore, the grant of a monopoly comes with a lot of strings attached. The rationale behind having a patent system is that inventors will simply keep everything they create a secret if not granted exclusive rights in their inventions. If every innovation is maintained in secret, then innovation as a whole suffers. Most governments have seen the value of trading a limited monopoly for the disclosure of important technology so that future generations of technologists can learn from, improve upon, and eventually use the off-patent inventions. It would be tragic for a powerful new medicine or an invention important to the

improvement of society to be forever lost because the inventor dies or the innovation was improperly documented.

You must fully disclose your invention in a patent application, and stopping
short of doing so could jeopardize your patent rights. Be prepared to file a comprehensive disclosure with the "secret sauce" if you want to enforce your issued
patent. This can be a challenge for inventors who are concerned about competitors and knockoffs. You may be faced with a tough choice between pursuing
patents and keeping your ideas confidential as a trade secret. Fortunately, there
are a number of strategies that allow you to maintain the patent option in addition
to keeping trade secret protection, at least for a time, as discussed in Chapter 19.

Once you've understood the policy objectives and tradeoffs associated with pursuing patent protection, and you are willing to make this contract with the government, it's important to understand the specific requirements for patentability.
There are many formal and administrative requirements that need to be satisfied to
secure a patent, but there are three core requirements for an innovation to be eligible for patent protection: The invention must be (a) useful, (b) novel, and (c) non-obvious. All three of these requirements *must* be met to secure a patent in nearly any
jurisdiction, though the terms used to describe these requirements may vary.

USEFULNESS (35 U.S.C § 101)

What can be protected with a utility patent? As it turns out, quite a lot. In *Dia-
mond v. Chakrabarty*, the U.S. Supreme Court summarized the standard succinct-
ly in holding that "anything under the sun made by man" can be protected with
a utility patent. Though it may seem self-evident, those last three words are
important. Only *human-made* inventions can be protected with a patent. Abstract
discoveries, scientific formulae, and natural phenomena cannot themselves be
patented because things of this nature are discovered, not invented. However,
applications of these discoveries may be patentable. For example, while Isaac
Newton couldn't patent gravity after purportedly being hit on the head with an

apple in the apocryphal tale, he could invent and then patent the cannon he invented to keep a cannonball perpetually in orbit that applies this theory. Discoveries alone are not inventions, but many discoveries have a subsequent practical application that may be patentable.

So, what does "anything under the sun made by man" look like in practice? The standard for usefulness has, for most types of inventions, been painfully low for a very long time. If you've made it this far in the book, then I'd like to give you a high five. Yes, what follows is a real U.S. Patent.

United States Patent [19]

Cohen

[11] Patent Number: **5,356,330**

[45] Date of Patent: **Oct. 18, 1994**

[54] **APPARATUS FOR SIMULATING A "HIGH FIVE"**

[76] Inventor: **Albert Cohen,** 176 N. Lake Ave., Troy, N.Y. 12180

[21] Appl. No.: **163,856**

[22] Filed: **Dec. 7, 1993**

[51] Int. Cl.⁵ A63H 33/00; A63H 3/36
[52] U.S. Cl. **446/491;** 446/390; 472/70
[58] Field of Search 446/390, 485, 491; 40/418, 490; 472/70; 482/83, 84, 85, 86

[56] **References Cited**

U.S. PATENT DOCUMENTS

1,425,945	8/1922	Congdon .
2,484,343	10/1949	Hawes .
2,585,780	2/1952	Johnson .
2,937,872	5/1960	Gilman .
3,252,242	5/1966	Zalkind .
3,427,021	2/1969	Donato 482/83
3,755,960	9/1973	Tepper et al. 446/299

3,804,406	4/1974	Viscione .... 482/83 X
3,877,697	4/1975	Lersch .
3,927,879	12/1975	Long et al. 482/83
4,381,620	5/1983	Panzarella .
5,171,197	12/1992	Healy et al. 482/83

FOREIGN PATENT DOCUMENTS

563984 7/1977 U.S.S.R. 482/83

Primary Examiner—Robert A. Hafer
Assistant Examiner—D. Neal Muir
Attorney, Agent, or Firm—Schmeiser, Morelle & Watts

[57] **ABSTRACT**

An apparatus for simulating a "high-five" including a lower arm portion having a simulated hand removably attached thereto, an upper arm portion, an elbow joint for pivotally securing the lower arm portion to the upper arm portion, and a spring biasing element for biasing the upper and lower arm portions towards a predetermined alignment.

12 Claims, 3 Drawing Sheets

Maybe you are one of those people that considers board games to be B-O-R-E-D games? If so, maybe I can interest you in a few rounds of this "Electrostatically Enhanced Game" invented by Ray L. Allen.

United States Patent [19]

Allen et al.

[11] Patent Number: **4,553,748**

[45] Date of Patent: **Nov. 19, 1985**

[54] **ELECTROSTATICALLY ENHANCED GAME**

[76] Inventors: **Ray L. Allen,** 204 Townsend Pl., Atlanta, Ga. 30327; **N. Cole Harrison,** 1438 Tullie Rd., Atlanta, Ga. 30329

[21] Appl. No.: **517,465**

[22] Filed: **Jul. 26, 1983**

[51] Int. Cl.⁴ A63F 9/00
[52] U.S. Cl. .... 273/1 E; 273/85 G; 273/DIG. 28; 361/232; 446/140
[58] Field of Search .... 273/311, 1 E, 1 GC, 273/85 G, DIG. 28; 128/783, 419 N, 419 R, 371, 375; 361/232; 446/140

[56] **References Cited**

U.S. PATENT DOCUMENTS

477,975	6/1892	Waite 128/783
2,404,653	7/1946	Plebanek .
3,819,108	6/1974	Jordan .
4,093,232	6/1978	Nutting et al. .... 273/121 A
4,149,716	4/1979	Scudder .
4,320,901	3/1982	Morrison et al. .

FOREIGN PATENT DOCUMENTS

2637250 2/1978 Fed. Rep. of Germany 128/783

Primary Examiner—Richard C. Pinkham
Assistant Examiner—Leo P. Picard
Attorney, Agent, or Firm—Jones & Askew

[57] **ABSTRACT**

An electrostatic enhancement apparatus for a video arcade or other game, including an electrostatic generator for generating a high voltage low current electrostatic charge, an electrode coupled to the generator for providing the electrostatic charge to a player, and control circuitry responsive to a control signal from the game for actuating the electrostatic generator to provide the electrostatic charge to the player upon the occurrence of a predetermined event in the game. The preferred embodiment includes an isolation booth for surrounding and electrically isolating the player during the electrostatic charging and preventing accidental discharge. Also included is a discharge arm mounted for electrical engagement with the electrode for removing charge from the electrode and the player under certain circumstances.

10 Claims, 4 Drawing Figures

Zowie, indeed. Shocking, right?

As recently as 30 or 40 years ago, the USPTO would actively weigh in on the morality of certain patent applications when deciding whether an invention was useful. The issue of usefulness was often evaluated subjectively by individual examiners. Whether the application's subject matter might have a detrimental effect on society was a relevant factor in determining patentability and the USPTO would frequently comment as to whether a given invention was socially acceptable to the point of being useful. Supposedly harmful technology such as gambling machines, it was argued, did not have any positive utility and thus shouldn't be patentable.

In 1999, *Juicy Whip, Inc. v. Orange Bang, Inc.* provided an unlikely battleground for moral judgements in patent disputes. The USPTO's subjective evaluation of what is useful subject matter came to a head in a dispute over, of all things, convenience store juice machines.

These machines, which were once ubiquitous, can still be seen in many gas stations and are immediately recognizable by the top-mounted transparent bin filled with a circulating liquid. Or, as I refer to it, the liar juice. Consumers naturally and understandably believe the juice dispensed from these machines comes from this visible circulating bin. However, this was an illusion and the liquid was actually dispensed from a tank of concentrate *beneath* the ma-

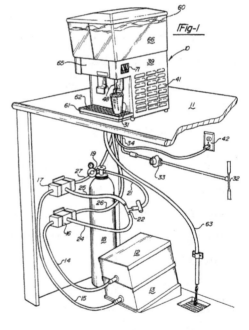

chine. It was argued that this was deceptive to the public and thus not eligible for patent protection. For better or worse, the owners of the machine prevailed and the USPTO has since stopped making moral judgments as a factor weighing against patentability. Despite cases like this, most would agree it's wise for individual USPTO examiners to refrain from using their own moral judgment to evaluate an applicant's technology.

Subsequent case law has further supported this notion that the USPTO should not engage in the subjective evaluation of an applicant's technology. A patent can be secured on almost any type of technology, and that includes illegal, impractical, dangerous, and/or deceptive innovations. The immoral invention of a decade ago may be viewed more favorably in the next decade. Previously illegal technology, such as the growth and harvesting of marijuana in the United States, may eventually become legal nationwide. As a result of this lower standard, however, the number of seemingly ridiculous, illegal, or impractical patents has skyrocketed. But this is an acceptable price to pay in order for the USPTO to maintain an objective approach to evaluating patent filings. A lot can happen in the 20 years of a standard patent term, including changes in the law that can make extremely valuable what was once impractical. If yours is a potentially dangerous or illegal invention, it's up to you to navigate any and all additional practical hurdles that might apply should you choose to commercialize your invention.

Usefulness is often an easy hurdle to overcome. As recently as 10 or 15 years ago this requirement was so easily satisfied that inclusion in this book would have been unnecessary. Except for traditionally-excluded subject matter, such as mathematical equations and natural phenomena, this type of rejection was practically extinct. Unfortunately, rejections under 35 U.S.C. § 101 (frequently called "101" rejections) have become more commonplace, particularly in the fields of software business methods and medical diagnostics. A basic understanding of the evolution of these 101 rejections and how they are currently being applied provides helpful background context for all patent applicants, particularly for those in the aforementioned technology fields.

In its most recent incarnation, 35 U.S.C § 101 has been interpreted to render inventions in the fields of software business methods and medical diagnostics — as well as others — as *patent ineligible* subject matter. Why is this type of rejection more commonplace for certain types of innovations? Unlike the requirements of novelty and non-obviousness, which focus on prior art developed before your invention, an invention facing a 101 rejection is considered subject matter that just flat-out can't be protected with a patent. Inventors with these types of inventions aren't even allowed to start the game.

If you end up facing a 101 rejection, you may find it extremely difficult to overcome. It's important to consult a patent attorney experienced in the specific subject field. They will be able to determine the best course moving forward and, if consulted before filing, can help you prepare the best possible patent application to give you the greatest odds of success. If you are innovating in one of these challenging fields, you should resist the temptation to throw up your hands and eschew the patent process altogether. Even if there might be some challenges with the patentability of your specific invention or inventions, you might still be able to create value with one of the many strategies in this book.

NOVELTY (35 U.S.C. § 102)

It should be intuitive that your invention must be new in order to be patentable. Once your application is filed, the USPTO will conduct a search for prior art, which includes patents and publications that predate your application's filing date. If a single existing patent or publication discloses every element of one of your claims, that claim will be rejected under 35 U.S.C. § 102 because it lacks novelty. These are commonly referred to as "102" rejections.

A patentable invention must be novel in view of every publication or patent, from anywhere in the world, available before the applicant's filing date. When you consider there are now more than 8 billion people on the planet, this is a very high standard to meet. If you try to re-patent the Twister concept, your

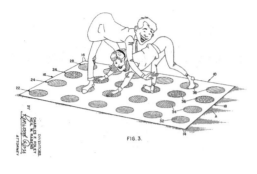

FIG. 3.

patent examiner will do a search, find the original patent from 1966, and determine that your newly filed application is "anticipated" or fully described in that prior, albeit expired, patent. Your examiner will cite the prior Twister patent against your application under 35 U.S.C. § 102 and you'll be out of luck. Remember, it doesn't matter that it has expired, it's still available as prior art against your newly filed patent application.

It's important to note that *brands* like Twister® are registered trademarks and the protectable brand name can last indefinitely. But you are free to make and sell your own version of this awkward game under a different name. The oh-so-cleverly named Don't Fall Down, which is the spitting image of Twister, is one such example of using almost the exact same concept, but with a different brand name.

You must be careful to avoid certain actions that will result in a loss of patent rights. Most inventors keep their inventions secret before filing because they are afraid the idea will be stolen, but there is another equally compelling reason for waiting to disclose the invention: In the United States, you are afforded a *one-year grace period* from the time you make a public use, a sale, or an offer for sale of your invention. If you fail to file a patent application within this one-year period, you will be barred for lack of novelty in view of your *own* activities. Most countries outside of the United States do not grant such a grace period, so a public disclosure even *one day* before you file a patent application could eliminate most of your foreign patent rights. It can be tempting to shop your invention before committing to an expensive patent filing, but waiting is a risky proposition, especially if you think there might be a global market for your invention. Your college isn't doing you any favors with that Invention Convention and your startup accelerator might be doing you more harm than good if you aren't patent pending before demo day.

NON-OBVIOUSNESS (35 U.S.C. § 103)

In addition to being useful and novel, your invention must be "non-obvious" to be patentable. Just because your invention isn't identical to a prior invention does not mean it's protectable. Minor variations on preexisting technology — such as inconsequential cosmetic changes — aren't enough to get you a patent. Non-obviousness requires your invention to be sufficiently different from the current state of the art to merit a monopoly. An obviousness determination can be made by a USPTO examiner based on a single prior art reference but is more commonly made based upon the combination of two or more references.

USPTO examiners start by trying to identify a single reference to reject your invention for a lack of novelty based upon 35 U.S.C. § 102. To make a 102 rejection, the USPTO examiner must find every element of your claimed invention within the four corners of a single reference, which can be challenging. If your patent examiner is unable to find *all* the elements for your claimed invention in a single reference, the examiner will then look to combine two or more prior art references to make an obviousness rejection under 35 U.S.C. § 103. This, staying consistent with the theme, is often referred to as a "103" rejection.

We discussed why your attempts to re-patent the Twister game concept would receive a 102 rejection, but could the Don't Fall Down "inventor" secure a patent on his iteration of the Twister concept? After all, as illustrated on the box cover, this version of the game uses dice instead of the spin wheel used in Twister. Genius, right? Although the original Twister patent never disclosed the use of dice, the USPTO examiner would likely still reject claims directed to the Don't Fall Down game under 35 U.S.C. § 103 as being obvious in view of the original Twister patent and one or more dice-related references.

Any USPTO rejection of a patent application — whether it's a 101, 102, or 103 rejection — is far from dispositive. It's quite common for new patent applications to initially have *all* of the claims rejected; in fact, it tends to occur for over 90 percent of first-filed applications. You may be disheartened when receiving this response from the USPTO, but you shouldn't be overly concerned — at least not yet. There are many tools and tactics that can be used to overcome these initial rejections. The patent applicant for the Don't Fall Down concept may be out of luck, but if your innovation is more inventive than this basic knockoff you might still have hope.

One of the most effective ways to overcome one or more rejections is the USPTO examiner interview. At various times during prosecution, you will be entitled to discuss your pending application in person or over the phone with the patent examiner. This is normally handled by your attorney or agent without the inventor present, but there are times when having the inventor participate can be helpful. Examiner interviews give you and your attorney an opportunity to make arguments, discuss prior art, propose amendments, and give evidence of secondary considerations (like a successful product or fulfilling a long-felt need) that could help you overcome any rejections. Examiner interviews are highly recommended for clarifying rejections, cited art, and proposed amendments while also potentially speeding up the prosecution of your application. Remember, examiners are not the enemy (usually...) and can even be helpful (sometimes...) in making suggestions that move your application closer to allowance. A collaborative relationship with your examiner can go a long way in helping you to expeditiously secure an issued patent.

CHAPTER 9

PATENT SEARCHING: MINESWEEPER

"PEOPLE DON'T WANT TO HEAR THE TRUTH BECAUSE THEY DON'T WANT THEIR ILLUSIONS DESTROYED."

– FRIEDRICH NIETZSCHE

Before the smartphone revolution, you might have wasted time in class or at work playing the PC game Minesweeper. Minesweeper originated in the 1960s, and this favorite pastime of procrastinators requires players to systematically clear a minefield without detonating any of the concealed bombs.

After clicking on one of the seemingly innocuous grey squares to start the game, players must try to deduce the location of a set number of bombs based upon the indication in adjacent squares as to how many bombs each safe space is touching.

As the game progresses, a flag can be placed on squares a player believes are concealing a bomb. If you successfully isolate all of the bombs you win, but accidentally detonate just one mine and you have to start this exercise in tedium all over again from the very beginning.

Patent searching is, in many respects, like playing a high stakes and global game of Minesweeper. In Chapter 8, I discussed the requirements of usefulness, novelty, and non-obvious required for an invention to be patentable. Your invention must meet these patentability requirements in view of *all* of the information, from anywhere in the world, which has previously been made publicly available. This patent-defeating information, referred to as "prior art" in patent legal jargon, is analogous to the hidden bombs in Minesweeper. Find just one of these prior art bombs and your game may be over. Having to meet the patentability requirements in view of everything publicly known prior to your application filing date is an incredibly high standard.

You are, however, generally not required to play the patent version of Minesweeper unless you choose to. It's a common misconception that the first step in the patent process must be a prior art search, but in most cases no such requirement exists. It may be perfectly acceptable and even advantageous to file a patent application directed to a purportedly novel and non-obvious invention without having done any patent searching whatsoever. It's the job of the USPTO and other international patent offices to conduct a prior art search and, if appropriate, make rejections based upon the findings. Conducting a patent search can be beneficial, but there are also potentially negative consequences of which you should be aware.

The patent process can be expensive and, for this reason, many inventors choose to conduct a patent search before committing to the filing of one or more patent applications. If you choose to play the patent version of Minesweeper, and you find a prior art bomb early, you may be thankful that your game ended before expending a considerably amount of time and resources going down a danger-ous path. Finding a patentability-defeating patent or publication can be dis-heartening, but many inventors would rather know sooner rather than later how likely they are to be successful.

Patent searches can also be very useful in defining critical whitespace. In Mine-sweeper, as you identify each bomb, large areas of safe space frequently open up between the bombs that present no threat to the player. Knowing where the bombs are can help you better define the unoccupied open spaces. In the patent game, an innovation may initially seem very broad, but after identifying and navigating through the prior art it may be become clear which features and as-pects of the invention are truly innovative. Focusing on these core features, rath-er than simply casting a wide net, can lead to faster and better issued patents.

In many jurisdictions, including the United States, you are required to submit to the patent office all of the information you are aware of that could be material to patentability. This includes, for example, prior patents and publications that you identify during the patent search process. This can be beneficial because a patent that has undergone a rigorous examination may be more difficult to at-tack in the future based upon undiscovered prior art.

What are the potential downsides to patent searching? Patent searches them-selves can be expensive and, if a technology is still in the early stages of devel-opment, it may be more cost effective to put those resources into a patent appli-cation instead of a search. Because establishing an early priority date is often critical, some inventors will choose to quickly file an initial patent application before engaging in a robust patent search.

Although an issued patent that has undergone rigorous examination is generally preferred, it's also possible that your patent examiner will improperly use some of the materials from your search to reject one or more patent claims. In my practice, I have worked with a number of overachieving inventors that have scoured obscure journals and publications, which must be submitted to the USPTO, only to have an examiner use those materials to make improper lack of novelty or obviousness rejections. Because most examiners search only a limited database of patents and publications, it is arguable, in these circumstances, that the inventor would have been better off not having found the references. Sticking your head in the sand can be dangerous, but handing the USPTO a lot of potential ammunition to reject your claimed invention can also be problematic. In the words of the Greek poet Hesiod, "moderation is best in all things."

An issued patent is presumed valid once issued, and because of this, it can be difficult to invalidate or otherwise challenge a granted patent. One strategy is to do little or no patent searching in an effort to avoid having to provide the USPTO and other patent offices with any information that could be used by an examiner to make improper rejections. Such applicants sometimes view aggressive patent searching as unnecessarily doing the examiner's job for them, but there is always the risk that there are the patent law equivalent of Minesweeper bombs lurking undiscovered.

Practically speaking, patent searches come in a lot of different shapes and sizes. Searches can be focused or limited to any number of categories such as jurisdiction, patents only, patents and published patent applications, journal articles, and more. For example, if you plan to pursue patent protection in the United States, you might limit your initial search to just issued U.S. patents and published U.S. patent applications. Although anything from anywhere in the world is fair game, this is the scope of the search likely to be conducted by your USPTO patent examiner. Patent examiners are given limited time to conduct searches, so it makes sense that in many cases they do not aggressively review art in other jurisdictions, particularly if it is not in English. It's also common to limit searches by cost where, for example, you might request the best search possible focused on a particular jurisdiction(s) and/or type of prior art at an agreed upon flat fee. Consult with your attorney to make sure that the cost and objective of a patent search meet your overall objectives before proceedings.

There are a number of websites, like patents.google.com and freepatentsonline.com that offer free patent searching resources. These websites are a great way for entrepreneurs or inventors on a budget to do a preliminary knockout search before engaging with an attorney. It's estimated that more than 90% of issued patents are never commercialized, so don't fall into the trap of believing that just because you've never seen your innovation on the internet or in stores that it must therefore be novel and non-obvious.

Many attorneys conduct internal patent searches on behalf of clients, but it can be more cost effective to engage with third party search services. You may still need to work with your attorney to request a search through one of these services, but third party groups that focus exclusively on searching can be more cost effective than a patent attorney with a high hourly rate. Startup technology companies, like AcclaimIP, are entering the patent searching game and provide search results combined with analytics that may be useful to inventors.

CHAPTER 10:
THE PIECES ON
THE BOARD

"THESE YOUNG GUYS ARE PLAYING CHECKERS.
I'M OUT THERE PLAYING CHESS."

– KOBE BRYANT

Like chess, the patent game includes a number of distinct pieces with specific movements, features, and abilities. Both games require you to use these foundational elements in combination to achieve your objective. It's important to understand these pieces, how they can be used, their limitations, and their strengths in order to execute the strategies I'll enumerate later in this book. There are three types of U.S. patents — utility, design, and plant patents — but this book will focus solely on utility and design patents. Plant patents only exist in a niche area of practice that, unless you are an orchid fanatic or are heavily involved in agriculture, you will likely never encounter. Foreign jurisdictions occasionally offer so-called "invention patents" which are an unexamined form of a utility patent. Infrequently used, they can be useful to minimize costs

The public's general understanding of patents has improved over time, but most people do not realize there are different types of patents and how each has very different requirements and functions. To understand these patent types (and sub-types), and how each can be used strategically, is paramount in the patent game.

To help you remember the differences and traits of these application types, this book will compare each patent application sub-type to a specific chess piece. By comparing chess pieces to patent applications, I'm not trying to go all John Nash in *A Beautiful Mind* on you and convince you that each application type is identical in every way to a particular chess piece. The goal is to reinforce comparisons that help keep various characteristics clear in your memory while also giving you a visual representation of how the patent game is played.

UTILITY PATENT APPLICATIONS

Utility patents are what most people think of when they hear that something is patented. They represent the vast majority of patents filed and issued—there have been approximately 10 million utility patents issued in the United States alone and the number grows every year, both in the U.S. and abroad.

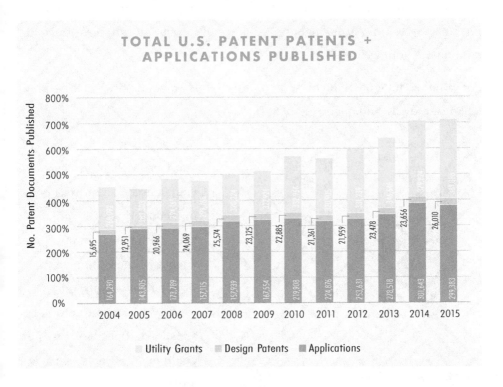

TOTAL U.S. PATENT PATENTS +
APPLICATIONS PUBLISHED

Utility Grants   Design Patents   Applications

A utility patent covers a new or improved product, process, article of manufacture, or machine. This is also known as a "patent for invention" and provides the negative right of exclusion I've discussed in prior chapters. Although ostensibly "anything under the sun made by man" can be patented, patentable subject matter is generally divided into four categories: compositions of matter, apparatuses, articles of manufacture, and methods.

These categories aren't perfectly segmented and many inventions fall into multiple categories, such as when both a device *and* a method of using or making that device are patentable. Being able to claim the same inventive concept with different claim formats gives you the opportunity to protect your innovation from different angles. In Texas Hold'em poker terms, you might evaluate your hand based upon the number of "outs" you have after the first three community cards have been shown (the "flop"), but before the last two cards are revealed (the "turn" and the "river," respectively). Your odds of winning the hand are improved if you can use a higher percentage of the community cards in combination with your current hand.

For example, imagine that your down cards — the two you're dealt at the start of a hand — are a 10 and queen of spades.

The flop is then revealed and you have a chance to evaluate your hand. You'll recognize immediately that, although you didn't make any pairs, you have the option to make *either* a flush or a straight when the next two community cards are shown. If a spade turns up, you'll make a flush, which is a great hand, and if a jack of any suit turns up, you'll make a straight, which is also a good hand. Having the flexibility to build a strong hand with either a spade or a jack of any suit gives you a better chance of winning the hand than if you needed one very specific card to win. The more outs you have, the better your odds are of winning.

In the patent game you can try to create additional "outs" by claiming your invention in different ways:

- Apparatus and article of manufacture claims
  are frequently used to protect physical products and devices.

- Method claims are typically directed to a series
  of steps that together result in a new process of some type.

- Composition claims can include chemical structures, monomers,
  polymers, drugs, and the like—situations in which a specific
  new compound has been invented.

There is generally overlap between these types, so if you can identify different approaches to claiming the same inventive concept then you can improve your chances of securing a patent with broad protection.

UNITED STATES APPLICATION TYPES

There are a number of patent applications associated with U.S. utility patents and these applications are some of the most important pieces in the patent game. To help you keep each application type clear in your mind, I'll refer to U.S. application types as the white pieces and foreign equivalent application types as the black pieces.

The Provisional Patent Application

A provisional patent application is a versatile tool used in a wide array of patent strategies. In chess terms, it's most similar to a pawn. Provisional patent applications are unique to United

States patent law and are without a true foreign equivalent. Because there is no foreign equivalent of a provisional application it can be said that there are only white pawns, and no black pawns, in the patent game.

Despite the lowly pawn's many limitations, the effective use of one or more pawns is frequently the key to victory in chess. In the patent game, effective use of one or more provisional applications can be powerful, particularly when they are used cooperatively like a pawn chain in chess. The effective use of multiple provisional applications can be seen in Chapter 16 on the Lean Patent Strategy. Though it cannot mature into an issued patent, a provisional application plays a critical strategic role in many, if not most, patent strategies. A provisional patent application is still a "real" patent application but, like the pawn in chess, it's a somewhat stripped-down game piece. These applications don't require claims to be included in the disclosure and the restrictions on what form it must take are less rigid than all other types of patent applications.

Like the pawn, provisional applications are frequently the first piece moved in the patent game. A provisional patent application is, for all intents and purposes, a *placeholder* patent application that starts the patent game by establishing your all-important priority date. But it cannot, by itself, mature into an issued patent. By filing a provisional application, you punch the chess clock to officially begin the patent game, but you'll need more powerful pieces to finish the game.

While it's true that something as basic as a PowerPoint presentation can be filed as a provisional application (see Chapters 21 and 22), many provisional applications are robust, complete disclosures of the invention that are filed strategically for a variety of reasons. For any patent application to support issued claims in a future patent it must be "enabled." This term is patent jargon for the patent applicant fully teaching how to make and use the invention in the disclosure of the patent application. You aren't permitted to omit critical disclosure and, if you don't yet have a workable solution to a problem, you should not be entitled to a patent. Provisional applications can vary dramatically in scope and how they are used tactically to achieve business objectives, but if you want the provisional application to support later filings this basic threshold of enablement must be met.

Regardless of how thorough they are, provisional applications are not substantively examined and thus require very little work by the USPTO. Because of that, this application sub-type has a relatively low associated filing fee. This should not be confused with provisional applications being an inexpensive type of application to draft and file—basic applications may be inexpensive, but more complete provisional applications may require substantial legal time to prepare. Fully teaching how to make and use a new technology, even in a provisional patent application, can take considerable time and effort.

Keep in mind why you might want to take the time and money to put together a thorough provisional application. Although there are less stringent filing requirements, you are only entitled to a priority date for what is disclosed in your application as-filed. Filing budget provisional patent applications can be useful in certain circumstances, but it's generally worth investing more in a better application that will give you more protection as you progress toward a bona fide patent.

Like a pawn, which is limited to forward movements of just one or two spaces, a provisional application has a limited range. The maximum pendency for a provisional application is 12 months from the date of filing, which is intended to give the applicant enough time to determine whether the invention is worth pursuing. If you want to continue the patent game in pursuit of an issued patent, you need to be prepared to file a subsequent non-provisional patent application, Patent Cooperation Treaty application, and/or foreign national stage application before this 12-month window closes. Each of these application sub-types are possible next moves in the patent game, and we'll discuss them in detail in the following sections. If you do not file one of these applications prior to the expiration of the 12-month deadline, your provisional application will become abandoned and its priority date will be lost forever.

Provisional applications are 100 percent confidential, which can be used to your advantage in a variety of circumstances. However, this confidentiality will not last if a subsequently filed non-provisional application, foreign national stage application, or PCT application publishes or issues. If your provisional application becomes abandoned without you completing these subsequent filings, then it can remain forever confidential. For companies with trade secrets, as discussed in Chapter 19, a provisional patent application containing proprietary information can be a valuable insurance policy if the trade secret is reverse engineered or inadvertently revealed.

Another beneficial feature of a provisional patent application is that it does not start the clock on your 20-year patent term. Provisional patent applications do establish the vital priority date for your invention, but the 20-year patent term will not begin running until your non-provisional, PCT application, or national stage applications are filed. A provisional application can effectively secure 12 months of priority without using any patent term, an extremely valuable feature if you are trying to maximize the time span of patent protection.

A provisional patent application entitles you to legally use the designation of "patent pending" for the technology covered in your application. This can be used as a deterrent and can create a positive perception for your business as it serves to notify the public and potential infringers that you are actively pursuing a patent on the technology. A patent infringement lawsuit can only be initiated after a patent has issued, but the patent pending label may make competitors think twice before copying your invention.

It's a common misconception that patent applications can't be monetized until an issued patent is secured. All patent applications — including provisional patent applications — can be licensed and sold, even while pending. Although you can't sue for infringement based upon a pending patent application, you can sell, license, or otherwise monetize a patent application long before issuance. In many cases, the patent process will take a long time. It's important to recognize that you do not need to wait until your patent issues to start monetizing your intellectual property.

The Non-Provisional Patent Application

If the provisional patent application is a pawn, then a good analog for the non-provisional patent application is a rook. Although provisional and non-provisional applications might sound quite similar, they're actually very different pieces and ones you should be careful not to get confused. Since a provisional can never mature into an issued United States patent on its own, the non-provisional patent application can step in to carry the ball forward.

Like a rook in chess, a non-provisional application is confined to a preordained set of moves. This application type permits you to claim only *one* inventive concept at a time, comparable to the linear moves of the rook on a chessboard. It's permissible and often beneficial to include multiple versions of your invention in the same application, but the USPTO will not evaluate multiple inventions claimed in a single application filing. For example, if you include claims in your application directed to a new type of golf club with claims for a jet engine, the USPTO will force you to choose one of these concepts to pursue in the present application.

A more common restriction made by the USPTO is between apparatus claims and method claims. As you'll remember, apparatus claims are generally directed to a physical invention, whereas method claims generally include a number of steps in a new process. In these cases, the applicant will be forced to initially choose one or the other of the apparatus or method claims to pursue in the non-provisional application. It may seem obvious to separate a golf club and a jet engine, and less intuitive to separate apparatus and method claims directed to the same product, but the USPTO has gotten very aggressive in making such restrictions. Fortunately, as I'll discuss in the next section, there are other pieces in the patent game that can be used to pursue unelected inventions while retaining the early priority date of the original application.

In most chess sets, the rook is a larger and more substantial piece than the pawn. This difference in size and shape helps to reinforce that the rook is a more powerful piece. Similarly, a non-provisional application is more robust, with even more content and requirements, than a provisional application. Non-provisional applications can issue as U.S. patents and are, therefore, required to contain formal drawings, at least one claim, and certain sections that are formatted in a particular manner. The filing fees for non-provisional applications are higher than for a provisional application at least partly because the USPTO will substantively review this application sub-type.

Meet the basic filing requirements and your non-provisional application will be accepted by the USPTO and you will receive an all-important filing date and serial number. You have now effectively placed your white rook on the board. Requirements like the payment of filing and examination fees can be completed after the application is filed, but these items must be completed before the non-provisional application will be examined by the USPTO. Other requirements, such as declarations from inventors affirming their inventive contribution, must be completed prior to patent issuance. It's generally prudent to have the non-provisional application as complete as possible at the time of filing, but the USPTO will still give you a filing date and serial number even if the application is deficient with respect to some non-essential items.

Although it's common to begin the patent game with a provisional patent application, it's perfectly acceptable to instead start the process with a non-provisional application. Many applicants prefer to take advantage of the benefits associated with a provisional application discussed in the prior section, but going straight to the non-provisional can be a good option if your invention is complete and you want to get the substantive patent process started as quickly as possible.

A non-provisional patent application is initially confidential, but will generally publish 18 months from the application's earliest priority date. For example, if you previously filed a provisional application, then the filing date of your provisional application will be used to calculate the timing of publication of your non-provisional. This pre-grant publication can have both positive and negative consequences. Once published, your application can be used by the USPTO to reject subsequently filed applications by your competitors. There are also provisional rights to which the applicant may be entitled if the claims of a subsequently issued patent match the as-published claims of the application. Provisional rights are rare, but can lead to enhanced damages during litigation if available.

There are some potentially negative consequences to publication. Any material in the now-published application will be publicly available, thus eliminating the option of keeping this technology a trade secret. Competitors may also use the published patent application to analyze your invention to begin plotting a workaround strategy. If continued confidentiality is important, there exist mechanisms for avoiding publication for as long as possible, as will be discussed in more detail in Chapter 19.

Continuation and Divisional Applications

The USPTO limits claims in a non-provisional application to a single inventive concept. However, it can be strategically beneficial to include many versions, features, and methods in a single non-provisional application despite the inability to claim all of those versions at the same time. There are three additional pieces in the patent game that are designed to protect these innovations: the continuation application, the divisional application, and the continuation-in-part

(CIP) application. These can be used to pursue initially unclaimed subject matter, to add new subject matter, or for other strategic purposes. Because these three application types share a lot of characteristics, we'll label them all as white bishops in our extended chess analogy. However, there are important nuances associated with each type that you should be aware of.

Although the USPTO does not want to examine more than one inventive concept in a single application, it would be unfair to force a patent applicant to choose just one invention and to forsake all others, particularly when the USPTO is aggressive in making such restrictions. If you do include multiple versions of your invention in a single application, the USPTO is happy to take your money to pursue the remaining inventive concepts in one or more spin-off patent applications. These spin-offs are non-provisional utility applications that can also mature into U.S. patents in their own right. The original non-provisional application may move forward like a white rook while these spinoff applications resemble the diagonal move set of a bishop.

As the original non-provisional is charging straight down the board toward an issued patent, these spin-off applications can be introduced on the board to cover different territory not protected by the original non-provisional application.

In chess, each side has two bishops that are restricted to moving diagonally on only one color of squares. If the first white bishop is restricted to the light squares then the second white bishop will be restricted to the dark squares of the chess board. Although both bishops have the same prescribed move set, they occupy mutually exclusive territory on the chess board. Analogously, continuation patent applications look very similar in content, but each can be used to protect a different inventive concept. If your original non-provisional application disclosed three inventive concepts — A, B, and C — you might be forced to choose just one to pursue in that first application. You could then introduce a first continuation patent application directed to B and a second continuation patent application directed to C to pursue all three of the originally disclosed concepts.

The priority date for your invention is critically important. Continuation patent applications would be far less appealing if you lost the ability to claim priority back to your original priority date. Fortunately, a continuation application effectively steps into the shoes of the first non-provisional application and is entitled to the *same* priority date.

A continuation is entitled to the priority date of the parent application — the non-provisional it is spun off from — but for this reason it's *impermissible* to add any new substantive material to this application sub-type. You can pursue anything *disclosed* in your original application, but you can't add new subject matter in a continuation application that wasn't part of the parent application. Continuation and divisional applications are like a hand in five card stud poker — you can shuffle those five cards around to make different combinations, but you can't draw any new cards. Because of this requirement, the body of most continuation applications is identical to that of the original non-provisional application, with only the claims being different. By keeping the specification and drawings the same, the applicant can be sure it isn't impermissibly adding any new substantive content.

Though chess only allows a player two bishops (at least at the start), the patent game allows you to introduce as many of these spin-off applications as you'd like. It's now very common for a large number of versions, methods, and features to be disclosed within a single non-provisional patent application, allowing for many continuation applications to pursue originally unclaimed subject matter. There are no limits to the number of spin-off applications — and subsequently issued patents — that can claim priority to a single parent application.

Divisional and continuation patent applications are nearly identical application types and, for practical purposes, I've combined them in this chapter. If you attempt to claim two or more inventive concepts in a single patent application you will, as I've discussed, be required by the USPTO to choose one of these inventions. You may be forced to cancel or withdraw claims directed to the unelected invention. A divisional patent application is a specific type of continuation application that is filed to pursue these cancelled or withdrawn claims.

Co-pendency is a concept that applies to many aspects of the patent game. Applicants are required to act—such as by filing a non-provisional application before a provisional application becomes abandoned—to maintain a chain of overlapping pendency in the application family. This is similar to the handoff in a relay race. The handoff must take place within a defined window or the runner will be disqualified and his race will end. So, too, must a non-provisional application be filed during the 12-month pendency of a provisional, and a continuation application must be filed while a non-provisional application or another application family member is still pending. Because of this co-pendency requirement, an applicant will not be permitted to file a continuation application if *all* pending family members become abandoned and/or issue as patents. Perfecting the timing of this handoff is important when building a robust patent portfolio.

Because patent applications frequently include a large number of embodiments, it can be important to maintain at least one pending application to keep open the option of filing one or more continuation applications. One frustrating scenario can arise where an applicant will file a robust application with numerous embodiments, receive a patent on just one of those embodiments, and fail to file a continuation application before the patent issues. In this circumstance, the applicant has effectively dedicated to the public any unclaimed subject matter disclosed in the originally filed patent application. It's therefore prudent, before a patent issues, to carefully review the disclosure of the application to determine if there is value in filing a continuation application. If the applicant fails to file a continuation application before the patent issues, it is forever barred from doing so. I've seen too many businesses that have left the patent equivalent of money on the table by not maximizing all available patent protection.

Continuation applications feature prominently in this book because they're a dynamic game piece that can be used effectively in a variety of different circumstances. Continuation applications can be used to attack infringers, to pursue claims of different scope, to patent technology from different angles, and to tailor claims to the needs of an acquiring company.

The Continuation-in-Part (CIP) Application

It frequently happens during the patent game that an inventor will develop a new feature, version, or use of a technology *after* the non-provisional application has already been filed. Continuation and divisional patent applications can be used to pursue disclosed but unclaimed subject matter, but these application types *cannot* be used to introduce improvements or anything substantively new.

A CIP application is a type of spin-off patent application that allows you to tack on newly-developed subject matter to your earlier-filed patent applications. If continuation applications are like five card stud poker, then a CIP application is more like five card draw. If you need something that's not currently in your hand, even after you've filed your non-provisional application, you still have the opportunity to add some cards from the deck. You get the equivalent of a draw pile from which to get new cards if you don't like the hand you're currently playing. There are, however, a number of strings attached to this proverbial draw pile.

A significant drawback to a CIP application is that any newly added material — subject matter invented and disclosed *after* the original filing date of the parent application — is *not* going to receive the earlier priority date of your parent application. We can't pretend that those newly added cards in your hand have always been there. That new material gets its own priority date when the CIP is filed, which could be months or years after the priority date of the original parent application. If you need to pull cards from the draw pile, then those new cards will be dated from the time you drew them.

But there's more. A CIP application's patent term is truncated to match that of your parent application. If the parent patent application had a patent term of 20 years from filing and the CIP application is filed three years later, then *both* the CIP application and the parent application will expire on the same date 17 years hence. Each child application, whether it is a continuation, divisional, or CIP, is tied to the parent with respect to patent term and expiration. A CIP application doesn't extend the 20-year patent term even if you are adding new subject matter. This double whammy of later priority date and truncated patent term might mean it's better to restart the process by submitting the subject matter in a new provisional or non-provisional application.

So why consider a CIP application? One potential benefit is versatility. Although your hand might have a combination of older cards and newer cards — some you were dealt initially and some you took from the draw pile — it might still be better to have more cards than fewer, particularly if your first hand was terrible.

Patents issuing from CIP applications can have claims that are each entitled to a different priority date within the same patent. Some of the issued claims may be entitled to the earliest priority date — these would be like the cards you were originally dealt. Others, directed to newly-added subject matter, may only be entitled to the priority of the CIP filing date. It can be very difficult for the other players in the patent game to know exactly when you drew the new cards and added the new information. You aren't required to tell the USPTO precisely when the subject matter in your application was first introduced, so under certain circumstances, you can use this lack of clarity to your advantage. CIP applications can be used strategically to obfuscate the priority dates for specific inventions contained within the same application. There are no limits to the number of CIP applications that can be filed, which is like having the unlimited ability to take cards from the draw pile. Although taking those additional cards has a cost, there are benefits to doing so that can make it worthwhile.

FOREIGN AND PATENT COOPERATION TREATY (PCT) APPLICATIONS

As stated earlier, there is no such thing as a worldwide patent and a patent must be procured in every country in which you want protection. The costs of international prosecution and patenting can add up quickly. This cost can be justified, however, if you are seeking protection in countries that are sales centers, manufacturing centers, or anywhere else you can otherwise benefit from a monopoly. Just like the game Risk, not all territories have equal value, are worth protecting, or are worth the cost of valuable resources.

Unlike a board game that has clearly defined territories of value, it can be difficult in the real-world patent game to know which countries or regions to pursue. It may be unclear where your invention will have commercial appeal, where knockoff products might originate from, and where you'll be able to enforce patents against infringers. Making these decisions can be particularly challenging if you are playing the patent game for the first time. It can be advantageous, therefore, to delay the deadline for making decisions regarding foreign applications for as long as possible. Fortunately, there are a number of different foreign application sub-types that can add flexibility to your decision-making process. You will recall, using our chess analogy, that the white pieces on the board are representative of U.S. patent application types. Now that we've discussed each of the U.S. application types, I'll move on to the different foreign application types, the black pieces.

Direct/Regional/National Stage Foreign Applications

One option in the international game is to file a patent application directly with a specific country's patent office. These national stage patent applications—

much like a non-provisional application in the United States — are substantively examined and can mature into an issued foreign patent. Almost every country in the world has its own patent office. The system, requirements, and terms of patents and applications in most of these jurisdictions share many similarities to U.S. non-provisional applications, though the finer points of the law may vary. As such, the black rook is representative of foreign national stage patent applications. The white rooks and black rooks have a very similar move set and are both powerful pieces that can mature into issued patents.

There are enough differences on a country-by-country basis that you'll need to consult with a patent attorney with expertise in each specific region. He or she will have a network of foreign associates to help navigate the rules and requirements in this sophisticated and multidimensional version of the patent game. Playing the U.S. patent game without a coach is challenging, but attempting to play the international patent game without professional help should be avoided entirely.

One consistent feature across most countries is that if you filed a domestic patent application — like a U.S. provisional patent application — in your home country, you can use that as a priority document for a subsequent national stage filing in another country. Most countries allow up to one year from the date of your domestic filing to complete one or more international filings. Doing so permits your international application to benefit from your earlier domestic application's filing date. For example, if a resident of the United States files a U.S. provisional application on January 1, 2018, a national stage application can be filed in most foreign countries on or before January 1, 2019, and that subsequent foreign application will be entitled to the filing date of the U.S. provisional application. This means filing a domestic patent application preserves your ability to pursue foreign patent rights for 12 months without requiring you to take any other action. This is extremely beneficial because that period can be used to evaluate the viability of your invention, determine if foreign patent filings are justified, or to raise additional capital. If you were required to file in *every* country from the outset, the cost and logistics would make international patenting inaccessible to most.

Most applicants interested in filing foreign national stage patent applications have already filed a domestic application in a home country, but this is not required. Residents of less-developed countries, for example, may see little benefit in securing a patent monopoly in their home country. If you live on Baltic Avenue, you might choose to skip purchasing that property and save your money for Boardwalk. Foreign applicants can first-file in a preferred country of which they are not a resident, but it's important to check the regulations of your home country before doing so. Certain countries, including the United States, require its citizens to receive permission from the government (which is called a foreign filing license in the U.S.) before filing a foreign patent application directly.

Once filed, your foreign national stage patent applications will be examined separately by the respective patent offices for each country in which your applications were filed.

Some countries have an equivalent of a U.S. continuation or divisional application—a black bishop—that allows you to spin off multiple patent applications from a first-filed patent application in that country. Check with your patent attorney to see what options may be available for additional protection in countries of interest. It's important to note the preparation of foreign national stage patent applications often takes considerable time. Give yourself and your attorney sufficient time to prepare if you're interested in national stage

applications so you don't inadvertently miss a key deadline. Playing speed chess can lead to mistakes and trying to play blitz chess against 10 opponents at the same time significantly raises the chances of making a blunder.

Direct national stage filings in specific countries can make strategic sense if you only plan to pursue patent protection in a limited number of foreign countries and you know exactly which countries are valuable. Direct national stage filings may be your only option in some regions, such as those which don't participate in the Patent Cooperation Treaty. Therefore, it's smart to create a list of target countries early in the process. Make a tentative list before starting the patent game, share this list with your patent attorney, and work together to determine if and when direct national stage filings should be pursued.

The Patent Cooperation Treaty (PCT) Application

At the beginning of the patent game it can be difficult to predict which countries and regions will drive the most value for your business. The high cost to pursue individual patents in multiple individual countries further exacerbates this problem, since choosing the wrong territories can waste a lot of time and money. Fortunately, there is a powerful patent game piece in the form of the Patent Co-operation Treaty (PCT) application, which can help buy you some much-needed time. The PCT application is so versatile, valuable, and essential to foreign protection strategies that it's earned the title of the black queen.

The PCT application is a commonly used option to facilitate foreign national stage applications, but on a *delayed* basis. The patent game includes a lot of different timers and the one-year deadline to file internationally can be particularly constraining, so opting to file a PCT application can buy you precious time to make expensive international filing decisions.

For many inventors and companies, the 12-month foreign filing deadline from the domestic filing date is not enough time to ascertain which countries have value, to develop a complete international filing strategy, and to complete national stage patent applications. Early in the process, you may be unclear as to whether international patents have any value. If your business is in the fundraising process, 12 months from your first domestic patent application filing may not be enough time to raise sufficient cash to pay for the considerable fees and costs associated with international patent filings. The Patent Cooperation Treaty, which includes approximately 150 jurisdictions (new countries are regularly added), gives you more time to consider your options. And, like the queen in chess, the moves available to you via the PCT application are numerous and formidable.

Although the queen is a very powerful piece, it's not the objective of the game. The objective of chess is to capture your opponent's king, and the queen can greatly help with that process, but the queen by itself is a means to an end. A PCT application itself can never mature into a patent. The PCT application can help you win the patent game, but you'll need to use this powerful piece in combination with other pieces to secure a monopoly and capture a U.S. or foreign patent—the white and black kings, respectively.

What makes this piece so powerful? Before the expiration of the 12-month foreign filing period, getting a PCT application on the board buys you another year and a half to decide whether to file in any or all of the approximately 150 PCT-participating jurisdictions. Your PCT application preserves your right to file in these countries for a total of *30 months* from your earliest filing date. If your first filed application was a U.S. provisional patent application and you file a PCT application 6 months after filing your provisional application, you will have another two years before you need to select one or more foreign countries in which to pursue protection. It's worth noting that in some jurisdictions—such as Europe (31 months) and China (32 months)—a PCT application gives you even more time beyond the base 30-month deadline. If you want to space apart national stage filings for financial or strategic reasons, you can read more about that approach in Chapter 30.

A PCT application is pricey, but it's nothing compared to the filing, translation, and legal fees associated with direct national stage applications. PCT application costs vary depending on a number of factors such as the searching authority you choose, your entity status (micro, small, or large), and the length of your patent application (fees are paid on a per-page basis). It's not uncommon for the filing fee for a PCT application to range from $2,500 to $5,000. This isn't insignificant, particularly for independent inventors or smaller companies, but each foreign national stage application filing can range from $1,500-$8,000 just to get the application filed. The added time to contemplate which foreign countries to choose, and to defer the associated filings costs, often justifies the fee for the PCT as a foreign placeholder application.

A PCT application is not a worldwide patent – again, there is no such thing. A PCT application is better described as a multinational placeholder since the PCT application itself can never mature into a patent. If you decide not to file national stage applications in specific countries that claim priority to the PCT, then your PCT application will simply become abandoned just like a U.S. provisional application. Although a PCT application is most commonly filed within a year of a domestic priority application, you can make your black queen the first piece you place on the board by leading with a PCT application.

In addition to serving as a foreign placeholder, your PCT application filing is entitled to an International Search Report (ISR) and Written Opinion (WO) regarding patentability. The PCT application fee includes the cost to prepare this report and, although not officially binding on most of your subsequent national stage filings, this report can help you identify potential issues impacting patentability. The rationale behind the ISR/WO is that many less developed countries don't have the resources to conduct their own comprehensive patent searches or justify a robust patent examination corps. Patent examiners from these jurisdictions will use the ISR/WO from your PCT application to help them more efficiently make a determination regarding patentability. If you happen to get a favorable review in your ISR/WO turn to Chapter 13 on how you might further expedite the patent process using the Patent Prosecution Highway.

The patent game is more global than ever and it's becoming increasingly rare to find inventors and companies interested only in domestic patent rights. Early stage companies may want to preserve the opportunity to file in foreign countries because an acquiring company, licensee, or partner may want these rights. Even for large companies, the ability to defer a decision on which countries to pursue can be very attractive. If you are unsure as to whether your innovation is valuable enough to justify the cost of foreign patent applications, or it is unclear where the key sales or manufacturing markets are located so early in the process, filing a PCT application can be a cost-effective stalling tactic and test of foreign patentability. Understanding the moves of the black queen in the patent game can be a key to victory.

DESIGN PATENT APPLICATIONS

Design patents are still patents, per se, but this application type is very different from the utility patent applications discussed in the prior sections. Design patent applications are the yin to the yang of utility patents. A utility patent is directed to *functional* devices and methods, whereas a design patent covers the *ornamental* features of a product, user interface, or the like.

Design patents are typically directed to three-dimensional objects — like the shape of a Connect 4 game — but can also be applied to various two-dimensional objects such as graphical user interface (GUI) designs.

There shouldn't be any overlap between what is claimed in a design patent and a utility patent, because if a feature is ornamental it cannot be protected with a utility patent and vice versa. Design patents *only* cover ornamental features and utility patents *only* cover functional inventions. Design patents and utility patents can be—and frequently are—found on the same article, where the ornamental features can be the subject of a design patent and the functional aspects can be covered by a utility patent. Using the Connect4® example, a novel chip release mechanism can be protected with a utility patent, whereas the ornamental shape of the Connect4® game itself can be protected with a design patent.

---

(12) **United States Design Patent**   (10) **Patent No.:**   **US D605,708 S**
Chapman et al.   (45) **Date of Patent:**   ** **Dec. 8, 2009**

---

(54) **STRATEGIC PATTERN BUILDING BOARD GAME WITH EJECTING FEATURE**

(75) Inventors: **Katharine Chapman**, Berkshire (GB); **Lee Lenkarski**, Belchertown, MA (US)

(73) Assignee: **Hasbro, Inc.**, Pawtucket, RI (US)

(**) Term: **14 Years**

(21) Appl. No.: **29/328,581**

(22) Filed: **Nov. 26, 2008**

(51) **LOC (9) Cl.** **21-01**
(52) **U.S. Cl.** **D21/337**
(58) **Field of Classification Search** D21/334–368; 273/236–288
See application file for complete search history.

(56)   **References Cited**

U.S. PATENT DOCUMENTS

3,149,842 A	9/1964	Cirrincione
3,506,267 A	4/1970	Taillie
4,381,112 A *	4/1983	Dupuy 273/239
5,154,428 A	10/1992	Woolhouse

6,533,277 B1	3/2003	Yin	
D535,703 S *	1/2007	Creech	.... D21/335
D544,548 S	6/2007	Miller	

* cited by examiner

Primary Examiner—Sandra Morris
(74) *Attorney, Agent, or Firm*—Perry Hoffman

(57)   **CLAIM**

The ornamental design for a strategic pattern building board game with ejecting feature, as shown and described.

DESCRIPTION

FIG. 1 is a perspective view of the strategic pattern building board game with ejecting feature of the instant invention;
FIG. 2 is a top plan view thereof;
FIG. 3 is a bottom plan view thereof;
FIG. 4 is a front elevational view thereof;
FIG. 5 is a rear elevational view thereof;
FIG. 6 is a right side elevational view thereof; and,
FIG. 7 is a left side elevational view thereof.

1 Claim, 5 Drawing Sheets

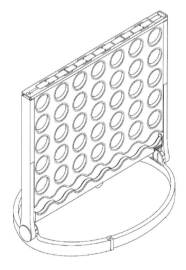

Connect 4® Design Patent by Hasbro®

Design patents have a number of other idiosyncrasies distinguishing them from utility patents. The patent number for a design patent will always start with a "D," making it easy to identify during a search. They also tend to be shorter in length than utility patents and rely heavily upon the figures depicting the inventive design. There isn't a need to discuss benefits or features as you'd commonly see in a utility patent. There aren't pre-grant publications with design patents as there are with U.S. non-provisional applications, so *every* published design application is an issued design patent. A design patent has only one claim which has a prescribed format that is markedly different from utility patents, which often have 20 or more claims with additional verbiage.

Design patents often include a drawing set with six orthogonal views (front, rear, right, left, top, and bottom) and a perspective view of the inventive design, so that the entire design is captured. The overall costs associated with a design patent application are typically less than that of a utility patent application. Additionally, design patent applications are often selected for substantive review by the USPTO more quickly than their utility counterparts. The scope of the design patent is defined by the *solid* lines shown in the drawings — solid lines are part of the claimed invention, while dashed lines are only environmental and do not limit the scope of the design patent. Generally, the fewer solid lines in your design patent, the broader it will be.

There are also some similarities between design patents and utility patents. Both are jurisdictional so, like utility patents, there is no such thing as a worldwide design patent. Both also have limited terms, but a U.S. design patent expires 15 years after issuance compared to the 20 years from filing afforded to U.S. utility patents. Design patents allow you to call the invention patented once a patent has been issued by the USPTO and patent pending prior to issuance.

As mentioned above, it's acceptable for the subject of the design patent to have some function, but the design patent cannot be directed to the functional aspects of the innovation. For an example of a product covered by both design and utility patents, we can look at a stylized video game console.

(12) **United States Design Patent**
Johnson et al.

(10) Patent No.: **US D673,620 S**
(45) Date of Patent: ** **Jan. 1, 2013**

(54) **USER INTERFACE FOR A GAMING MACHINE**

(75) Inventors: **Bradley W. Johnson**, Austin, TX (US); **Travis Bussey**, Austin, TX (US); **Juan Salazar**, Austin, TX (US); **Clint Owen**, Austin, TX (US); **Frank DeSimone**, Austin, TX (US); **Michael Kolodziej**, Austin, TX (US); **Leroy H. Gutknecht**, Las Vegas, NV (US)

(73) Assignee: **Multimedia Games, Inc.**, Austin, TX (US)

(**) Term: **14 Years**

(21) Appl. No.: **29/402,578**

(22) Filed: **Sep. 23, 2011**

(51) **LOC (9) Cl.** **21-03**
(52) **U.S. Cl.** **D21/369; D21/385**
(58) **Field of Classification Search** D21/324–329, D21/369–370, 385; 463/17, 20, 46–47
See application file for complete search history.

(56) **References Cited**

U.S. PATENT DOCUMENTS

D450,094 S	* 11/2001	Hedrick et al.	.... D21/369
D557,748 S	* 12/2007	Jumper	.... D21/333
D627,008 S	* 11/2010	Bruzzese et al.	.... D21/385

* cited by examiner

Primary Examiner — Sandra Morris
(74) Attorney, Agent, or Firm — Russell D. Culbertson; JP Cody

(57) **CLAIM**
The ornamental design for a user interface for a gaming machine, as shown.

DESCRIPTION

FIG. **1** is a left front perspective view of a gaming machine including a user interface embodying the ornamental design according to the present invention.
FIG. **2** is a right front perspective view of the gaming machine and user interface shown in FIG. 1.
FIG. **3** is a left side view of the gaming machine and user interface shown in FIG. 1.
FIG. **4** is a right side view of the gaming machine and user interface shown in FIG. 1.
FIG. **5** is a front view of the gaming machine and user interface shown in FIG. 1; and,
FIG. **6** is a top view of the gaming machine and user interface shown in FIG. 1.
A user interface for a gaming machine embodying the ornamental design disclosed herein is intended to be part of a gaming machine and to be used by a player to participate in wagering or other games at the gaming machine and to participate in other features or activities available at the gaming machine.

1 Claim, 6 Drawing Sheets

This Multimedia Games, Inc. design patent is directed to the ornamental shape of the body of a game console. This patent does not and cannot protect the operation, gameplay, electronics, or any other functional aspect of the console. If you look closely, you'll also note a portion of the body is shown in dashed lines, meaning those features are environmental only and aren't part of the claimed design.

A design patent can also be used to protect limited animation in a user interface. If you have a particular feature or an animation distinctive to your business or your product, this may be something to consider.

One example of this is U.S. Design Patent D670,713 to Apple, protecting the iBooks page-turn animation.

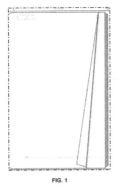

FIG. 1

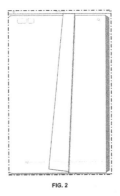

FIG. 2

Apple Design Patent — First Stage of a User Interface Design

Apple Design Patent—Second Stage of a User Interface Design

As will be discussed in Chapter 32 in the second half of this book, many different types of companies can sometimes benefit from incorporating design patents into their overall patent strategy. Although design patents can sometimes offer narrower protection than a utility patent, if the underlying design is distinctive and/or is commonly associated with your business, then this application type can have tremendous substantive value. Design patents can be a great counterpart to utility patents as infringement claims may be easier to assert and may be less susceptible to attacks on validity or enforceability. Especially when paired with utility patents, design patents can help to build a robust patent portfolio, protect innovative designs, and function as a deterrent to would-be competitors. The relatively low cost and high speed of examination and allowance for design patents can make this application type a useful option in a variety of circumstances.

CHAPTER 11:
PATENT CLAIMS: THE GAME WITHIN THE GAME

"THE GAME WITHIN THE GAME IS THE GAME THAT ONLY THE PLAYERS SEE. THEY EXPERIENCE IT IN RELATION TO ONE ANOTHER ON THE FLOOR AT A PARTICULAR TIME AND IN THE MIDDLE OF THE ACTION. IT IS ONE OF THE NUANCES OF THE GAME OF BASKETBALL."

– WALT FRAZIER

Many games, particularly video games, incorporate a game within the game. These minigames are often played by the avatar characters competing in the larger game. Some of my classmates in college nearly didn't graduate because of Nintendo's *Mario Party*®, a classic party game in which Mario and other characters compete in a series of minigames, with names like Balloon Burst and Magical Mushroom, within the game itself. Each minigame requires a particular skill set, has its own specific challenges, and must be mastered for a player to be successful in the larger game.

Patent claims are, in many respects, the minigame being played within the overarching patent game. It's impossible to win or even to fully understand the patent strategies discussed in this book without at least a basic understanding of how this minigame is played. Both utility and design patents are divided into three basic sections: The specification, the drawings, and the claims. The specification and the drawings typically make up the bulk of most patent applications, but the claims are generally the *most important* part. These legalistic haikus are often dense, but they form the basis for infringement lawsuits and truly define the patentee's monopoly. I referred earlier to patent claims as "nerd poetry," and if you've already tried to read a set of claims for a complicated invention, you'll probably agree with that description.

It's permissible — and even encouraged in many cases — to include a wide range of embodiments, features, and processes all within the same patent application. All of this content goes into the specification and drawings, which is why patent applications now more commonly have over 100 pages of material. However, for all of this robust disclosure, you have to hone in on one inventive concept that you want to pursue in each specific patent application. The USPTO has imposed the practical limitation of requiring you to further define this sought-after monopoly with one or more claims directed to a single inventive concept. Crafting and prosecuting successful claims is as much art as it is science. I'm not trying to turn you into the patent equivalent of Emily Dickinson, but you should have a basic understanding of this key element of a patent.

A patent claim is the legal instrument upon which infringement is determined. The specification and the drawings support the claims, but it's the claims which truly define your invention. A claim of a patent defines the invention's scope and, to infringe, a third party must perform or include *every* element listed in that claim. If a claim requires elements A, B, and C and a third party is able to make the apparatus or perform the method by eliminating just one of these elements, then there is no infringement. A broader claim typically has fewer elements so that it's much harder for third parties (such as your competitors) to make the apparatus or perform the method without using *all* the required elements. A narrower claim requires more elements to infringe, which can make that claim easier to design around.

Imagine a Monopoly board where the properties themselves aren't pre-defined perfect squares with set purchase prices. The game gets infinitely more complex when you have the ability to claim one of these properties and also *define* the borders of the property. Under the standard rules, you can buy Boardwalk for $400 and if someone lands within the four corners of your defined space they have to pay you a set amount of rent. Now, imagine you can secure Boardwalk and Park Place, but also craftily expand the borders of your monopoly to catch players that land on the Luxury Tax space between your two properties. The broader your monopoly, the more players you will catch, and the more rent you will collect. Conversely, poorly managed borders might mean you miss the opportunity to charge someone rent (e.g., grant them a license or sue them for infringement). It's great to have a lot of properties in the patent game, but much of your success will be based on how well you define and broaden the properties comprising your monopoly.

Using only words, a patent claim attempts to precisely define the exact boundary of your Monopoly territories and to expand this area to the greatest extent possible. Because words are inherently imperfect, and because the exact bounds of what may be patentable are often challenging to define, patent claims are considered one of the most difficult legal instruments to draft. If your patent claims are too narrow, or require more elements than were necessary to be patentable, then a competitor might not have to pay you the "rent" you might otherwise be owed. If you are too aggressive with your borders, your attempted monopoly may be rejected by the USPTO or invalidated after it has been granted. Striking the perfect balance between what is narrow enough to be patentable, but broad enough to have business value, can be like bending a soccer ball through a small window on a free kick.

Fortunately for inventors and patent practitioners, the patent systems of most countries are more of a negotiation than a pass/fail system. Many inventors assume that the determination is binary—your invention is either patentable or it is not—but the reality is much more nuanced. When filing a U.S. non-provisional patent application, the fee for up to 20 claims is included in the cost of the filing fees. You can file additional claims for an extra charge, but many applications maximize the 20 "free" claims without going over. Each of these claims is a minigame within the larger patent game. Each claim is a "shot on goal" that will often range in scope from very broad to very narrow.

The set of claims included in your first-filed patent application is, in many cases, very broad. There can be advantages to going a bit narrower, as discussed in Chapter 24, but many applicants will include as few elements as possible in the claims in an attempt to expand the borders of the monopoly as much as possible. You might be pretty sure you can secure Boardwalk and Park Place, but if you can also cover the Luxury Tax square then why not try, right? In response, a USPTO examiner will be assigned to conduct a search to identify prior art references — existing patents or publications that exactly describe your claimed invention or render your claimed invention obvious. You have a lot of shots on the goal with your 20 or so claims, but you'll have to get at least one past the metaphorical goalie, your USPTO patent examiner, to secure an issued patent. Your initial set of claims may be so broad that your USPTO examiner is easily able to deflect the shots such that nothing scores. It's very common for all your claims, on your first attempt, to be rejected.

However, just because you took a few ineffective shots it doesn't mean that you've lost the game. Don't take your ball and go home just yet. In response to the USPTO, you can tweak, add, or cancel claims. Maybe this time you'll target them a little more narrowly to avoid the goalie and the relevant prior art. You can learn a lot from those first shots, including how good your goalie is, which way he or she leans, and what areas of the goal seem the most open. If you are new to the patent game, you may be disheartened by an initial rejection, but experienced practitioners know that you're just getting warmed up.

After receiving a USPTO rejection, you have the opportunity to further refine your claims, submit new claims, and make arguments about why your examiner's conclusions were incorrect. You also have the opportunity to "huddle" with the goalie — in the form of an in-person or telephone interview with your patent examiner — to try and expedite the process. Interviews can be an invaluable tool in advancing your patent claims and coming to an understanding with your examiner about acceptable claim scope. Unlike soccer, the goalie in the patent game is happy to let you score if you are deserving of a win. In fact, the goalie might even coach you on the best approach, but you'll still need to take a great shot. Just bend it like Beckham and you'll be fine.

Your USPTO examiner can feel like the enemy, but he or she really isn't. Like many board games — especially Monopoly — no one likes to do deals with or help jerks. The minigame of negotiating patent claims requires more interpersonal skills than most people realize. In many cases, your USPTO examiner is the sole gatekeeper, the goalie between you and the goal of a patent. If you anger your USPTO examiner with arrogance, lack of preparation, or with sloppy play, it's going to be a lot easier for them to block your shots and to want to block those shots. Telling an examiner that they're an idiot or otherwise disrespecting them, even if you feel strongly they're wrong, is ill-advised. This minigame requires strong patent law skills, but also an element of emotional intelligence that's often overlooked. If your goalie knows that you are a strong player and there is mutual respect, you are likely to score more often than not.

Typically, after one or more rounds of this back-and-forth, your USPTO examiner will finally agree that you have some patentable subject matter. In the famous words — well, word — of Andres Cantor: "Goooooooaaaaaalllllll!!!" If your USPTO examiner continues to reject your patent claims and you have reached an impasse, there are procedural ways to bring in a referee (e.g., the examiner's supervisor) for additional review, but it's better to work with your assigned examiner to the greatest extent possible.

With that as background, you are ready to start kicking some balls! Or something like that. Like the broader patent game, the minigame of patent claims has its own component pieces. As mentioned, you are allotted 20 claims in a utility patent application as part of your standard filing fee, but these claims are not all of the same type. While only one claim is required in a utility patent application, most applications have more than one claim and many utilize all 20 of these allotted claims. In a utility patent application, there are two important types of claims: independent claims and dependent claims. You have a few different types of shots from which to choose in order to give yourself the best chance of scoring.

INDEPENDENT CLAIMS

Independent claims are the foundational claims of any utility patent. Claim 1 is always an independent claim and, of the allotted 20, up to *three* of these can be independent claims without requiring additional fees. An independent claim stands on its own and includes a number of elements that will define your invention. Independent claims are the broadest claim type and can be easy to spot because they do not reference any other claims. They are, fittingly, independent.

Claims are the key building blocks of patent protection, so I will use the original Lego® patent as an illustrative example. The original Lego patent, entitled TOY BUILDING BLOCK, was invented by G.K. Christiansen and received U.S. Patent 3,005,282 on October 24, 1961.The original Lego patent has seven total claims. Claim 1, the first independent claim, is reproduced on the next page.

All patent claims are numbered in sequential order starting with Claim 1 and, taken as a whole, are referred to as a claim set. This nerd poetry can be challenging to read due to a number of specific requirements by which all claims must abide. Namely, claims must be a *single* sentence (albeit a painfully run-on one) that starts with a capital letter and ends with a period. This single sentence rule is often pushed to the extreme, with many claims running on and on while using awkward punctuation. Each claim includes a preamble (in this example, "a toy building set") introducing the subject matter of the claim and sometimes the

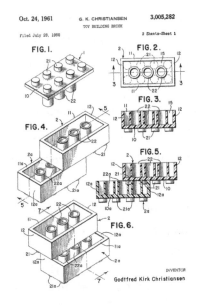

Oct. 24, 1961   G. K. CHRISTIANSEN   3,005,282

TOY BUILDING BRICK

Filed July 28, 1958   2 Sheets-Sheet 1

FIG. I.

FIG. 2.

FIG. 3.

FIG. 4.

FIG. 5.

FIG. 6.

INVENTOR

Godtfred Kirk Christiansen

1. In a toy building set, a hollow building block of rectangular parallelopiped shape comprising a bottom and four side walls, at least four cylindrical projections extending normally outwardly from said bottom and arranged in two rows of opposed projections to define a square, a tubular projection extending normally from the inner face of said bottom, and parallel to said side walls, the longitudinal axis of said tubular projection passing through the center of said square, and the peripheries of said cylindrical projections contacting said tubular projection and at least one side wall when said peripheries are geometrically projected normally to said bottom, whereby the cylindrical projections on one of said blocks may be inserted into clamping engagement with a tubular projection and a wall of another of said blocks.

type of claim (such as whether it is an apparatus, composition of matter, article of manufacture, or method). The preamble is followed by a transitional phrase using a word such as "comprising," and then the body of the claim.

The body of the claim includes the elements or required features of your invention. There are few rules about how elements must be presented or organized, leaving room for flexibility for the claims drafter. Many patent poets, if you will, have a style all their own. Importantly, every word in a patent claim has meaning, so anything that limits or defines the scope of your invention could be considered a narrowing element. If you are trying for the broadest possible claims, you should be careful to include only those elements you feel are necessary for your invention to be patentable. Adding too many elements, features, or steps can make your patent simple to design around. But, on the other hand, having too few elements can make your patent insufficiently distinct from the prior art. You need to curve your shots past the goalie, but keep them inside the boundaries of the goal.

Each listed feature or element of the Lego claim can be viewed as a requirement.

For example, Claim 1 of the Lego patent requires a "rectangular parallelepiped shape comprising a bottom and four side walls." Because *four* side walls are required by the claim, a triangular shaped building block would not infringe this Lego patent. Other required elements include "at least four cylindrical projections extending normally outwardly from … and arranged in two rows of opposed projections to define a square" and "cylindrical projections on one of said blocks may be inserted into clamping engagement with a tubular projection and a wall of another of said blocks." Claim 1 of the Lego patent is outlining shape requirements, structural requirements, and even requirements as to how individual Lego blocks fit together. To infringe, a competitor needs to include every one of these required elements in its knockoff blocks.

Because you get up to three independent claims included with your filing fees, it's common to include three independent claims and to vary the language of each independent claim to target a slightly different characterization of the overall inventive concept. Harkening back to my earlier poker analogy with respect to "outs," claiming the same innovation differently (such as with composition, process, apparatus, or article claims) can give you a better chance of winning. You are hoping at least one of these claims will be viewed by the USPTO examiner as innovative and worthy of patent protection.

DEPENDENT CLAIMS

A dependent claim, as the name suggests, depends upon an independent claim for support. Clever, right? Dependent claims are easily spotted because they *always* refer to at least one other claim, whether that's an independent claim or another dependent claim. Claim 2 of the Lego patent references Claim 1, which tells us it's a dependent claim, and adds an additional element. Specifically, Claim 2 adds a Lego block where "the inside diameter of said tubular projection is equal to the diameter of said cylindrical projections."

A dependent claim incorporates *all* of the limitations from the referenced claim (in this case, Claim 1) upon which it depends and adds at least one *additional* element or limitation. For this reason, dependent claims are *necessarily* narrower than the claim(s) upon which they depend.

> 2. A building block as set forth in claim 1, wherein the inside diameter of said tubular projection is equal to the diameter of said cylindrical projections.

It's a fair question to ask why we have both independent and dependent claims. If dependent claims are narrower, then why not just rely upon the broader independent claims? Having both types of claims serves a number of different purposes. During prosecution or negotiation with a USPTO examiner, independent claims and dependent claims form "claim trees" that move in scope from broader to narrower. Because dependent claims incorporate all of the limitations from reference claims, the format of a dependent claim saves you from having to rewrite the preceding claims in their entirety.

Dependent claims play a significant role during patent infringement proceedings. The USPTO is not infallible, and your goalie will sometimes let shots score that shouldn't have. Said differently, your patent examiner might allow claims that are overly broad and should have been rejected. Frequently, this is because the examiner was constrained by time during his or her search and did not discover a relevant publication, patent, or journal article. Although issued claims have a presumption of validity, it's possible to overcome this presumption.

When you attempt to assert an issued claim against an infringer, the infringer has a variety of mechanisms by which they can attack the supposed validity of your claims. Broader independent claims are the most vulnerable to attack by undiscovered prior art and may be invalidated during litigation or post-grant proceedings. However, every claim is independently evaluated. So, if a broader independent claim is invalidated, a narrower dependent claim may still be upheld. If a third party also infringed the narrower dependent claim, then infringement will still be found. For this reason, when asserting a patent against an infringer, it's helpful to identify both broad and narrow claims you believe have been infringed upon. In many cases, you want your goalie—the USPTO examiner—to be at the top of his or her game. You might rejoice if you score some easy goals at first, but you may realize your shots aren't nearly as good as you thought when you move up to the big leagues.

CHAPTER 12:
WHAT'S YOUR LEVEL?
(MICRO, SMALL, AND
LARGE ENTITIES)

**"GET THE FUNDAMENTALS DOWN AND THE LEVEL
OF EVERYTHING YOU DO WILL RISE."**

– MICHAEL JORDAN

Many games have some form of handicapping to allow players with different levels of experience, skill, or resources to compete on the same playing field. Marathoners have age groups, chess tournaments have Elo-based rating brackets, boxers have weight classes, and golfers have stroke handicaps. Games incorporating a handicap implicitly suggest that some players have an unfair advantage over others. A handicap evens the playing field to create more competitive games.

In the patent game, the USPTO recognizes that larger companies are better equipped to bear the expenses associated with the patent process than their smaller counterparts. For this reason, patent application fees are handicapped according to entity status. There are three categories for which an applicant can qualify – a micro, small, or large entity. The playing field is leveled by reducing the fees for smaller organizations making filings, extensions, and other associated actions. Patent offices are government-administered bodies and, not surprisingly, almost every filing, petition, and extension associated with the patent process requires payment of a fee. The USPTO is no exception – its current fee schedule can be found easily on the USPTO website. However, this three-tiered entity system and associated fee schedule can help applicants of different sizes better compete with one another.

As one may expect, large entities pay the highest fees, followed by small entities, and then micro entities. To be characterized as a large entity, a company generally needs to have more than 500 employees. Smaller companies, however, may still need to pay fees at large entity rates if the applied-for or patented technology is licensed to a company that qualifies as a large entity. Qualified small entities pay an amount reduced by 50 percent for nearly all USPTO fees and micro entities, in turn, pay only 25 percent of the large entity rates. Fee reductions based upon entity status apply to almost every USPTO fee, including application fees, Track One Prioritized Examination fees, extension of time fees, issue fees, and so on.

Micro entity status was first introduced on March 19, 2013 as part of the America Invents Act (AIA). The patent process can be cost-prohibitive for independent inventors and entrepreneurs, so this new status category was created to make patent-related government fees more palatable. If you qualify as a micro entity, the associated discount might open up patent strategies that otherwise would be impractical. A qualified micro entity must check four boxes: First, it has to qualify as a USPTO-defined small entity, which I will discuss in more detail shortly. Second, inventors cannot be named on more than four previously filed non-provisional applications or patents. Third, inventors cannot have a gross income *more* than three times the national median household income (this total is presently around $150,000). Last, an inventor cannot be under an obligation to assign, grant, or convey a license or other ownership interest to another entity that does not meet the same income requirements as the inventor.

Financially, you can qualify for micro entity status if your gross income was below the threshold for the prior year (obviously subject to change as median incomes change). This gross income calculation is not the total for an entire household, but is instead calculated for the *individual* inventor's income—a married inventor would not take a spouse's income into account when making this calculation. The income calculation also does not refer to revenue from your business if it's not accruing to you as taxable income. The income requirement is directly tied into what the inventors, individually, earned as income in the prior year. For example, three inventors on a patent application that each made $100,000 in the prior year—and otherwise qualify—would be eligible to pay micro entity rates, even though the cumulative amount exceeds $150,000.

Let's illustrate this with another Monopoly example. The reduced fees for micro entity status are like having the ability to buy properties on the board at a 75 percent discount if you are a new player. Similarly, if you are struggling financially, but still want to play the game, this discount might help you secure territory you otherwise couldn't afford. Remember, though, that all four requirements must be met to qualify for micro status. If someone in Monopoly was buying up reduced-priced properties at a fast clip to the detriment of other players, at some point, continuing to give that player a discount would seem unfair. As for the patent game, you can no longer take advantage of micro entity rates for any new patent applications once you have five or more non-provisional patent applications or patents. The USPTO is *not* going to count inventions you developed for an employer against this number, so prolific inventors who are obligated to assign their work to their employer might still qualify for micro entity rates for independently developed inventions.

Those unable to take advantage of micro entity status may still qualify for the 50 percent discount afforded a small entity. The small entity discount applies to any small business concern—any company that has no more than 500 employees, as defined under Section 3 of the Small Business Act—as well as to an independent inventor or nonprofit organization. Universities qualify as small entities, regardless of size. As above with micro entities, a small business concern can lose its small entity status if it has assigned, granted, conveyed, licensed, or is under an obligation to assign, grant, convey, or license any rights in the invention to any person or entity that would *not* qualify for small entity status itself.

CHAPTER 13:
POWER UP CARDS: EXPEDITED PATENT TOOLS

"POWER AND SPEED BE HANDS AND FEET."

– RALPH WALDO EMERSON

From PacMan® pellets to Super Mario® mushrooms, many games include some type of "power up" that can help you, the hero, achieve your objectives more easily. Sometimes these power ups are found in the wild and, other times, you need to expend resources to purchase one. Games will also impose limitations on when power ups can be used and there may be ideal times in which to use a power up to achieve maximum benefit. The patent game has its own power ups and, in many cases, these are related to speeding up the game.

 The patent process can be quite slow and it's not uncommon for three or more years to pass from when you first file a patent application to when a patent is issued. Because of the current USPTO backlog, it can sometimes take years before a newly filed application is substantively reviewed. You may like that the patent process tends to be slow — and there are strategies in Chapters 28, 29, and 30 that can help the process move even slower — but many applicants would like to get their applications examined and granted as quickly as possible. This is particularly true when an invention has a short shelf life, where competitors are infringing, or where an issued patent is critical to the valuation of the business. In these cases, you need a power up and the strategies incorporating these power ups can be found in Chapters 18, 25, 26, and 27.

In response to pressure from patent applicants, the USPTO has developed a number of mechanisms that can be leveraged to advance prosecution of a patent application ahead of the other applications in line. It's like playing a Skip card in Uno® that allows you to jump ahead of the other players. Some of these power ups are free of charge, but require you to meet specific requirements, whereas others are pay-to-play. Expedited examination results in a speedier examination process for your application, meaning your patent will likely issue faster than a regularly filed application. The key power ups I'll describe include Track One Prioritized Examination (also just known as "Track One"), Accelerated Examination, and the Patent Prosecution Highway (PPH).

How effective are these power ups? Typically, applications under the Track One, Accelerated Examination, and PPH programs will receive a first Office action on the merits in less than five months and a final disposition from the USPTO within about 12 months. The benefits of expedited prosecution may be somewhat obvious, but there are a number of situations where expedited examination and acquiring a patent quickly can add tremendous value. You might want to grab that mushroom if any of these motivations apply to your situation:

- Targeting infringers, as an infringement
  lawsuit cannot be brought until a patent has issued

- Excluding or discouraging competitors under threat of an issued patent

- Improving investment prospects by making your company
  or entrepreneurial entity more attractive with an issued patent

- Improving acquisition prospects with a portfolio of issued patents

- Improving your company's valuation with a protectable monopoly

- Maximizing the value of your patent term
  by getting an issued patent as quickly as possible

- More quickly securing foreign patents

These are just a few of the reasons you should consider expedited examination. If your budget and circumstances allow, securing a patent more quickly can have significant advantages.

"TRACK ONE" PRIORITIZED EXAMINATION

In many games, some of the most valuable power ups require "payment" of some type. In *Sonic the Hedgehog*®, if you want to activate Super Sonic mode (which grants you flight, speed, and invulnerability), you'll need to have acquired all seven Chaos Emeralds and collected at least 50 gold rings. That's pricey in the context of that game's economy. While Track One Prioritized Examination will not grant you flight, it's definitely the Super Sonic mode of the patent game. And it comes at a cost. Track One is a fairly recent development and became law with the implementation of the America Invents Act. Track One designated applications are intended to receive a final disposition (hopefully a notice of allowance) within 12 months. Contrast this with non-Track One patent applications where, in many art groups, the current backlog of unexamined patent applications means your regularly-filed application will not be reviewed for years. That is one very slow hedgehog.

Track One applications have a number of specific requirements that must be met at the time of filing. A Track One application must be a utility application (this includes non-provisional applications, continuation applications, divisional applications, and CIP applications) and can include no more than four independent claims and no more than 30 total claims. Traditional non-provisional applications can include any number of claims so long as you pay an excess claims fee, but for Track One applications the maximum number is capped. Other specific requirements include an electronically filed application and the inclusion of formal drawings. If your application does not meet these requirements when you file, your application will not be accepted into the Track One program. Also, the USPTO has the option to limit the number of Track One applications it handles per year, but this program seems to be working and is a win-win for both inventors and the USPTO. I.e., you get faster patent examination and the USPTO gets more of your money.

The Track One program is a pay-to-play option anyone can take advantage of, although this approach can be cost prohibitive for some inventors and entrepreneurs. However, even for cash-strapped startups, the cost may still be justified given the associated benefits. On top of the standard filing fees for a non-provisional application, you must pay an additional fee for Track One status (approximately $4000 for large entities, $2000 for small entities, and $1000 for micro entities). But also take note that using the Track One will result in much faster USPTO Office actions, which used to be spread over years, that will now be highly compressed. This is like doing speed drills with your shots on the goal and it can be a drain on resources if you aren't prepared.

ACCELERATED EXAMINATION

Accelerated Examination or "Petition to Make Special" practice is another power up, but one more akin to Mario finding his power up mushroom rather than having to buy it. Accelerated Examination, which is discussed at length in Chapter 26, can provide many of the benefits of the Track One program, but at low or no monetary cost to the applicant. Inventors 65 years of age or older and applicants with health issues can, for free, file a petition to request his or her patent application be examined more quickly. If you think one or more of the inventors associated with your invention may qualify, be sure to consult with your patent attorney or agent to see if this no-cost option is available.

The age and health-related reasons for accelerated examination are particularly desirable because you get the benefits of expedited prosecution at no cost. There are separate accelerated examination procedures for inventions that improve the quality of the environment, contribute to the development or conservation of energy resources, help to counter terrorism, or other altruistic benefits of that ilk, but these are not commonly used, so I won't be discussing these in any level of detail. Unfortunately, accelerated examination in these other categories requires a search and the submission of a document pre-emptively distinguishing your claimed invention from the references identified in the search. The associated costs (such as those for the search and report preparation), and the potential damage to patent scope, have left categories other than age and health largely unused. Said differently, this juice is not usually worth the squeeze. If you want expedited handling, but do not qualify for the age or health-related petition to make special, consider the Track One program instead.

A Petition to Make Special for age or health-related considerations can be filed at any time during the pendency of a patent application. If an inventor did not initially qualify, but during prosecution of the application becomes eligible, he or she can still take advantage of this program. If the petition is submitted at the time of filing, the goal of the USPTO is to examine and reach a final disposition of a patent application made special within 12 months of filing.

THE PATENT PROSECUTION HIGHWAY (PPH)

The Patent Prosecution Highway or PPH was developed to expedite the review and allowance of patents between participating countries, as the name suggests. Many countries have similar patent laws and patent applicants frequently pursue multiple, similar patent claims in the countries where protection is desired. Rather than duplicate the examination process for every country, the PPH provides reciprocity between many jurisdictions once an applicant has secured allowable subject matter. Not every jurisdiction offers this reciprocity, but many of the most commonly pursued countries have adopted the PPH. An overall increase in patent applications has put pressure on governments to quickly prosecute and rid themselves of significant backlogs. The PPH is an effective tool for these overwhelmed patent offices to reduce the backlog while giving patent applicants a faster path to issuance in multiple regions.

The PPH may be available when you are granted a patent or have an indication of allowable claims in one country and you want to obtain a patent on those same claims in a different PPH-participating country. If one patent office has found your claims to be patentable, then the other countries in the PPH network will expeditiously review your application and are more likely to grant an early allowance. Referring back to our extended chess analogy, like the knight in a game of chess, the PPH is the only piece in the patent game that allows you to effectively jump from one jurisdiction to another.

Allowable subject matter in the United States can jump via the PPH — the white knight — to the foreign track in order to expedite issuance of one or more foreign applications.

Similarly, allowable subject matter in a foreign country can jump via the PPH — the black knight — to the U.S. track to expedite issuance of a U.S. patent.

In order for you to employ a knight, you *must* have an issued patent or allowable subject matter in a PPH-participating country. You can then use this allowable subject matter to jump into other countries, such as from the United States to Japan, from Australia to Mexico, or wherever the PPH is recognized.

The favorable review that triggers your ability to use the PPH can start with a specific country, such as allowable claims in a U.S. non-provisional application, but it can also originate with your PCT application. As I discussed in Chapter 10, you will receive an International Search Report and Written Opinion as part of your PCT application filing and, if this review comes back without any patentability issues, you can jump from your PCT directly into a participating country. This PCT-PPH program, like the country-to-country PPH program, can significantly speed up the patent process and improve your odds of securing an issued patent.

The PPH can result in significant cost savings while helping you quickly secure patents in a wide range of countries. The odds are good that the process will go faster and that it will result in a favorable outcome, but be aware that the PPH is not a rubber stamp—just because you have allowable subject matter in one country does *not* mean that all other countries will automatically grant you a patent. That being said, statistics associated with the PPH program are very applicant-friendly in terms of allowance rate and speed of examination. Once you jump into a PPH-participating country, examination of your application will often begin within two to three months from the grant of your PPH request. In the patent game, this is lightning fast.

The PPH, like the knight in chess, is unique in its ability to jump across lines and quickly further your objectives in the patent game. There are an ever-increasing number of countries from which you can initiate this jump and an equally growing number of places where your knight can land.

CHAPTER 14:
HITTING THE PAUSE BUTTON: DELAYING TACTICS

"SLOW PAPER IS BETTER THAN NO PAPER."

– LIL WAYNE

Almost every video game controller has a pause button. In the middle of your efforts to save a princess, you might need to run to the restroom, make some nachos, or call your mom. The amount of time that you need might vary, but the idea behind the pause button is that you have other non-game needs that require attention. Video games, in particular, typically incorporate a pause button because the mission you are on could take a very long time to complete.

The patent game, like many of these video games, can be an incredibly long process, and there are times when you may need to pause the game to take care of other business-related needs. Although the patent game can be ploddingly slow if you aren't using power ups, there may be times when it's advantageous for you to make the game go even *slower*. Fortunately, because of its immense backlog, the USPTO is willing to accommodate certain requests to delay prosecution.

LIMITED SUSPENSION AFTER A REQUEST FOR CONTINUED EXAMINATION (RCE)

After you've received a second Office action from the USPTO—which is generally a Final Office Action—you have the ability to continue negotiating with your USPTO examiner by filing a Request for Continued Examination (RCE). A Final Office Action is a bit of a misnomer because, in reality, it's not at all final. If you think you have room to work with your USPTO examiner, you have more arguments to make, or you have new amendments that might be successful, then filing an RCE will start the process with your current examiner all over again. When submitting this RCE, you can request a suspension of action by the USPTO for a period not exceeding three months without specifying a specific reason. Any request for suspension of action must be filed with the RCE, specify the period of suspension, and include the processing fee.

DEFERRAL OF EXAMINATION

Do you really need to hit the pause button for a *long* time? Like enough time to go to college, start a family, or write an entire book? If so, you can request that the USPTO grant you a deferral of examination for as much as *three years* from your earliest filing date. In addition to requisite fees, your request will only be accepted if all the following conditions are met:

- Your patent application is an original U.S. utility patent application

- You have not filed a nonpublication request

- Your application is in condition for publication

- The USPTO has not issued either an Office action or a notice of allowance.

Once your deferral of examination has been granted, your application will not be taken up for action by a USPTO examiner until the suspension period expires. If you file a request for deferral of examination for the maximum period permitted, the action by the USPTO on the application will be suspended and the application will automatically be placed in a regular new case status on the examiner's docket 36 months from the effective filing date of your application.

SUSPENSION FOR CAUSE

In limited circumstances, if you have good non-business reason why you need a pause in the patent game, then the USPTO will consider such a request. The USPTO can grant a suspension of action for good and sufficient cause, but it should be noted that the USPTO will not suspend action if you have a reply due to an outstanding Office action. Any petition for suspension of action for cause must specify a period of suspension not exceeding six months and must include both a showing of good and sufficient cause for suspension of action and the required fee, unless such cause is the fault of the USPTO. An example of what can qualify for this suspension includes the temporary, but unavoidable, unavailability of a party whose participation in the patent prosecution process is critical. Importantly, this cannot be requested for a mere business reason.

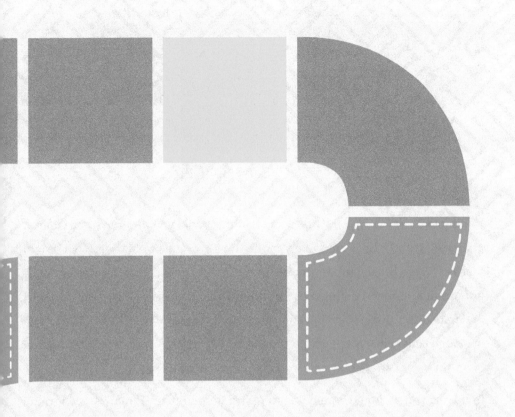

ART 2:
LAYING THE GAME

2

CHAPTER 15:
PLAYING THE GAME

"A FEW MOMENTS TO LEARN, A LIFETIME TO MASTER."

— ANCIENT PROVERB

Having made it through the first section of this book, you deserve some congratulations — your IP IQ is now likely in the top 2% of the population! That's right, Mensa level. Understanding the players, the board, and the pieces is critically important to understanding how to successfully play the patent game. By fully understanding these principals and dispelling any of the misinformation and mistaken beliefs that often plague neophyte players, you are now ready to select the right patent strategy for your innovation or business.

In this second section, we're going to play patent Plinko®. Plinko is one form of a game called pachinko that originated in Japan, a type of mechanical game that is used as both a form of recreational arcade game and, much more frequently, as a gambling device. In Japan, pachinko fills a niche similar to that of the slot machine in Western gaming.

A pachinko machine resembles a vertical pinball machine. The player loads a ball into the machine and releases a spring-loaded handle to launch the ball into a metal track. The track guides the ball around the edge of the playing field and, when the

ball loses momentum, it falls into the playing field from the top. The ball enters a field populated by a large number of brass pins and several small cups into which the player hopes the ball will fall. The ball bounces from pin to pin until, hopefully, it lands in a desirable cup or slot.

Plinko, the most popular game in the history of the *Price Is Right*, is one version of Japanese pachinko. This crowd-pleasing game requires a player to place circular Plinko chips against a large vertical board containing a number of evenly spaced pegs. Each chip makes its way down the board toward a number of spaced-apart slots representing a dollar amount. The goal of the game is to land each Plinko disc in the slots with the highest cash award. While pachinko is typically a passive game where players have no control over the path of the balls, Plinko allows contestants to drop each disc from a starting point of his or her choosing. This starting position will, hopefully, give the chip the best chance of reaching the most desirable slot. Of course, Plinko chips don't always cooperate and frequently infuriate contestants by traveling unpredictably across the entire length of the board.

When searching for a patent strategy, it's possible to use one or more decision trees to help you navigate towards an optimal solution, not unlike a Plinko board. Aside from the original starting position, the original Plinko game is completely dependent upon luck. But in our version of patent Plinko, you control the process throughout every decision point. You'll choose a starting point from which to drop your chip, with the chip representing your invention. The slots at the bottom of the board represent the strategies that might best protect your innovation and drive value for your business. Along the way, your chip will encounter decision points, which can guide your chip in one direction or another, much like the pegs in Plinko.

To begin, I'll ask you to climb the stairs of the patent Plinko board and pick an initial position from which to drop your chip. The board below you is divided into three sections, where each section corresponds to one of the resource considerations from the Project Management Triangle—scope, budget, and timing. The top of the board might look something like the drawing below.

After reading the first section of this book, hopefully you now have a better sense as to where you should start the process and which of the three considerations is most important. One of these three factors often stands above the others in terms of importance when searching for an optimized patent strategy. If there are multiple compelling considerations, such as timing and budget, then I recommend you try dropping your patent Plinko chips from multiple different points on the board to see where each lands. In Patent Plinko, you have an unlimited number of chips to drop. Just like Plinko on the Price is Right, you may be surprised how far your chip travels across the board once it has been dropped. Keep in mind that your chip can easily cross over into other sections based upon your answers to subsequent questions, but like a Plinko chip, it can be helpful to at least aim in the right general direction.

The following sections on scope, budget, and timing describe in more detail why each might be an optimal starting point. After selecting a starting position for your patent Plinko chip, you will find a decision tree in each section that will guide your chip towards one or more strategies. Of course, part of the fun of Plinko is playing the game repeatedly to see where each chip lands based upon where you start and how the chips bounce through the pegs. It's worth running multiple simulations by choosing different starting positions and by making different decisions as each chip falls. After you've run this process a number of times, you're bound to find one or two strategies that stand out. One of those might be a winner.

If you're already hooked on the patent game you are welcome to read through each strategy in this book, cover-to-cover, and doing so will certainly increase your overall IP IQ and make you ready for anything. But if it's more efficient to jump directly to the strategies optimized for your business, please feel free to treat this like a Choose Your Own Adventure book. Once your patent Plinko chip has landed on a strategy in the decision tree, you can turn directly to the corresponding chapter for an overview, a description of benefits and drawbacks, a step-by-step description, and a real-world example. And, because I love analogies, most strategies include a game-related title and comparison to make them more memorable.

As a final caveat (and, as a lawyer, it's impossible for me to write anything without at least one caveat), you should know there are, of course, *many* more strategies in the patent game than those outlined in the forthcoming pages. Claiming to have listed every strategy would be like teaching you a few chess openings and proclaiming you a grandmaster. The approaches to follow are some of the more commonly-used strategies for small to mid-sized businesses, and they are certainly applicable to businesses of all sizes, but the complexities of some patent strategies used by Fortune 50 companies are somewhat beyond the scope of this book. That being said, once you have assimilated knowledge of the board, pieces, and players in the patent game, and have navigated your way through patent Plinko, you should possess the skill, background, and confidence to adapt your play to whatever patent game you might choose to play.

It's vital to be adaptable to your environment—be aware that what began as a cost, timing, or scope-focused strategy may suddenly change based upon internal or external factors. The patent game is dynamic and it's prudent to *regularly* rerun the game of Patent Plinko to make sure that your strategy of choice is still optimal. You may need to move from a slow to a fast approach based upon market conditions. What started out as a budget-focused strategy may be sub-optimal once you've raised a round of Series A financing. If you are forced to abandon trade secret protection, then you might want to go all-in on patent protection. There is no one-size-fits-all strategy for patents and the best strategy today might not be the best approach tomorrow.

15a SCOPE OVERVIEW
AND DECISION TREE

"TOO MUCH OF A GOOD THING CAN BE WONDERFUL."

— MAE WEST

All businesses rely upon budgets and want deliverables as quickly as possible, but if these are secondary to breadth of protection or a substantive consideration, then this should be your starting position in Patent Plinko. Selecting this as a starting point does *not* mean you will skip or miss strategies that have budgetary or timing benefits, but it will start you down a path more likely to satisfy your most compelling initial needs. This can be a great starting position if you have a particularly novel innovation, you have a lot of financial resources, the field of interest lends itself to strong patent protection, the valuation of the company is tied closely to intellectual property, or the loss of intellectual property and patent rights would materially damage your business.

Scope, of course, should not be confused with the "best" or "highest quality" strategy for your business. Because scope is a somewhat abstract term, you'll find a number of specific considerations below that, if applicable, should make you lean towards this as your initial starting point. You should start your patent Plinko chip down the scope section of the board if one or more of the items below are particularly important to your business:

- Maximizing substantive domestic and international patent coverage

- Maximizing protection for a large number of versions or embodiments of your invention

- Maintaining patent claim flexibility over the life of a patent family

- Maximizing patent term

- Balancing confidentiality and trade secrets with patent rights

- Effectively capturing and patenting iterative technology developments

If one or more of these factors is the primary objective for your business or innovation, then you should proceed through the Patent Plinko board below on your way to finding an optimal solution.

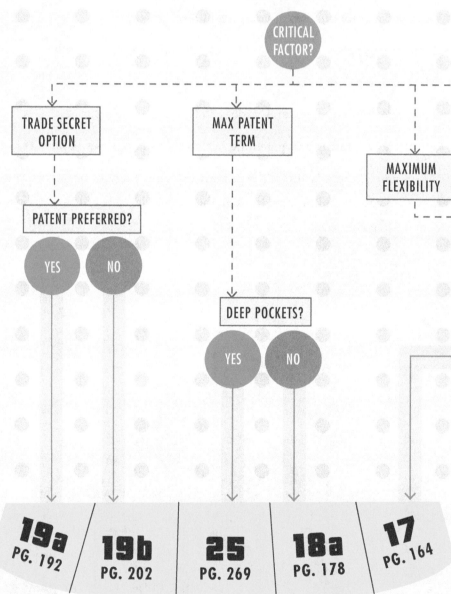

PATENT PLINKO
SCOPE

START HERE

CRITICAL FACTOR?

TRADE SECRET OPTION

MAX PATENT TERM

MAXIMUM FLEXIBILITY

PATENT PREFERRED?

YES   NO

DEEP POCKETS?

YES   NO

19a PG. 192 / **19b** PG. 202 / **25** PG. 269 / **18a** PG. 178 / **17** PG. 164

Selecting the scope section of the patent Plinko board as a starting point does not mean you will skip or miss strategies that have budgetary or timing benefits, but it will start you down a path that will ensure the final strategy satisfies your most compelling initial needs.

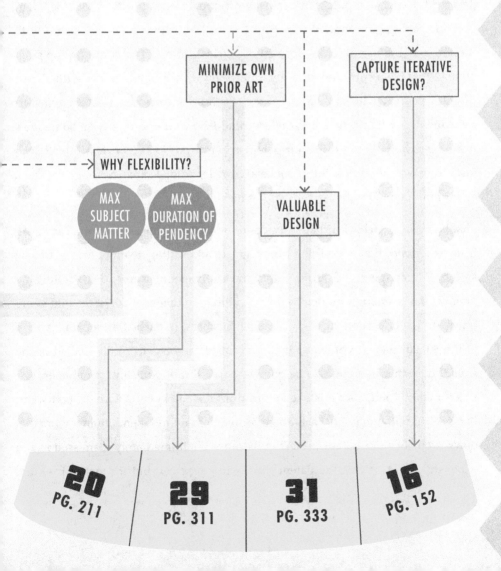

15b BUDGET OVERVIEW
AND DECISION TREE

"BEING BROKE IS A TEMPORARY SITUATION. BEING POOR IS A STATE OF MIND."

— RICHARD FRANCIS BURTON

Patents have a reputation for being a rich man's game, which is not entirely undeserved. Expensive patent attorneys with hourly rates north of $600 per hour, ever-increasing government fees, and the multiplicative costs associated with pursing patents in numerous foreign countries can be a real drain on the pocketbook. I've been cornered at many a party by would-be inventors with a "million-dollar idea" who can't stomach the fees it takes to secure a patent and start a business. If I had a nickel for every time I was offered equity in someone's business to help them write their patent applications in lieu of cash... well, let's just say I would have a lot of nickels. And by a lot I mean Scrooge McDuck swimming in an Olympic-sized pool of nickels.

That being said, I feel your pain. I've co-founded three companies and I can speak from experience that everything from legal, to accounting, to engineering, to marketing, to managing and hiring....and the list goes on, seems to cost a fortune. There is never enough money to do everything 100 percent correctly, and sometimes, difficult decisions need to be made. Startups, in particular, seem to live off of the 80/20 rule—if you can get 80 percent of the benefit for 20 percent of the spend, then that may have to be good enough. But, if you think patents are too rich for your blood, it's a mistake to throw out the patent baby with the bathwater. I've spoken with too many early stage companies and independent inventors that don't even consider patent protection because it's immediately dismissed as too expensive. It's true that the patent game can get pricey, but it's just as true that meaningful value can be secured for much less than you might think. There are trade-offs inherent in a reduced-cost approach, but if desperate times call for desperate measures, something is generally better than nothing at all.

There are varied reasons why budget might be especially constraining for a particular innovation. I've seen cost considerations equally impact Fortune 500 companies and garage inventors. The reasons may be different, and the scale might differ, but the need to squeeze as much value as you can out of an inexpensive strategy is not limited to the guys wearing tinfoil hats and living in mom's basement. For example, a groundbreaking invention may have tremendous patentable potential, but the startup that developed the technology may not want to divert resources from the prototype or miss payroll. A company with deep pockets may have a new technology development, but because the innovation has dubious patent or commercial value, there is an unwillingness to invest heavily in protection. Universities and technology transfer offices are frequently flooded with requests from professors and graduate students asking for financial resources to pursue patent protection, but often there is a limited amount of funds available for these pursuits. Budget-conscious strategies can allow for at least some protection while commercial, technical, funding, and other considerations are further explored.

Some technology fields, such as software business methods and medical diagnostics, are currently a quagmire of patent-ineligible subject matter. However, with the law in flux, there can be substantive or perception-related benefits to filing a patent application if the price is right. For "me too" companies, or companies operating in a dense technology field where securing patents is difficult, filing a cost-effective patent application solely for the deterrent value or positive perception can still have tremendous value relative to the cost.

Whatever the reason for your budget constraints, you might consider dropping your Patent Plinko chip down this section of the board if financial considerations are, at least initially, more compelling than scope or timing.

PATENT PLINKO

BUDGET

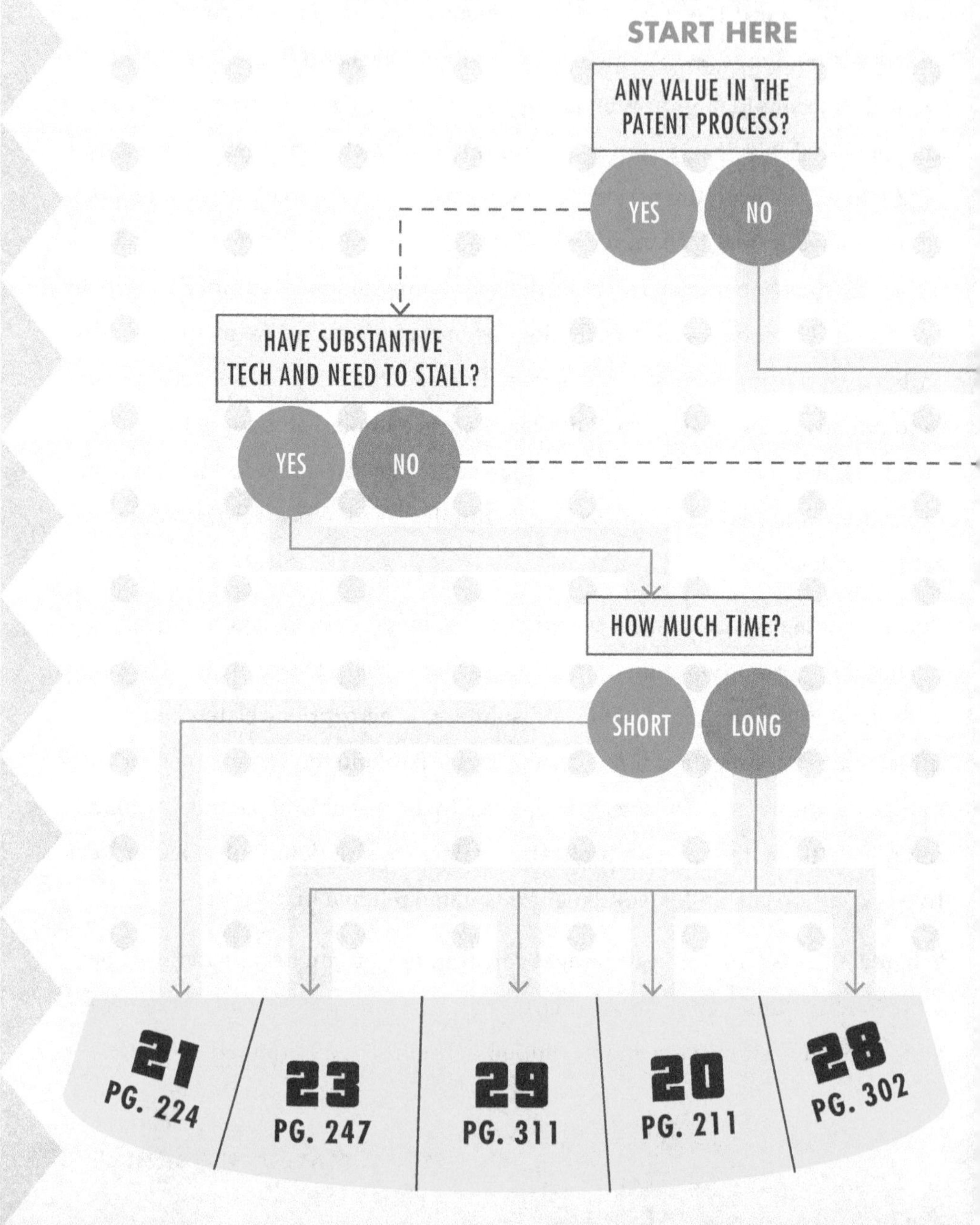

START HERE

ANY VALUE IN THE
PATENT PROCESS?

YES   NO

HAVE SUBSTANTIVE
TECH AND NEED TO STALL?

YES   NO

HOW MUCH TIME?

SHORT   LONG

21 PG. 224 / **23** PG. 247 / **29** PG. 311 / **20** PG. 211 \ **28** PG. 302

Whatever the reason for your budget constraints, you might consider dropping your patent Plinko chip down this section of the board if financial considerations are initially more compelling than scope or timing.

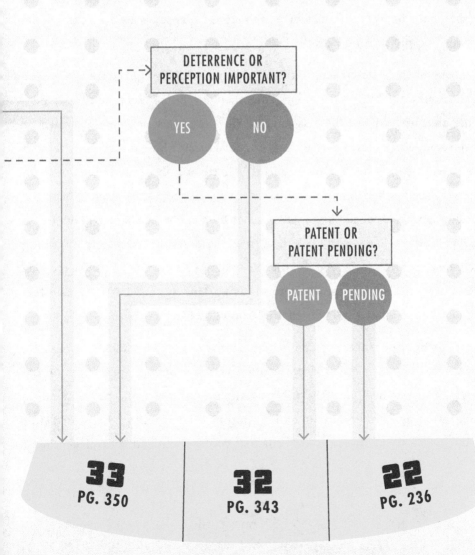

DETERRENCE OR PERCEPTION IMPORTANT?

YES   NO

PATENT OR PATENT PENDING?

PATENT   PENDING

33
PG. 350

32
PG. 343

22
PG. 236

"TIME IS AN ILLUSION. TIMING IS AN ART."

— STEFAN EMUNDS

There is someone out there making a fortune selling those tiny sand timers that are included in Boggle, Scattergories®, Catch Phrase®, and many other games we've played from childhood through adulthood. Those anxiety-inducing hourglasses make us feel as if our world is about to collapse because we can't name a school supply starting with the letter "O".

In most games, faster is better. Athletes and gamers play against a clock or race against one another. In the patent game, there are numerous time constraints — some are imposed like the classic sand-filled hourglass, others are a race between competitors, and some are a race against diminishing resources. Although the patent process has a reputation for being painfully slow — which is sometimes justified — there are now several mechanisms that can be used to expedite various aspects of the patent process. As we touched on in Chapter 13 on power ups, you might want to go really fast, or as discussed in Chapter 14 on hitting the pause button, maybe you'd rather the patent process move at a glacial pace. Either way, if a timing consideration is important to your business then this section of the Patent Plinko board might be a good starting point.

Most patent applicants want the patent process to move as quickly as possible, but the reasons for expedited prosecution vary. Getting an application on file quickly can establish an early priority date, permit use of the patent pending designation, and can be a useful tool in warding off competitors. Expedited strategies may be a good fit for your business if you've identified an infringer, investors are pressing the company to secure an issued patent, or you want to maximize your patent term. Because patent applications and issued patents can materially improve the valuation of a business, if you are raising capital or planning to sell the company, then securing these assets as quickly as possible can be beneficial.

On the other hand, there are circumstances where patent applicants want the process to move as *slowly* as possible. We've all heard the phrase "it's a marathon, not a sprint" in reference to games that require a player to conserve resources in an effort to win the long game. There are scenarios in which an optimal patent strategy moves as slowly as possible. Sometimes, the ability to outlast your competitors and to be the last one standing will lead to victory. Think of a car dealership or radio station promotion awarding a car to the person who can keep at least one hand on a vehicle for the longest period of time. Preparing in advance for the long haul — whether that includes wearing diapers or not — will give you a leg up over your competitors. Reasons for moving slowly can include a lack of sufficient short-term financial resources, concerns about the patentability of a given technology, or being in a technology field subject to patent eligibility questions. When you file your application, and you still aren't 100 percent sure which version or features of your invention will have significant commercial value, going slowly can give you time to experiment. Delaying prosecution of a patent application can conserve resources while ascertaining commercial demand and viability. The strategies in this section place more value on timing, whether expedited or delayed, than the competing factors of cost and scope.

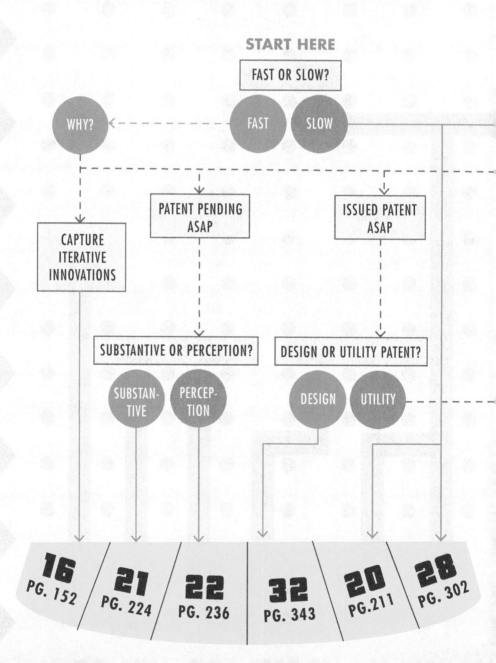

PATENT PLINKO

TIMING

START HERE

FAST OR SLOW?

WHY? ← FAST   SLOW

PATENT PENDING ASAP

ISSUED PATENT ASAP

CAPTURE ITERATIVE INNOVATIONS

SUBSTANTIVE OR PERCEPTION?

SUBSTANTIVE   PERCEPTION

DESIGN OR UTILITY PATENT?

DESIGN   UTILITY

16 PG. 152 / **21** PG. 224 / **22** PG. 236 / **32** PG. 343 / **20** PG.211 / **28** PG. 302

The strategies in this section place more value on timing, whether expedited or delayed, over the factors of cost and scope.

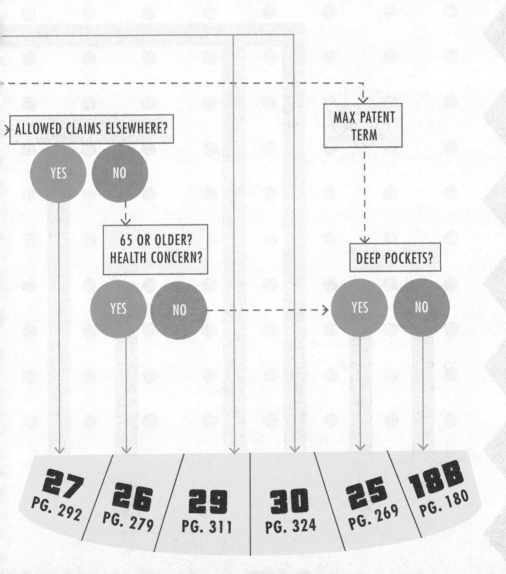

ALLOWED CLAIMS ELSEWHERE?
YES   NO

65 OR OLDER?
HEALTH CONCERN?
YES   NO

MAX PATENT TERM

DEEP POCKETS?
YES   NO

27 PG. 292
26 PG. 279
29 PG. 311
30 PG. 324
25 PG. 269
188 PG. 180

CHAPTER 16

THE LEAN PATENT STRATEGY—ITERATIVE PROTECTION FOR DEVELOPING TECHNOLOGY

"THE LESSON OF THE MVP IS THAT ANY ADDITIONAL WORK BEYOND WHAT WAS REQUIRED TO START LEARNING IS WASTE, NO MATTER HOW IMPORTANT IT MIGHT HAVE SEEMED AT THE TIME."

— ERIC RIES, *THE LEAN STARTUP*

Why this strategy might be for you...

- You are a Lean Startup believer

- You need to plant the flag on a workable invention

- Your invention works, but it's not nearly finished

- You anticipate learning a lot as you iterate over the next few years

- Being patent pending could help you

- You want to disclose your invention to investors or customers

A business strategy and book created by Eric Ries called *The Lean Startup*, seen as the new mantra for many early stage businesses, provides a scientific approach for developing products with strong product-market fit. This model encourages companies and, particularly, startups to create a minimum viable product (MVP) and then iterate technology development in sync with customer feedback. At its core, this model recognizes the inherent risks in trying to guess what your customer wants while maximizing flexibility and minimizing the resource and time costs associated with failed assumptions. The goal is to achieve a strong product-market fit as quickly as possible with little concern for anything that doesn't inform or improve the prospect of achieving that objective.

The Lean Startup methodology was groundbreaking, in part, because up to that point many companies would spend massive resources and lots of money in an attempt to make a product perfect before introducing it to the market. Not surprisingly, this approach frequently led to sub-optimal results or outright failure. Companies using this approach were more likely to see product launches as a binary success or failure result rather than as a valuable learning experience. Lacking any "dry powder" in the form of capital or other resources once a failure did inevitably happen, these companies were unable to effectively learn from mistakes, improve upon the technology, and try again. Failed project launches of this nature can be one and done.

Many of these same issues negatively impact the ability to develop an optimized patent portfolio. Businesses often unnecessarily postpone intellectual property protection because inventors or business leaders want the technology to be perfect before starting the patent process. Sometimes highly focused patent applications are filed on one specific version of the technology that later prove to have no commercial value. In many cases, a workable invention was developed long before the commercial embodiment was finalized, but the filing is postponed until the decision makers believe the project to be done and the innovation perfect. In a first-to-file patent system, this delay can mean that competitors beat your all-important filing date by years, months, or even days. Filing a first application quickly to establish an early filing date, followed by subsequent applications that reflect new versions and improvements to your innovation, can capture the earliest possible filing dates without you having to guess which features or embodiments will be the most valuable.

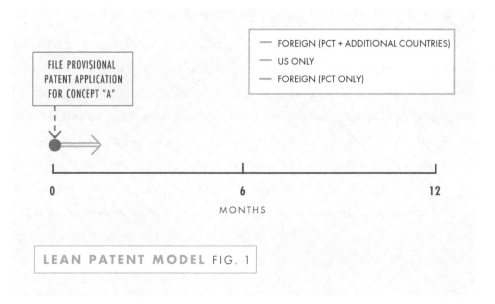

FILE PROVISIONAL
PATENT APPLICATION
FOR CONCEPT "A"

— FOREIGN (PCT + ADDITIONAL COUNTRIES)
— US ONLY
— FOREIGN (PCT ONLY)

0   6   12

MONTHS

LEAN PATENT MODEL FIG. 1

The Lean Patent strategy opens with the filing of a provisional patent application. In keeping with the theme, we'll refer to this as the minimum viable provisional, or MVP, application.

The objective of this first application is to quickly and efficiently establish an early priority date for an invention even if the innovation is not yet optimized. Much like the Minimum Viable Product introduced by Erie Ries in *The Lean Startup*, the Minimum Viable Provisional should be filed as soon as an initial workable solution to a problem has been identified.

Provisional patent applications can run the gamut in terms of quality and some are filed more for perception than substantive protection (such as those described in Chapter 22), but it's important to remember that enough time should be taken to prepare the MVP application such that it teaches and supports at least one *workable* solution for the invention.

Like any provisional patent application, your MVP has a 12-month pendency during which a non-provisional application, foreign national stage application, or PCT application should be filed. Any provisional application is 100 percent confidential, so you have the option to let it become abandoned such that it never sees the light of day if you are worried that an early filing could later become an embarrassment. It's better to have the *option* to claim priority to an early application than to be in a position where you wish you had a chance of securing an earlier priority date.

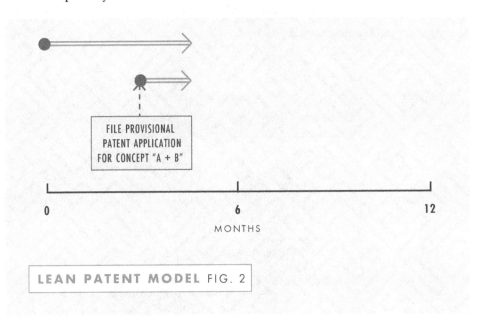

LEAN PATENT MODEL FIG. 2

Once the MVP application has been filed, you should get back to developing and testing the technology. As new solutions, features, applications, or methods are developed, as shown in Figure 2, consider preparing and filing a *second* provisional application directed to these iterative improvements. This second provisional—which may be filed months, weeks, or just days after your MVP application—can build upon the disclosure of the MVP application by adding this new subject matter. For the new features or applications, you will be entitled to the priority date set at the filing of the second provisional application. Because newly introduced subject matter is not entitled to the earlier-filed MVP application, you'll want to get this second provisional application on file as quickly as possible.

As shown in Figure 3, you can continue to file additional provisional applications — each building upon the previous — as you iterate the technology, develop improvements, and optimize your invention.

Continually building upon the MVP with other provisional applications will ensure that each improvement is captured as it is developed such that it receives the earliest possible priority date.

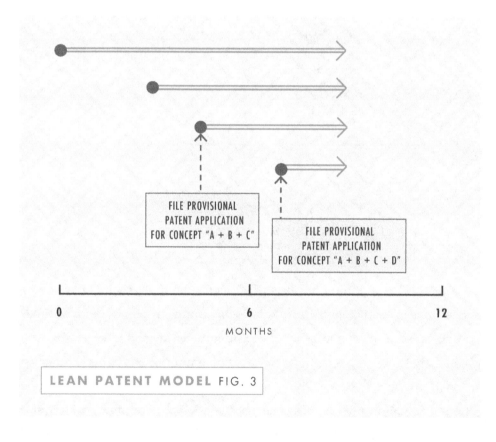

FILE PROVISIONAL
PATENT APPLICATION
FOR CONCEPT "A + B + C"

FILE PROVISIONAL
PATENT APPLICATION
FOR CONCEPT "A + B + C + D"

0   6   12

MONTHS

LEAN PATENT MODEL FIG. 3

Remember that a U.S. non-provisional application must be filed within 12 months of the MVP's filing if priority to that first application is still desirable.

This strategy does *not* wait the entire 12-month available term from the MVP application to file another application. Although it's permissible to add material at the time of the non-provisional filing, you may lose valuable months of priority if you wait that long. If your MVP application proved to be too anemic or off course in light of further testing and development, you could choose to allow the MVP application to become confidentially abandoned and, instead, calculate the 12-month period for filing a non-provisional application or PCT application from your second provisional application filing. You can see in Figure 3 what it looks like when you file multiple provisional applications to include new iterations. Any number of provisional applications can be filed within the 12-month period from the MVP application, as we'll see in the real-world example at the end of this chapter.

Here's the kicker — if the MVP is still viable and you've successfully captured all pertinent developments in the subsequent provisionals, a U.S. non-provisional can claim priority to *all* of the preceding provisional applications. As shown in Figure 4, it is perfectly acceptable to claim priority to *multiple* provisional applications in a single, subsequently filed non-provisional application as illustrated above. Just make sure that if you want to claim priority to the MVP application and the subsequent provisional filings in the same non-provisional application, your non-provisional application must be filed within 12 months of the *MVP application* filing date. Although each subsequently filed provisional technically gets its own 12-month period of pendency, the earliest filing date will control if you want to bundle your provisional applications as described and shown above.

If you continue to iterate and improve your technology during preparation of the non-provisional application, it's perfectly acceptable to add new subject matter to that application that was not included in your prior provisional applications. It's yet another opportunity to capture iterative developments. Like the provisional applications, new subject matter in the non-provisional application will only be entitled to the priority date of the non-provisional application when it was first introduced.

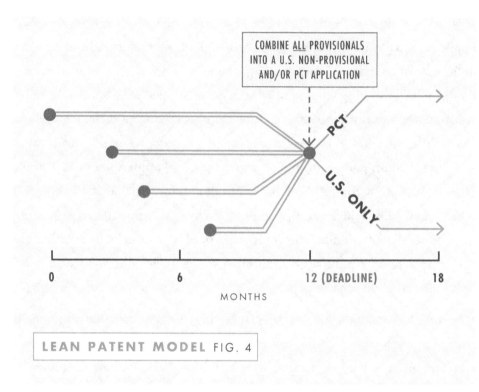

COMBINE <u>ALL</u> PROVISIONALS INTO A U.S. NON-PROVISIONAL AND/OR PCT APPLICATION

PCT

U.S. ONLY

| 0 | 6 | 12 (DEADLINE) | 18 |

MONTHS

LEAN PATENT MODEL FIG. 4

Your non-provisional application, with the bundled disclosure of one or more prior-filed provisional applications, can eventually mature into a U.S. patent. Each of the claims of the patent might be entitled to the MVP application or to one of the subsequently filed provisional applications. If the patent has multiple claims, it's possible for these claims to have *different* priority dates based on when the subject matter was first introduced. The claims of the issued patent will be entitled to the priority date of the application in which *all* of the subject matter of that claim was first disclosed.

It may be useful in some circumstances to file spinoff applications — such as continuation or divisional applications — to pursue subject matter not covered by the claims of the first non-provisional application. Using the Lean Patent approach results in a many-to-one relationship between a number of provisional applications and a single non-provisional application. Once the non-provisional application has been filed, you can use a one-to-many approach to spin off multiple applications, and eventually patents, from a single non-provisional application filing.

Of course, iterative development likely won't stop after 12 months from your initial provisional application filing. What happens when you develop improvements after your non-provisional application has been filed? As shown in Figure 5, you can't use a continuation or divisional application to introduce new subject matter, but you can utilize a Continuation-in-Part (CIP) application, as discussed in Chapter 10, to *further* build off the disclosure of the non-provisional application as shown above.

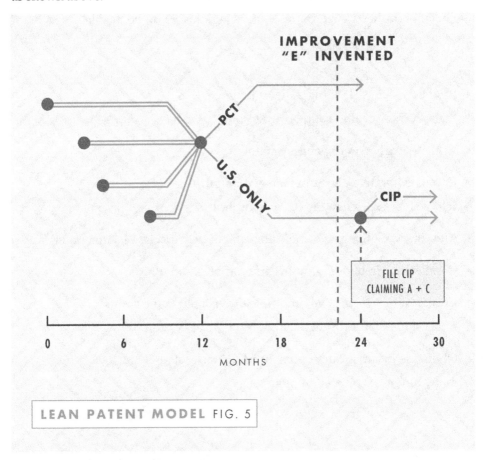

LEAN PATENT MODEL FIG. 5

The Lean Patent strategy can apply to protecting your innovations in foreign countries as well. You'll still have to abide by the 12-month deadline from your earliest patent application filing to pursue foreign patent protection, but if you choose to file a PCT application, you can consolidate any prior filed provisional applications in much the same way you can with a U.S. non-provisional.

Unfortunately, there is no easy way to append new technology developments to a PCT application in the same way it is possible to do so with a CIP application. At the 12-month foreign filing deadline you can, of course, also file directly in specific foreign jurisdictions of interest. Some countries have mechanisms by which you can continue to add subject matter, but you will need to check with you patent attorney to determine if and when this might be doable.

BENEFITS OF THE LEAN PATENT STRATEGY

- Establishes an early filing date for the invention that can be critical in competitive technology fields

- Achieves early patent pending status

- Captures iterative developments with multiple, relatively inexpensive provisional applications

- After the MVP filing, the applicant can publicly disclose its invention

- Cost savings in building upon earlier application filings

- Cost savings in combining multiple provisional applications into a single non-provisional and/or PCT application

- Obfuscate priority dates of newly added technology with many different application filing dates

DRAWBACKS TO THE LEAN PATENT STRATEGY

- Fully-formed inventions, such as inventions for chemical compositions, may not be a good fit for this approach

- Lean does not necessarily equate to inexpensive — iterative application filings can add to the overall cost

- Preparing a fully-enabled MVP application can be costly as this should not be confused with a basic provisional application used primarily for perception and deterrence reasons

REAL WORLD EXAMPLE: SELF-DRIVING SHOPPING CARTS BY WALMART INC.

There are no limits to the number of provisional applications an applicant can file to capture the iterative development process. Although perhaps not well-known for its intellectual property, Walmart Inc. has been developing a patent portfolio around self-driving shopping carts.

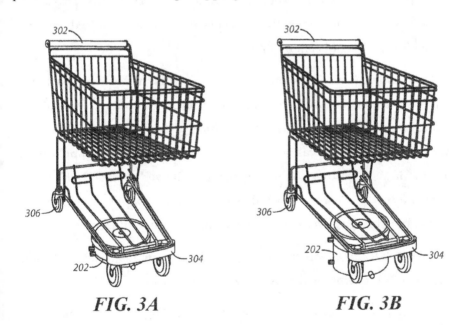

FIG. 3A   *FIG. 3B*

Its first provisional application (U.S. App. No. 62/129,726) — the MVP application — was filed on March 6, 2015 and, during the 12-month pendency of this first application, Walmart filed another 36 provisional patent applications!

Just before the end of the 12-month term of the MVP provisional, a non-provisional patent application (U.S. App. No. 15/061,980) was filed by Walmart claiming priority to all 36 subsequent filings in a *single* application. The initial provisional application was fairly robust, with 26 pages of written description and five accompanying drawings. But Walmart added more and more to each subsequently filed provisional application and by the time Walmart filed its non-provisional application almost one year later, the application had almost doubled in size. The non-provisional application included 45 pages of description and 10 accompanying drawings directed to the same general autonomous shopping cart concept. In addition to the new disclosure, Walmart's non-provisional filing included the exact same first five drawings as the first provisional application, meaning those inventive concepts are likely entitled to the priority date of the first MVP application filing.

But Walmart didn't draft a new provisional application from scratch each time an iterative improvement was made. Its patent attorneys used the foundational provisional application as the basis upon which subsequent applications were drafted and new material was added. Rather than filing separate applications directed to different features, Walmart generally followed a strategy of building upon the original disclosure to include subsequent developments. Taking this approach can help reduce the cost of preparing subsequent filings.

On January 3, 2017, Walmart Inc. was granted U.S. Patent 9,534,906, claiming priority to the aforementioned provisional applications.

With so many priority documents having different filing dates, Walmart's competitors may have found it difficult to ascertain the exact priority date to which each of the issued claims in the '906 patent is entitled. Divining each claim's true

(12) **United States Patent** (10) Patent No.: **US 9,534,906 B2**
High et al.   (45) Date of Patent: **Jan. 3, 2017**

(54) **SHOPPING SPACE MAPPING SYSTEMS, DEVICES AND METHODS**

(71) Applicant: **Wal-Mart Stores, Inc.**, Bentonville, AR (US)

(72) Inventors: **Donald R. High**, Noel, MO (US); **Robert C. Taylor**, Rogers, AR (US); **Michael D. Atchley**, Springdale, AR (US)

(73) Assignee: **Wal-Mart Stores, Inc.**, Bentonville, AR (US)

(*) Notice: Subject to any disclaimer, the term of this patent is extended or adjusted under 35 U.S.C. 154(b) by 0 days.

(21) Appl. No.: **15/061,844**

(22) Filed: **Mar. 4, 2016**

(65)   **Prior Publication Data**

US 2016/0258763 A1   Sep. 8, 2016

Related U.S. Application Data

(60) Provisional application No. 62/129,726, filed on Mar. 6, 2015, provisional application No. 62/129,727, filed (Continued)

(51) **Int. Cl.**
G01C 21/20   (2006.01)
(52) **U.S. Cl.**
CPC **G01C 21/206** (2013.01)
(58) **Field of Classification Search**
CPC G01C 21/206
(Continued)

(56)   **References Cited**

U.S. PATENT DOCUMENTS

1,774,653 A   9/1930   Marriott
2,669,345 A   2/1954   Brown
                 (Continued)

FOREIGN PATENT DOCUMENTS

CA   2524037   5/2006
CA   2625885   4/2007
                 (Continued)

OTHER PUBLICATIONS

U.S. Appl. No. 15/061,325, filed Mar. 4, 2016, High.
                 (Continued)

Primary Examiner — McDieunel Marc
Assistant Examiner — James F. Stroud
(74) *Attorney, Agent, or Firm* — Fitch, Even, Tabin & Flannery LLP

(57)   **ABSTRACT**

Systems, apparatuses and methods for mapping a shopping space are provided. A system for mapping a shopping space includes a plurality of motorized transport units, a store map database, and a central computer system. The central computer system being configured to divide the map of the shopping space into a plurality of sections, assign a unique section identifier to each of the plurality of sections in the shopping space, associate a blocked tag with each section inaccessible to the plurality of motorized transport units, associate an accessible tag with each section accessible by at least one of the plurality of motorized transport units, for each section having an accessible tag, allow an access restriction setting to be configured, and provide navigation instructions to the plurality of motorized transport units based on access restriction settings of each section of the shopping space stored.

20 Claims, 8 Drawing Sheets

priority date can take a lot of effort. Each claim must be evaluated separately to determine when *all* the elements from that claim were first introduced in a prior application filing. Some elements may have been disclosed in the MVP application, others in later provisional application filings, and perhaps some were introduced only when the non-provisional application was filed.

This uncertainty can certainly benefit the patentee if a third party wants to challenge the validity of one or more claims. The Lean Patent model can help capture an iterative design process, but it can also present challenges to competitors or third parties in litigation giving them fits trying to determine the exact priority date for each claim in a given claim set.

CHAPTER 17
SUPER BIG BOGGLE® AND THE BUCKET OF LEGOS® STRATEGY

"WHENEVER THERE'S A DROUGHT GET YOUR UMBRELLAS OUT BECAUSE THAT'S WHEN I BRAINSTORM."

– JAY Z

Why this strategy might be for you...

- You have a lot of ideas and versions of your invention

- You are not sure which features or versions
  of the invention will have the most value

- You anticipate competitors will try to design around your patents

Growing up, I was always the kid on the block with the biggest bucket of Legos. On Christmases or birthdays, I'd start by spending time diligently following the directions. But in a matter of hours that perfectly-built Millennium Falcon would be piloted by samurai laying siege to a medieval castle.

Before

After

By the end of the day, after a valiantly fought battle, the dismantled pieces would end up mixed together in an 18-gallon storage bin. The intended Lego builds are great, but the instructions didn't hold a candle to the freedom to build whatever my heart desired from the thousands of now mixed-together pieces. A five-winged dragon with wagon wheels for legs taking off from an aircraft carrier to attack my sister's Barbie collection? Sure, I have the pieces for that.

One of my personal favorite strategies in the patent game — and the one I find myself using most frequently — is the equivalent of having the largest bucket of Legos. The patent application itself is the "bucket" and the "Legos" are anything and everything that you can jam into that bucket. As you add more of these Legos to the bucket, the possibilities increase dramatically to the point that you can build whatever you want, whenever you want. The more you put into your initial application filing — even if you aren't sure you'll ever want or need it — the more options you'll have in the future to build what your heart desires. If those items aren't in the bucket and you later need them to build valuable claims, you'll be out of luck.

Another way of thinking about this, in game terms, is a bit like playing the game Super Big Boggle®. As you may recall from rainy days with your family, traditional Boggle® involves a random set of letters being laid out on a four-by-four grid. Players race to make as many words as they can from contiguous strings of the visible letters. Super Big Boggle is fundamentally the same, but the game is expanded to include a six-by-six grid of letters. This larger board has more letters — and thus, more possible words — in play. Because there are more possible permutations on a six-by-six board, there exist more opportunities for the players to make winning combinations. A robust patent application gives you the opportunity to make your patent game version of the Boggle board as large as possible, providing more options and improving your chances of winning.

The equivalent of a large grid is helpful in the patent game, but the quality of the letters you have to choose from is equally important. A key element in Boggle is that players are forced to form words from a random selection and orientation of letters. After each round the letters and the orientation of those letters change such that no two rounds are ever the same. Not every letter is easy to use with its neighbors and a board with a lot of vowels might be more favorable than a consonant-heavy one with difficult letters like X, V, and Q sprinkled in.

In your patent application, each feature, application, or version of your invention represents a letter on your board. Including half-baked or non-functional elements in your application can be like seeding a Boggle grid with multiple Qs and Xs. Having a larger board or grid can be helpful in its own right, but the benefits are magnified greatly by having letters within the grid that are valuable and easily used in combination. It can be beneficial to include a lot of elements in your patent application, but quality needs to be considered in addition to quantity.

There can be benefits to focusing on only a single inventive concept (See Chapter 31), but the downside of such a focused application is that you'll have just a few Legos in your bucket from which to choose. There are *no* limitations on the number of versions, embodiments, or features that can be included in a single patent application. A common misconception — and a sign of a low IP IQ — is the belief that a vague patent application is a broad one. In reality, it's actually the opposite. The more versions, elements, ranges, or details that are included in your patent application, the more pieces you'll have available to build with in the future.

HOW THE BIG BOGGLE OR
BUCKET OF LEGOS STRATEGY WORKS

As shown in Figure 1, the Big Boggle/Bucket of Legos strategy, like many approaches in this book, begins with a provisional patent application. But the provisional application in the Bucket of Legos strategy is no ordinary provisional.

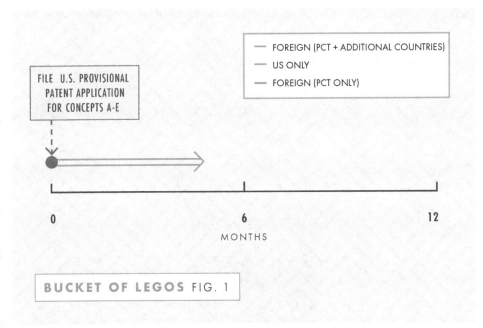

FILE U.S. PROVISIONAL
PATENT APPLICATION
FOR CONCEPTS A-E

0

6

12

MONTHS

BUCKET OF LEGOS FIG. 1

It can — and, for the purposes of this strategy, almost always should — be a gigantic application including numerous embodiments, features, functions, and methods.

This is the patent game equivalent of a Big Boggle board or having the largest bucket of Legos. Other strategies (See Chapter 16) use multiple provisional applications to introduce iterative technology improvements as they are developed. But if you can brainstorm improvements to your invention ahead of time, even if you've never built those versions, you can dump them all into a single provisional patent application at the outset. At the time of filing, you may be unsure as to which features and what combination of these elements will eventually provide the most business value. Why choose if you don't have to? By including all potential features in your provisional application, you preserve the ability to later claim or build whatever you like from these myriad elements.

With reference to Figure 2, this approach often maximizes most or all of the 12-month pendency of the provisional application before filing a non-provisional or PCT application because priority for all of the Legos in the bucket has already been established. Remember, your 20-year patent term doesn't begin until the non-provisional application or PCT application is filed.

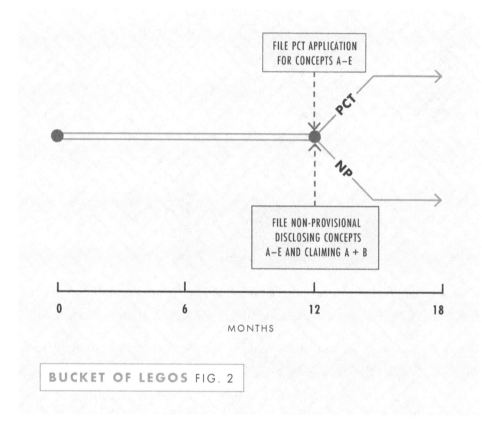

FILE PCT APPLICATION
FOR CONCEPTS A–E

PCT

NP

FILE NON-PROVISIONAL
DISCLOSING CONCEPTS
A–E AND CLAIMING A + B

0   6   12   18

MONTHS

BUCKET OF LEGOS FIG. 2

You will recall that the USPTO only allows applicants to claim one inventive concept at a time. Does choosing one initial combination to claim mean that you have to give up the unselected features or versions? Of course not. Your first selection is merely a starting point and might be the first of many variations that you protect with a patent family. The Bucket of Legos strategy preserves your ability to later pursue unelected features and combinations of those elements in continuation and divisional applications.

Imagine that you are going along your merry way, perfectly happy with your pending application, but then something significant happens. This significant event could be an infringer selling something from your application that you disclosed but have not yet claimed. Maybe the combination of elements you initially chose to pursue has proven to be worthless. As long as your original patent application included support for whatever combination proves valuable, you still have a chance to protect it. I've had plenty of clients that grudgingly included seemingly off-the-wall or sub-optimal versions of an invention in a patent application, only to later frantically search its applications to see if there is enough support to protect the concept once it has proven to have value.

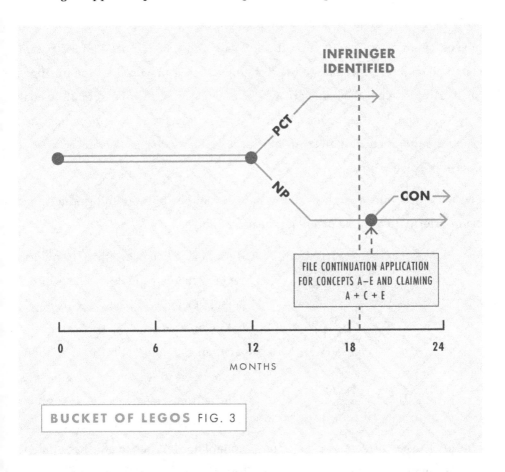

BUCKET OF LEGOS FIG. 3

To build something new from this bucket of Legos you started with, the disclosure in your original application as shown in Figure 3, you can use a continuation application or divisional application to spin off claims covering the desirable elements. As discussed in Chapter 10, a continuation application steps into the shoes of the parent application and is entitled to its same priority date. Just because you didn't initially claim everything of value doesn't mean you will be penalized with respect to priority date in continuation or divisional applications that are filed subsequently.

Your continuation filing, like your original non-provisional application, can be prosecuted before the USPTO until it becomes a patent. As shown in Figure 4, with a granted patent you can now threaten or initiate a patent infringement lawsuit against your competitor. It can be advantageous to have issued patent claims that closely correlate to the technology being practiced by the infringer. Such claims, even if they are narrower or more specific, may be difficult to challenge as invalid or unenforceable for being overly broad. Broad claims in a granted patent can be powerful, but there is also value in the precision of a laser-scoped sniper rifle.

There are no limits as to how many patents can be spun off and granted that claim priority to a single patent application filing.

It's estimated that more than 16 million people alive today are descendants of the Mongol, Genghis Khan. Like Genghis Khan, your initial patent application can spawn an unlimited number of children. It is common to see ten or more patents originate from a single parent application in some fields, building what is sometimes referred to as a "picket fence". I prefer "Mongol horde," personally. Each patent that originates from the same original filing can target a different combination of elements to help create an impenetrable patent portfolio.

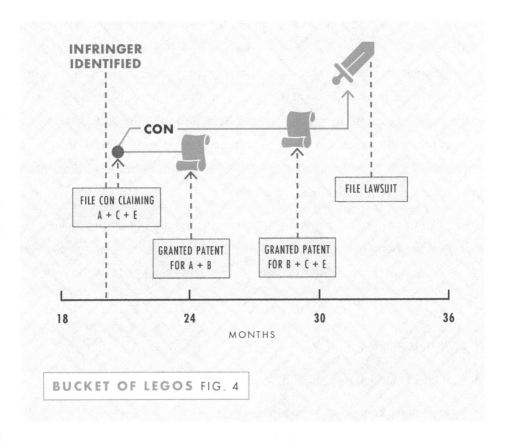

INFRINGER
IDENTIFIED

CON

FILE CON CLAIMING
A + C + E

GRANTED PATENT
FOR A + B

GRANTED PATENT
FOR B + C + E

FILE LAWSUIT

18   24   30   36

MONTHS

BUCKET OF LEGOS FIG. 4

Although not discussed in detail in this chapter, the Bucket of Legos strategy often includes a PCT application or one or more direct foreign national stage filings that can lead to one or more foreign patents. Check with your patent attorney to see if foreign jurisdictions of interest have the equivalent of a divisional or continuation application. For more details on the PCT process and foreign protection look to Chapter 10.

This approach is one of my personal favorites because it can be used effectively in a number of different scenarios. It can be a great fit for you or your business if you have a lot of embodiments, features, or methods related to a foundational concept, especially if you are unsure which ones will ultimately have the most value when you start the patent game. If you have multiple versions with different features or uses, you might want to create a Frankenstein's monster version of your invention. That's another scenario where this strategy can come in handy. Sometimes the increase in available permutations can make the sum greater than the mere addition of the parts. The Bucket of Legos strategy can be effective as a deterrent by giving you the flexibility to target, with laser focus, competitors arriving on the scene. Additionally, a robust application with a large number of published variations can block future patent applicants from improving upon the underlying technology.

If you like this approach but want to go faster, consider one of the power ups described in Chapters 18, 25, and 26. If you want to go even slower, consider one of the techniques for going more slowly described in Chapters 14,28, 29, and 30.

BENEFITS OF THE BUCKET OF LEGOS STRATEGY

- Lots of flexibility for future continuation or divisional applications

- Can lead to a huge patent family domestically and internationally

- Great when a commercial version of the embodiment has not been determined

- Great for targeting competitors attempting to design around patented technology

- Establishes an early filing date for a large number of features, embodiments, methods, and combinations

- After the provisional application filing, the applicant can publicly disclose the invention

- Can maximize patent term by establishing an early provisional filing date and waiting much of the 12-month pendency before filing a non-provisional and/or PCT application

- Published application and patents can be expansive prior art that blocks competitors filing applications in the technology field

DRAWBACKS TO THE BUCKET OF LEGOS STRATEGY

- A robust provisional application can be costly

- Half-baked ideas included in the disclosure can become damaging prior art

PRACTICAL EXAMPLE – JOHNSON & JOHNSON, INC.

Earlier in my career, I had the privilege of working at Ethicon Endo-Surgery, a subsidiary of Johnson & Johnson, Inc. I cut my teeth in the patent trade by working with several truly exceptional patent attorneys and agents from whom I learned a great deal about patent strategy, working with inventors, and how to build formidable swords and shields using a patent portfolio. The deep pockets of Ethicon—combined with an intense focus on patent strategy and R&D—have driven its value up substantially. The Bucket of Legos strategy is particularly well-suited to medical device applications and is often used by Covidien, Medtronic, and other big names in the industry.

There are many examples of product platforms to choose from that demonstrate the Bucket of Legos strategy in action. We'll be taking a look here at a particular patent family from Ethicon directed to surgical staplers. Ethicon is the assignee—or owner—of at least 3,124 United States and international patents. The diagrams below represent a snapshot of this ownership and the distribution of Ethicon's patents across the world.

As illustrated, Ethicon has secured at least 2,115 patents in the United States alone at the time of this writing. The U.S. is where Ethicon is based and the charts suggest that this is also its key market for medical device sales. But another takeaway from these diagrams is that even companies with the deepest of pockets are judicious in the choices it makes when it comes to filing foreign patent applications. That there are no worldwide patents means even the largest of applicants need to weigh the pros and cons of pursuing protection in secondary markets. Foreign patent fees can add up quickly—particularly when ongoing annuity fees are taken into account—and the chart should illustrate why smaller businesses might want to be even more careful with where they choose to file.

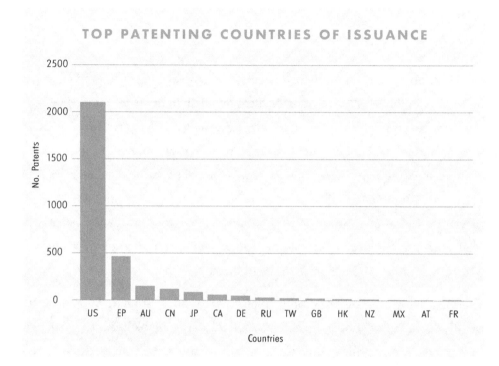

TOP PATENTING COUNTRIES OF ISSUANCE

For our practical example, we'll look at one of the many product lines of Ethicon; the surgical stapler. The global surgical stapling market is expected to reach USD 6.8 billion by 2024, according to a report by Grand View Research. This demand is attributable, at least in part, to the growing market for bariatric applications, endoscopic operations, and powered surgical devices. As the application of stapling in medical procedures has gradually moved from open surgery to endoscopic surgery, established companies and medical device startups alike are racing to develop and define the next standard of care.

The primary goal of the Bucket of Legos strategy is to file a robust disclosure that includes a wide range of versions, features, and uses for the patent applicant to exploit in later-filed spin-off applications. Remember what I discussed earlier—there are no limits to the number of continuation patent applications that can be spun off a single parent application, and the chief benefit of these continuations is that the spin-off filings are entitled to the very same priority date as the parent. You can file one application which in turn results in a hundred (or more) patents with the same priority date.

On September 30, 2010, Ethicon filed a *massive* non-provisional patent application with 324 pages of disclosure including 139 sheets of drawings. To date, the "simple" family related to this early filing (that is, the original and spin-off filings *not* adding new matter) include over 125 cases in the United States and abroad. Of these application filings, 19 have already become U.S. patents. Patents entitled to the parent filing date have issued every year starting with the first patent issuances in 2008.

These patent issuances, based upon new application filings, may continue for the entire duration of the family's available patent term. The most recent continuation for this family, at the time of this writing, was filed on January 12, 2017 and there may yet be more before the term expires.

CHAPTER 18

PLAYING THE LONG GAME— CIVILIZATION AND MAXIMIZING PATENT TERM

"THE EMPIRES OF THE FUTURE ARE THE EMPIRES OF THE MIND."

– WINSTON CHURCHCHILL

Why this strategy might be for you...

- You want a protectable monopoly for as long as possible

- Your invention has a long commercial life

- Your technology field lends itself to strong patent protection

- You want to maximize royalties or patent litigation damages

Sid Meier's *Civilization* is a multiplayer computer game where players start a settlement with rudimentary resources, skills, and tools then attempt to grow this inauspicious colony into a powerful and long-lasting empire. The scope of *Civilization* is larger than most other games, with the possibility of starting in 4000 BC and lasting through AD 2100 in its version of society on Earth. While many other games are focused on speed, or at least making the most of the time available, ones like *Civilization* are about the long game and players have to position themselves for longevity in order to be successful.

As a player's settlers build in-game knowledge, they will invent new technology, find new resources, and grow in strength. The civilization, however, is constantly under attack by others developing at the same time. These competing societies constantly challenge the settlers' defenses and technology. If you stay in the game long enough, you might even get nuked. The goal is to establish dominance over one's territory and to do so for as long as possible.

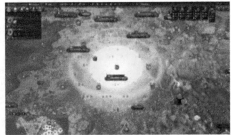

There are many circumstances in the patent game where it can be immensely valuable to establish protection for as long as possible, which commonly takes the form of maximizing your patent term. Pharmaceuticals companies, for example, seek to maximize every possible *day* of a patent's available term. If you're in a technology field where every day counts, there are tactics for maximizing patent term you should consider, whether that means capturing every available day within the 20-year patent term or securing an additional patent monopoly beyond the initial 20 years.

Big Pharma has a bit of a bad reputation for trying to extend patent term by any available means to preserve market share and ward off generic drug manufacturers. There is a lot of misinformation around this subject that implies large pharmaceutical companies use nefarious or illegal techniques to preserve a monopoly. In reality, much of the supposed patent extension actually refers to newly filed applications and granted patents that cover different variations or delivery mechanisms for a blockbuster drug. These new application filings restart the patent clock, but the technology covered by a now-expired patent is in the public domain. The new patent application filings must be novel and non-obvious in view of the company's *own* prior invention. There is nothing wrong with improving on a technology and patenting those improvements, particularly if those improvements become the new standard of care.

That being said, there are a few limited circumstances where additional time can be added to an existing patent. The government acknowledges that it can take years to secure Federal Drug Administration (FDA) and other clearances and wants pharmaceutical companies to continue developing new medicines. For that reason, there are mechanisms by which companies can claw back patent term lost while awaiting the proper approvals. Applicants not in fields subject to such regulatory clearances may still be able to regain lost patent term if the delay in securing a U.S. patent was the fault of the USPTO. The USPTO is notoriously backlogged and — in order to continue encouraging applicants to apply for patents — it tends to be willing to grant additional patent term to compensate for USPTO-caused delays.

18a TOOLS TO EXTEND PATENT TERM

A chess player in a timed game has a set amount of time to win. Each player is on the clock during each turn. The players then punch the clock when they've made a move to start the timer on the opposition. If one player uses all the allotted time before checkmate is achieved, that player loses. Trying to maximize patent term can feel a bit like playing the USPTO in a game of chess, where *your* clock is running even when the USPTO is making its moves. Because the 20-year patent term starts when a non-provisional application is first filed, delays by the USPTO are ticking valuable days, months, or even years off of your clock. Fortunately for many applicants, there are mechanisms by which patent term can be supplemented due to governmental delays.

PATENT TERM ADJUSTMENT (PTA)—USPTO DELAYS

Patent prosecution before the USPTO can be painfully slow. Applicants tend to be rightfully concerned that these delays will negatively impact valuable patent term. In response, the USPTO established a number of timing thresholds that, if exceeded by the USPTO, can add additional time to your term. Any time added to your patent term can be offset by your own delays in prosecution, however, so you'll need to respond as quickly to the USPTO as possible to maximize the available Patent Term Adjustment (PTA). The specific PTA calculations are beyond the scope of this book, but you should be aware this is available for you and your patent attorney to consider. For example, you may be entitled to additional patent term if the USPTO sends you an Office action or restriction requirement after 14 months from your filing date, fails to issue a patent within three years from your filing date, or does not issue your patent within four months from payment of the issue fee.

PATENT TERM EXTENSION (PTE) REGULATORY DELAYS

The USPTO is not the only government agency that can negatively impact your patent term with delays. Many products and methods — including human and veterinary pharmaceuticals, food additives, color additives, and medical devices — require approval from a regulatory body before being commercialized. In most cases, patent applications directed to key technologies will be filed and/or issued before trials or review under the appropriate regulatory agency have begun. Patent term extension (PTE), which can extend your patent monopoly beyond 20 years under certain circumstances, is available under the 1984 Drug Price Competition and Patent Restoration Act, also known as the Hatch-Waxman Act ("The Act").

According to the Manual of Patent Examining Procedure (MPEP), The Act sought to eliminate a distortion to the normal patent term caused by the requirement for premarket regulatory approval of certain products. 50 percent of the time spent in clinical testing and 100 percent of the time spent in regulatory review can be added back to your patent term, but the total patent term extension cannot be more than five years. This PTE will not be granted automatically and, if you think you qualify, your application for patent term extension must be filed with the USPTO within 60 days of the regulatory approval of the product.

18b BLITZ CHESS VARIATION

A more common way to maximize patent term is to speed the patent game up so as to secure an issued patent as quickly as possible. There are two tactical approaches to discuss here—the Blitz Chess approach and the Track One approach. These two techniques can be used together to maximize the speed of the patent process. Prior to the America Invents Act, which introduced Track One Prioritized Examination as a filing option for applicants, the Blitz Chess approach was often the best and only way to maximize all available patent term in addition to any PTA or PTE to which you might have been entitled. What's now the poor man's strategy, so to speak, may still be the strategy best suited to your needs.

Picture a chess clock with two timers, one for your patent term and the other for the time it takes the USPTO to take actions such as reviewing your application, evaluating your responses, and issuing you a patent.

Once the USPTO has made a move— for example, an Office action reject-

ing some or all of your patent application claims — you need to quickly respond with your response, punch the timer, and put the USPTO back on the clock. The faster you can respond, the better — every day that passes can negatively impact your patent term. Think about your next move while the USPTO is still on the clock so that you're able to respond immediately once they act. You might use the Blitz Chess approach from start to finish, but you can always speed up or slow down your moves during the patent process depending on your needs, objectives, or available resources.

This approach can optionally begin with the filing of a U.S. provisional application to get the game started. As mentioned previously, a provisional application has a maximum 12-month pendency, during which a U.S. non-provisional application, PCT application, or foreign national stage application, should be filed. **Filing a provisional application or a foreign national stage patent application is a smart way to buy an extra year of priority without losing valuable patent term.**

Once a U.S. non-provisional application has been filed, it will enter the queue at the USPTO to be picked up for substantive examination. This starts the 20-year patent clock. The timing until you receive a first Office action varies depending on the USPTO's backlog, but the wait is frequently a year or longer. The longest delay I've personally experienced was *56 months*, which is brutal if you are trying to quickly secure a patent and maximize patent term. Remember, this delay is just the wait for the *first* substantive Office action in a process where multiple rounds with the USPTO might be — and typically are — required before you ultimately secure an issued patent.

With the timer started and the 20-year clock running, it's important for you to do *everything* in your power to promptly respond to USPTO communications to keep the game moving. If you elect not to use one of the expedited prosecution tools, then there is little that can be done with respect to USPTO delays. But you and your attorney can control how quickly you respond to the USPTO when the ball is in your court.

You may be able to claw back some time via PTA if the USPTO takes too long to prosecute your patent application, but you should assume that every day of delay, whether it's on you or the USPTO, is taking away valuable patent term. A couple week's delay here and a month there can quickly add up. USPTO Office actions allow for a *maximum* of six months to respond, but there is no reason to wait this long if time is of the essence. Putting the USPTO back on the clock by responding quickly gives you the greatest possible opportunity to maximize patent term.

Playing blitz chess with the USPTO is a simple way for you to try and maximize your patent term. There are, of course, attorney fees to prepare Office action responses and to take other actions, but there are no additional fees for responding promptly to the USPTO. Speed is important, but you should also manage your expectations because preparing responses, conducting examiner interviews, and other quality legal work takes time. You want to make your move and punch the clock quickly, but not at the expense of a crucial blunder. The goal is to get a patent quickly and have *useful* protection for the life of your patent.

The Blitz Chess approach for foreign patent protection progresses in much the same way. A PCT application, like a provisional application, functions primarily as a placeholder application for future filings. It can be a useful mechanism to delay expensive national stage applications for 30 months or more from your earliest priority date, but this delay will correspondingly shorten the patent term of any granted foreign patents. If you want to maximize the term of your foreign patent portfolio, consider filing direct national stage applications instead of a PCT application or — if you do choose to file a PCT application — file your national stage applications as quickly as possible well in advance of the 30-month deadline. Once these foreign applications are picked up for substantive review by each respective patent office you should, again, be prepared to take action as quickly as possible.

If you do receive notice of allowable subject matter, whether that's in the United States or abroad, be sure to review Chapters 13 and 27 on the Patent Prosecution highway to see if you can use that good news to expedite patent applications in other jurisdictions.

BENEFITS OF THE BLITZ CHESS APPROACH

- A relatively inexpensive means to secure an issued patent as quickly as possible

- Faster patent issuance generally equates to a longer patent term

- A patent infringement lawsuit cannot be brought until a patent has issued

- Infringement damages generally only begin once a patent has issued

- Aggressive prosecution will help you more quickly understand the patent landscape

- Can help ensure that you receive all of the PTE and PTA to which you may be entitled

DRAWBACKS TO THE BLITZ CHESS APPROACH

- You might want the patent process to go even faster than this approach will permit

- Responding quickly to the USPTO can result in higher overall costs, less efficiency, front-loading of costs, and diminished quality.

A second option for maximizing patent term, the Track One approach, is even faster than Blitz Chess and often more effective. Coined after the namesake Track One Prioritized Examination (which is also discussed in Chapters 13 and 25), this tactic uses a special request available to all inventors following the enactment of the America Invents Act (AIA). Applicants that qualify for free expedited examination for age or health-related reasons, as discussed in Chapter 26, can also take advantage of this strategy without paying the added fees associated with a Track One filing.

Because prosecution time tends to be inversely proportional to patent term, an expedited approach gives you a better chance at achieving a longer monopoly. In the best-case scenario, this approach may result in significantly more patent term than you might expect when using only the Blitz Chess approach. If you're feeling particularly aggressive, you can combine the tactics of the Blitz Chess approach with your Track One filing to compound the efficacy of these approaches.

HOW THE TRACK ONE MAXIMUM
PATENT TERM STRATEGY WORKS

There is a lot of overlap between this approach and Blitz Chess. We often begin with the filing of a U.S. provisional application. Thus begins the standard 12-month pendency for filing your U.S. non-provisional application and/or foreign application. As with the Blitz Chess approach, you should try to maximize most or all of the available 12 months because this will not negatively impact patent term. The crucial difference with Track One is the U.S. non-provisional application, *at the time of its filing*, should include a request for Track One Prioritized Examination. The non-provisional must include the fee for the Track One program and must also comply with several administrative and content requirements described in more detail in Chapters 13 and 25. These additional require-ments, unique to utilizing Track One, are necessary so the non-provisional is ready for patent issuance as-filed.

When you file your complete non-provisional with a Track One request, it will enter the expedited queue at the United States Patent and Trademark Office to be picked up for substantive examination. You can expect about three to six months to pass before a first Office action is mailed by the USPTO. It's up to you to respond promptly to any USPTO action or else you'll be removed from the Track One program.

As discussed in Chapter 13 on power ups, the USPTO's objective with the Track One program is to give you a final disposition on your application within 12 months. The optimal scenario is that this final disposition includes allowable claims so that you can secure an issued patent. During the Track One process, the USPTO will give you two substantive rounds of examination within this 12-month period, a process which normally would take years following the fil-ing of a standard track application. Assuming your invention is useful, novel, and non-obvious — and that the various USPTO formalities have been satisfied — your non-provisional application can then issue as a U.S. patent.

With respect to foreign patent protection, few jurisdictions have the equivalent of Track One Accelerated Examination or similar accelerated examination for health or age-related reasons. Your patent attorney should be able to determine if there are analogous strategies in countries of interest to your company.

However, as discussed in Chapters 13 and 27, many countries are now partici-pants in the Patent Prosecution Highway (PPH). The PPH allows your applica-tion to be examined out of turn and, in some cases, issued more quickly if there are corresponding claims that are allowed or issued in a participating country or jurisdiction. The PPH can be a great tool for expediting issuance of foreign pat-ent applications if you are able to secure allowable subject matter in the U.S. or other participating countries. If you do receive indication from the USPTO or other PPH-participating patent office that claims are allowable, turn to Chapter 27 to see about taking advantage of the powerful PPH. Through use of PPH, you can often parlay that allowance into quick and efficient allowances of similar claims in other PPH-participating countries.

BENEFITS OF THE TRACK ONE APPROACH

- Can help secure as much patent term as possible

- A patent could issue within 12 months of filing

- A lawsuit can only be brought once a patent has issued

- Damages often only begin to accrue once a patent has issued

- Allows you to use the "patented" designation more quickly

- Allows you to see how prosecution progresses in the U.S. before deciding whether to invest in foreign patent applications

- Enhances likelihood of applicability of PPH process to expedite foreign applications

DRAWBACKS OF THE TRACK ONE APPROACH

- Track One filings can be costly

- Prosecution may be more costly because of the compressed timeline

- Frontloads patent filing and prosecution costs

- Can lead to receiving bad news faster if the USPTO finds relevant prior art

For a real-world example of this approach, turn to Chapter 25 illustrating how the Track One process functions in practice.

CHAPTER 19

HEDGING YOUR BETS— RISK® AND RETAINING THE OPTION FOR BOTH PATENTS AND TRADE SECRETS

"THEREFORE, JUST AS WATER RETAINS NO CONSTANT SHAPE, SO IN WARFARE THERE ARE NO CONSTANT CONDITIONS."

– SUN TZU, "THE ART OF WAR"

Why this strategy might be for you…

- You are interested in both trade secret and patent protection

- Your invention may not be patentable,
  but a patent is your first choice if at all possible

- You'd prefer the longevity of a trade secret, but you have
  concerns about premature disclosure of the proprietary innovation

- Competitors may actively try to reverse engineer your technology

When playing a board game like Risk®, it's important to have a strategy, but having a Plan B in case your initial plan goes sideways is every bit as crucial. Having too rigid of a game plan can be as dangerous as having no plan at all. You can control which pieces you place on the board in the patent game and how you move those pieces, but always keep in mind that your competitors are actively playing against you. Their moves might directly impact how you can best achieve your objectives. Circumstances can change based on factors outside of your control, making your original plan unappealing or even impossible to execute. Planning for the potential failure of your original plan can leave you in a better position should the worst-case scenario come to pass.

As discussed earlier in this book, trying to take and hold all of Asia early in the game is a Risk strategy doomed to fail. But there are many approaches to the game that can lead to successful global domination. The success of tried-and-true strategies, like targeting Australia or North America early in the game, are heavily dependent on the flow of the game and the strategies of the other players. The strategy that worked in the last game might fail miserably in a subsequent one.

One of my favorite strategies in Risk is to secure and hold North America quickly. That continent is large enough to earn a player five bonus soldiers for a successful hold of the territory, but it's not so large (like Asia) that holding it early in the game is practically impossible. This is generally my Plan A and I'm always hopeful that I'm the only one with this strategy. Once secured, it becomes relatively easy to reinforce the three incursion points and build a sizeable army.

When playing with more experienced players, however, this approach can be much more challenging to execute and can even lead to crushing defeat early in the game. I'm often not alone in North America being my Plan A, which becomes painfully obvious as other players begin actively claiming and reinforcing territories on the continent early in the game. As this unfolds and players start reinforcing positions, a storm begins brewing that can quickly turn into a battle of attrition. If two or more players are 100 percent committed to this territory, long and bloody battles will ensue that leave both sides weakened and lacking a continent to call their own. As Sun Tzu said in *The Art of War*: "He who wishes to fight must first count the cost." He also clarified that thought in greater length and eloquence, writing: "Now, when your weapons are dulled, your ardor damped, your strength exhausted and your treasure spent, other chieftains will spring up to take advantage of your extremity. Then no man, however wise, will be able to avert the consequences that must ensue." Two players exhausting one another early in the game are likely to *both* be overrun by a more patient player lying in wait to attack the weakened forces.

If North America is shaping up to be a bloodbath, I'll keep a close eye on Australia, which is my Plan B. Australia is a smaller continent worth only two bonus soldiers per turn if held; however, there's only one access point to Australia, making it easier to hold and difficult to attack. There are downsides to holding Australia. In addition to only earning two extra soldiers per turn, the closest accessible continent is the untenable Asia. But if North America is shaping up to be the venue for an ugly and protracted conflict, a pivot to an Australia-focused strategy can still be a winner.

I've been in games with multiple parties playing a game of chicken with one another, trying to secure North America before someone finally capitulates and falls back to a Plan B. At some point during this standoff, however, discretion becomes the better part of valor. Knowing when to abandon Plan A in favor of Plan B is of critical importance. Players with only one strategy or those that stubbornly engage in a pissing match will rarely emerge victorious. A single-minded approach can look brilliant when it works but, if the conditions and other players don't facilitate the execution of the original plan, you're likely to be the first one knocked out of the game.

Like Risk, it can be incredibly valuable in the patent game to hedge your bets on a Plan A strategy with a solid Plan B. It's common for patent applicants to commit to just one strategy, like being dead set on controlling North America in Risk, without any thought of a backup if this initial plan fails. Sometimes the failure to develop a contingency plan is attributable to overconfidence, but in many cases I find it's a lack of IP IQ that leaves players in this position. Nowhere is this more apparent than in the preservation of patent rights *and* trade secret protection. A common misconception is that patent applicants can't have the proverbial cake and eat it too when it comes to both trade secrets and patent protection. It's true that you cannot keep both options forever with respect to the same subject matter — an issued patent must publish and will terminate any trade secret protection for that subject matter — but it's possible to keep your Plan A and Plan B as open options far into the patent game.

Fields such as the mechanical arts generally aren't great candidates for trade secret protection because the technology is easily reverse engineered once it hits the market. However, inventions such as manufacturing methods, chemical formulations, and firmware or backend software that are not easily reverse engineered may present the inventor or business owner with two seemingly mutually exclusive choices. This inquiry usually begins and ends with a question: "Should I file a patent application and completely disclose the invention in exchange for the *chance* at a 20-year monopoly, or should I keep this as a trade secret and hope that my competitors don't discover it?"

A patent is not a guarantee, of course, and so many prospective applicants are concerned they will end up with the worst of both worlds by having the technology published while also failing to secure a valuable patent. A trade secret can theoretically last forever, but inventors considering this route may be nervous that, shortly after the innovation is a success, a competitor will discover the secret. If a competitor reverse-engineers your trade secret—as impossible as that might seem at the outset—*all* of your protection is lost. If a disgruntled employee steals trade secrets and makes them public or gives them to a competitor, your trade secrets are lost. There are numerous circumstances in which trade secrets become part of the public domain, even when business owners are trying to be diligent.

On the other hand, you may have an invention for which you prefer patent protection but securing that patent may be difficult. For example, securing a monopoly for 20 years on a novel backend software development may be valuable, but its patent eligibility may be uncertain given the current state of the law. If pursuing a patent fails, the invention might make for a good trade secret given the behind-the-scenes nature of the innovation. Manufacturing methods, certain chemical formulations and methods, and software-related technology may fall into this category. The trade secret option can also provide value in a technology field that is dense with a lot of patents and published patent applications, making it uncertain whether sufficiently broad claims can be secured. A carefully kept trade secret may be more valuable than a very narrow patent.

Fortunately, in the patent game, there are strategies that can help you keep both the patent and trade secret option available for as long as possible. Regardless of an inventor or company's initial preference, the choice between patent and trade secret does not have to be binary. Technology that can be protected with a patent can, in many cases, also be maintained as a trade secret. I'll start with the scenario below where a trade secret is preferred and you want to keep the patent option as an insurance policy. In the second section of this chapter, I'll walk you through an approach where a patent is your Plan A, but a trade secret is a viable Plan B.

19a TRADE SECRET IS PLAN A AND THE PATENT IS PLAN B

The 20-year monopoly associated with a patent might seem too short for some innovations such as, for example, a chemical formulation that could have value for decades or more. In such circumstances, a trade secret may be the more valuable option. The formulation for Coca-Cola® is, arguably, the most famous trade secret in the world. If a patent had been pursued on the formulation this knowledge would have entered the public domain long ago. Whatever your reasons for preferring a trade secret, the first section of this chapter will demonstrate an approach where this protection is paramount, but the realities of the marketplace suggest that a patent fallback is a prudent insurance policy. The Plan A: Trade Secret; Plan B: Patent strategy presents one option for inventors who don't want to immediately make the decision to pursue only patent protection or a trade secret for the invention.

HOW THE TRADE SECRET IS PLAN A AND A PATENT IS PLAN B STRATEGY WORKS

As shown in Figure 1, our example scenario begins with the filing of a U.S. provisional application. It's a common misconception that merely filing a patent application means you have fully committed to only the patent process. Because a provisional application is 100% confidential, this application filing will not jeopardize trade secret protection. Provisional applications are a great way to keep your trade secret intact while still establishing a filing date for future patents. Remember, a provisional application only lasts for 12 months and if you decide to let it become abandoned, it will never become publicly available. You could learn a lot in the first year after you've developed an invention, such as whether your technology can be reverse engineered or otherwise discovered.

Taking the simple step of filing a provisional application can be a relatively cost-effective way to maintain a Plan B option. And if you forget about your provisional application or otherwise do nothing to further the patent process, the application will become automatically abandoned and will never become public. You can set it and forget it.

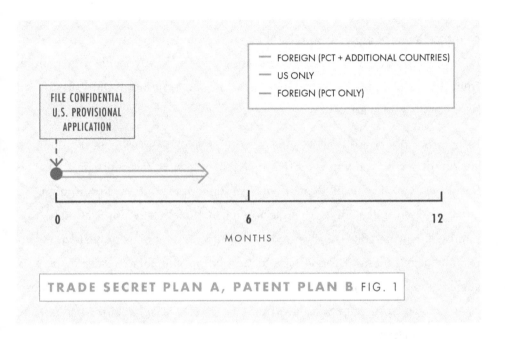

FILE CONFIDENTIAL
U.S. PROVISIONAL
APPLICATION

— FOREIGN (PCT + ADDITIONAL COUNTRIES)
— US ONLY
— FOREIGN (PCT ONLY)

0   6   12

MONTHS

TRADE SECRET PLAN A, PATENT PLAN B FIG. 1

Another benefit to this early provisional application filing is that this single application filing can be used as a single priority document for *each* of your U.S. non-provisional patent applications, PCT applications, or foreign national stage filings if Plan A fails during the first year. Your ability to keep both your Plan A and Plan B in place is greatest during this initial 12-month period.

Just as the coverage in insurance policies varies, so does the variation in quality of provisional applications. If the technology is highly valuable and you want maximum protection if you do need to rely upon your provisional application filing, then spending resources at the outset on a quality provisional application filing is important. Alternatively, you may decide that an insurance policy has only limited value, thereby dedicating a smaller portion of resources to the backup plan.

It's relatively easy to keep both the trade secret and patent option in play during the first year, but beyond that you'll need to make some difficult decisions. After 12 months from filing, if you choose to pursue a PCT or a patent in a foreign country, then your patent application will be on a path towards publication. PCT and foreign national stage applications will typically publish 18 months from the earliest priority date. Obviously, once an application publishes, trade secret rights will evaporate.

If the 12-month deadline is upon you, you've been successful in maintaining your trade secret, and you want to keep a patent backup insurance policy henceforth, then you'll typically have to give up the opportunity to seek foreign patent protection. Even filing a single foreign national stage application at this point will require your U.S. non-provisional application to be published. It's up to you to determine if foreign protection is too valuable to sacrifice at this stage. If you do forego foreign patent protection, there is still a way to keep your U.S. non-provisional application as a confidential backup for domestic patent protection.

With reference to Figure 2, keeping the trade secret option intact in the United States simply requires you to check the box on your non-provisional application to request non-publication. This designation *must* be made at the time of filing or the USPTO will publish your application in accordance with normal procedures 18 months from your earliest priority date.

☐ **Request Not to Publish.** I hereby request that the attached application not be published under 35 U.S.C. 122(b) and certify that the invention disclosed in the attached application **has not and will not** be the subject of an application filed in another country, or under a multilateral international agreement, that requires publication at eighteen months after filing.

Bear in mind that this request for non-publication specifically requires you to acknowledge you *have not* and *will not* be filing an application in another country that requires publication.

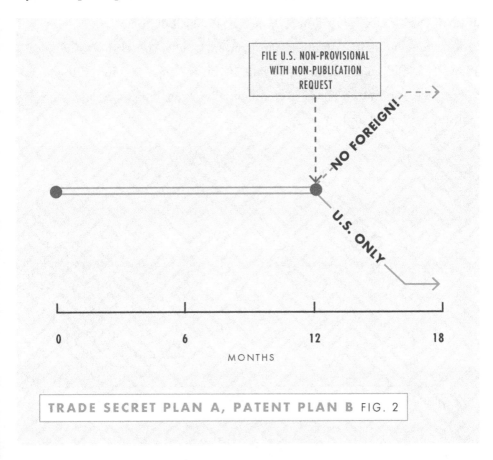

FILE U.S. NON-PROVISIONAL
WITH NON-PUBLICATION
REQUEST

NO FOREIGN!

U.S. ONLY

0   6   12   18

MONTHS

TRADE SECRET PLAN A, PATENT PLAN B FIG. 2

If you correctly make this designation, your non-provisional application will eventually be examined by the USPTO, but every communication will be just as confidential as the application itself. In this case, the entire patent prosecution process takes place confidentially and if you let your patent application become abandoned, it will never become publicly viewable. The USPTO's backlog and the year or more it may take for it to review your application may work to your advantage. Let the slowness of the process play to your benefit and use this time to gain clarity on which of patent protection or a trade secret holds more value in the long run.

If you receive a notice of allowance from the USPTO, you don't have to accept its offer. Once a patent is granted, it must be public. But up until that point, you control the confidential status of the pending application entirely. Even with allowed claims you can continue to stall. If you are interested in stalling tactics to keep the application pending confidentially for as long as possible, have a look at Chapters 14 and 28.

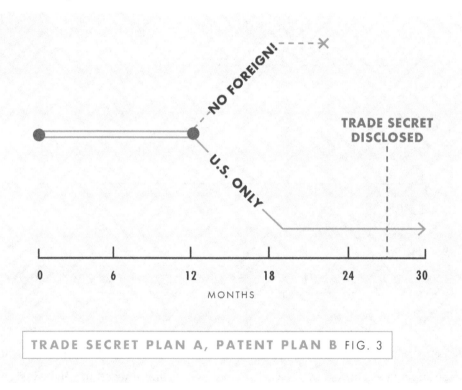

TRADE SECRET PLAN A, PATENT PLAN B FIG. 3

But an event may occur, as shown in Figure 3, while your patent application is lurking in the dark that makes your Plan B for patent protection valuable or necessary. This event could be the accidental disclosure of the trade secret by an employee, a competitor successfully reverse-engineering the technology, or an infringer using the technology. Once this trigger has occurred, you might then decide to pursue an issued U.S. patent in earnest. If you want to pursue a patent as fast as possible, take a look at Chapters 13, 18, and 25 for a few options.

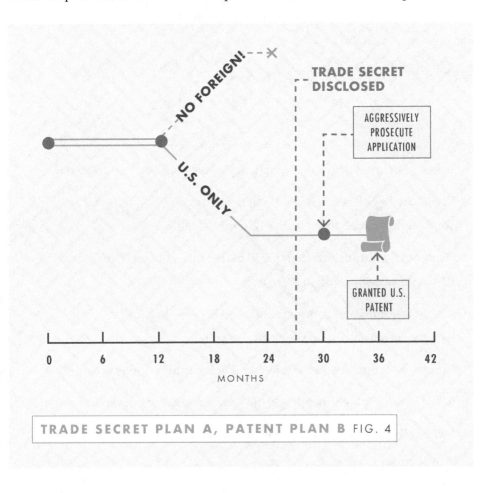

TRADE SECRET PLAN A, PATENT PLAN B FIG. 4

If you are successful in securing a granted patent, as shown in Figure 4, all prior filings and the prosecution history for each will become publicly available. That means everything involving the USPTO associated with your patent—from your provisional application to USPTO correspondence—will now be publicly available to any third party. This formally and permanently nullifies your trade secret option. You may have lost some patent term while your application was lurking, but you'll be thankful you kept this insurance policy in place if your

Plan B is needed. And if you want to make up some of that lost time, look at Chapter 18 for tactics for maximizing patent term. Losing a trade secret to the public can be disappointing, but having the fallback position of patent protection can keep you in the game.

BENEFITS OF THE TRADE SECRET PLAN A, PATENT PLAN B STRATEGY

- Maintain both trade secret and patent option domestically and internationally for 12-month pendency of the provisional application

- Provisional application will automatically become confidentially abandoned at the 12-month deadline

- Maintain both trade secret and U.S. patent option beyond the initial 12-month period for up to 21 years

- Ability to confidentially prosecute the U.S. non-provisional to allowance before committing to a patent

- Competitors unable to ascertain whether an application was ever filed

- Ability to use "patent pending" and "proprietary" on marketing materials

- Potentially infinite life of trade secret protection if Plan A is effective.

DRAWBACKS OF THE TRADE SECRET PLAN A, PATENT PLAN B STRATEGY

- Insurance policy of a provisional patent application may be an unnecessary expense if trade secret can be maintained

- Preparation of provisional application may require significant resources to have value if needed as Plan B

- After the 12-month pendency of the provisional expires, if maintenance of trade secret and a U.S. provisional application are desired, the opportunity to seek foreign patent protection must be forfeited

- Maintaining a pending U.S. non-provisional
  over the life of the patent term can be costly

- Half-baked ideas included in the patent disclosure can become
  damaging prior art in the event the patent is allowed to issue

REAL WORLD EXAMPLE: INDUSTRIAL COATINGS

A Colorado-based corporation, to remain unnamed, formulates various industrial chemicals for manufacturing. Many of the proprietary chemistries developed by this company are difficult to reverse engineer. For this reason, trade secrets are particularly appealing because of the potential to maintain newly developed innovations as proprietary well beyond a 20-year patent term. A trade secret has a theoretically infinite duration as long as the innovation is kept confidential and is not reverse-engineered or independently developed by a competitor.

In 2014, the company invented a potentially valuable coating composition that produced highly durable and effective coating layers in a single-step curing process. Coating layers incorporating this chemistry displayed beneficial properties. The formulations associated with this invention appeared to be novel and non-obvious and, thus, would qualify for patent protection. However, the initial reaction was that trade secret protection could have more value to the company over the long term. Like many companies, it was initially under the impression that it would have to choose very early in the process whether to try and patent the new invention or proceed only with trade secret protection.

The decision was made by management that, although a trade secret was the preferred option, the new innovation had sufficient value that an insurance policy in the form of a provisional patent application was justified. A provisional patent application was filed on behalf of the company directed to the novel coating composition and methods of applying the coating. This provisional application was 100% confidential—thus, a record of the application was *not* available on the USPTO website or any other publicly available search engines. Unless the company actively chose to disclose its newly-filed provisional application, the innovation would remain invisible to the public.

During the 12-month pendency of this provisional application, the company began to commercialize the coatings while taking steps to maintain the invention as though it were a trade secret, despite having a provisional application on file. At the end of the 12-month pendency of the provisional application the company had the opportunity to reevaluate whether the trade secret route or patent protection had more business value. If there had been an accidental disclosure of the technology or a competitor had reverse-engineered the proprietary composition, it could have switched gears and invested heavily in a domestic non-provisional application as well as foreign patent protection. The first year of commercialization for a new technology can teach a company a great deal about market potential, efforts by competitors to independently develop the innovation, and how robust internal protections are to maintain the composition as a trade secret.

As the 12-month deadline approached, the company felt strongly that trade secret protection was still the best course of action. The company, though, had concerns that some employees—particularly in the sales department—had access to the proprietary information and was therefore at risk of accidental disclosure. Thus, the company opted to file a U.S. non-provisional application. If its confidence level in the trade secret option had been higher, the company could have chosen to let its provisional application become abandoned but lose the option of a patent as Plan B. But by taking this route, and filing a U.S. non-provisional application, it kept alive the trade secret option while hedging against accidental disclosure, since this newly-filed non-provisional application was also kept confidential by checking the "non-publication request" box at the time of filing. The company was also required to give up any foreign filing opportunities, but the option to protect the U.S. market with a patent justified the cost of the confidential non-provisional application filing.

Despite the company's best efforts, it was discovered in 2017 that several salespeople had inadvertently disclosed proprietary composition information at a trade show in order to make a sale, justifying the company's initial concerns. Such a disclosure, even if unintentional, likely eliminated any trade secret protection associated with the proprietary chemistry. Had the company relied only upon trade secret protection, it would have been left without any intellectual property around a now highly-valuable product. Instead, its insurance policy in the form of the pending non-provisional application was picked up for substantive review by the USPTO in August of 2017. With the trade secret protection lost, the company turned its attention to securing a patent as supported by the original provisional application filing.

The company was thrilled to secure its first issued patent on the proprietary coating in 2018. A continuation patent application was filed in advance of this issuance to pursue additional claims and to keep the disclosure of the patent family available for future continuation filings. Although having a trade secret well into the future might have been the first option, it turned out to be wise to have a pending patent application as a backup option. The protection associated with the patent might not be the duration of a trade secret, but having protection through at least the patent's expiry is much better than having lost all intellectual property protection because of a rogue salesperson trying to make a deal.

19b PATENT IS PLAN A AND THE TRADE SECRET IS PLAN B

It can seem counterintuitive to keep a trade secret as a backup to patent protection, particularly in view of the common misconception that the two concepts are entirely mutually exclusive. However, there are useful techniques that can be used to pursue patent protection while keeping the disclosure of your patent application proprietary in the event where your plan A fails.

Patentability in certain technology fields, like medical diagnostics and software business methods, is in flux, and patent eligibility of this subject matter may be dubious. Dense technology fields where the scope of available protection is difficult to ascertain can also call patentability into question. Before capitulating and resigning yourself to the fact that it will be *impossible* to secure a patent, it may still be worth exploring the option. Patent claims run the gamut in terms of scope and quality, so there may be circumstances where no patent at all is better than an extremely narrow one. Instead of guessing how the USPTO will examine your claimed invention, you should consider exploring the scope of protection you might be able to secure before falling back to trade secret protection.

HOW THE PATENT PLAN A, TRADE SECRET PLAN B STRATEGY WORKS

Unlike many strategies in this book, this approach generally does not open with a provisional patent application.

We begin, instead, with the filing of a *non-provisional application* as shown in Figure 1. And this isn't just any ordinary non-provisional application; it's a Track One Accelerated Examination filing that is intended to add rocket fuel to the patent process. For more details on using Track One as a power up, have a look at Chapters 13 and 25. Expediting your filing by designating it as Track One is available for a fee, but if you qualify for accelerated examination for health or age-related reasons as discussed in Chapter 26, you can use that approach in lieu of a Track One application to achieve the same objective.

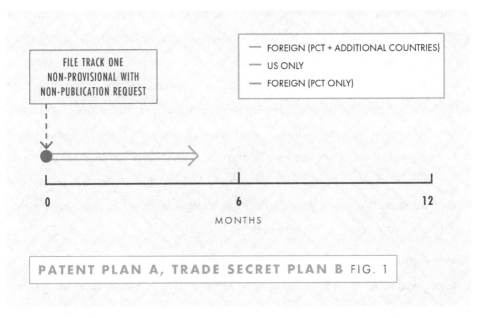

PATENT PLAN A, TRADE SECRET PLAN B FIG. 1

The objective of this approach is to get your claimed invention examined by the USPTO as quickly as possible. Starting with a provisional application would delay that process, as would filing a standard track non-provisional application. Only by going as fast as possible can you ascertain whether your invention is patentable or better suited as a trade secret while still keeping the option open to pursue patent protection in the United States *and* internationally. You will recall that there is a 12-month deadline to pursue international patent protection once you've filed a U.S. patent application. Without adding a power up to this process, given the USPTO's backlog, there is only a small chance that you'll receive even a *first* response from the USPTO before this 12-month deadline passes. Once you decide to pursue foreign patent protection, your patent application *must* publish. The race is on to learn as much as you can about patentability during that first year long window.

When filing your Track One non-provisional application it's very important to ensure that the request for non-publication is selected on your application data sheet, which will keep your non-provisional application from publishing 18 months from the time of filing. You'll still have 12 months to determine the scope of what is protectable by confidentially and aggressively pursue patent protection. The request for non-publication must contain a certification that the invention disclosed in the application has not been and *will not* be the subject of an application filed in another country. Fortunately, the USPTO has contemplated the scenario where you change your mind on foreign filing. Prior to filing foreign applications, you can *rescind* the nonpublication request or, if one or more foreign patent applications have already been filed, you can notify the USTPO of such filings no later than 45 days after the filing date of the counterpart foreign or international application.

This non-provisional application, with a Track One petition and non-publication request, will enter the expedited queue at the USPTO to be picked up for substantive examination, leading to a first action by the USPTO for a Track One application within four to six months. That's a lot better than the year or more you should expect with a non-expedited application. Once you receive an Office action from the USPTO, you need to respond as quickly as possible to keep the process moving. For a more detailed discussion of expedited prosecution you can refer to Chapter 18 on the Blitz Chess approach to the patent process.

It's unlikely that you'll get a notice of allowance on the USPTO's first review of your claims. This means that you'll want time for not one, but at least two substantive Office actions from the USPTO *before* the 12-month deadline expiration. That sand timer will feel like it's draining quickly! However, the USPTO's objective with the Track One program is similar to yours to provide you a final disposition on your application within 12 months from filing. The ideal is to give you two substantive rounds of examination within this 12-month period, hopefully enough to get you a notice of allowance or to sufficiently clarify the prospects of patentability. The second action, or final disposition, can be the notice of allowance that you're hoping for.

As shown in Figure 2, if you receive a notice of allowance or an indication of some allowable subject matter from the USPTO within 12 months from your initial filing, then Plan A is a success and you can proceed as hoped. You can make the decision to forego a trade secret and pay the issue fee to secure a granted patent, provided the claims you included hold sufficient business value. Now that you know you can secure valuable patent protection, you might want to consider additional spin-off continuation or divisional application filings as discussed in more detail in Chapters 10 and 17. Once the trade secret option has been surrendered, consider maximizing the scope of your patent protection.

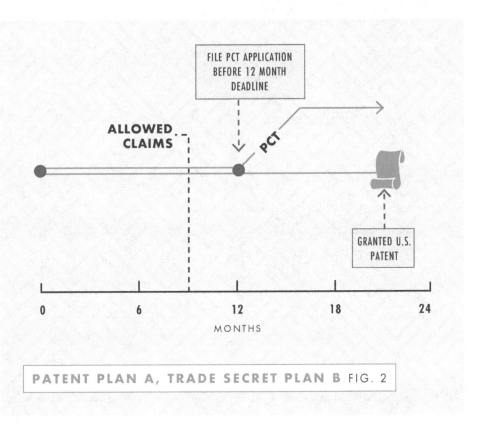

PATENT PLAN A, TRADE SECRET PLAN B FIG. 2

Because you're choosing the patent route by securing an issued patent, and because you've done so within 12 months from the original filing date of the non-provisional, you can also choose to pursue foreign patent applications. Remember that you must rescind the original non-publication request from your non-provisional application to do so, as it prohibits international filings. You may then choose to file a PCT application and/or direct foreign national stage applications that claim priority back to the Track One non-provisional application. Your PCT application and foreign national stage applications must be filed within 12 months from the non-provisional filing for this approach to work.

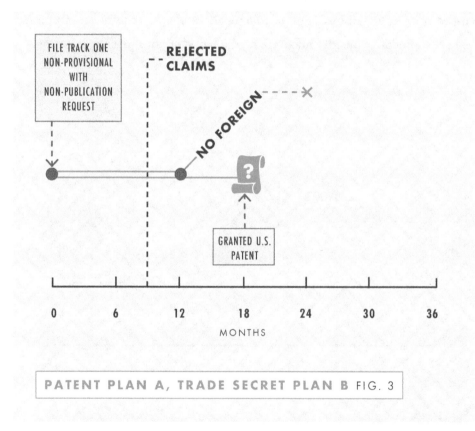

PATENT PLAN A, TRADE SECRET PLAN B FIG. 3

But not everything always goes to plan. As shown in Figure 3, you may need to fall back on Plan B because of patentability or prior art issues. Before relying completely on trade secret protection, you could choose to continue to prosecute the U.S. application for U.S.-only protection. The 12-month deadline to pursue foreign protection will have passed, but because of the non-publication request you can continue to confidentially prosecute your U.S. application with the USPTO.

If you no longer see value in pursuing the patent process, you may choose to simply let the Track One non-provisional application become abandoned. Doing so will maintain the confidentiality of this filing such that you can maintain the innovation as a trade secret. Merely failing to respond to any outstanding action will cause this non-provisional application to become abandoned, so you don't need to take any specific action to bury it. Because the non-publication request option was selected at the outset, your application and the associated prosecution history will never become publicly available.

BENEFITS OF THE PATENT PLAN A, TRADE SECRET PLAN B STRATEGY

- Maintain both trade secret and patent options while aggressively pursuing patent protection

- Possibility of securing U.S. and international patent protection if Plan A is successful within 12 months

- Possibility of securing U.S. patent protection if Plan A takes longer than 12 months

- Ability to use patent pending and proprietary on marketing materials

- Potentially infinite life of trade secret protection if Plan B is necessary

- Long patent term if Plan A is successful because of how quickly patent is secured

- Ability to file spin-off continuation and divisional applications if Plan A is successful

- Applicant retains control of whether disclosure of the patent application becomes public

- Ability to use patented designation more quickly

- Potential to use Patent Prosecution Highway (PPH) for allowed claims if Plan A is successful

DRAWBACKS OF THE PATENT PLAN A, TRADE SECRET PLAN B STRATEGY

- Expense of preparing and filing a Track One non-provisional application may be cost-prohibitive

- Speed of USPTO Office actions and required response can be a drain on time and financial resources

- Lacks the advantage provided by a provisional application to establish 12 months of priority without starting the patent term clock

REAL WORLD EXAMPLE: POLYMERIZATION SYSTEMS AND METHODS BY SIRRUS, INC.

Sirrus, Inc., which started as a small venture-backed startup company in Cincinnati, OH., developed a new chemical platform to reduce the time, energy requirements, and environmental footprint of many chemical processes. The materials that Sirrus manufactures are being incorporated into the next generation of high-performance coatings, adhesives, sealants and binders.

Polymerizable compositions are useful components in a number of applications and products and can be used as adhesives, coatings, and sealants. Sirrus believed this technology to be novel and non-obvious — and therefore patentable — but it had some concerns about a worst-of-both-worlds scenario that could result if the claimed technology was rejected by the USPTO *after* the 18-month pre-grant publication of its patent application. The published application would reveal what could possibly have been maintained as a trade secret and would amount to a roadmap for competitors should a patent not be secured. Sirrus saw value primarily in securing a patent for the new technology but, if that option failed, maintaining the specifics of the invention as a trade secret was an acceptable Plan B.

It can be difficult to ascertain the odds of securing a patent until you prosecute the claimed invention before the USPTO. Searches of prior patents and publications can be instructive, but even comprehensive searches could still miss a key piece of prior art that could be used to reject some or all of the applicant's claims. A USPTO examiner may identify art not considered, particularly when making obviousness rejections that combine multiple different references, such that you can never be sure your technology is patentable until you receive a notice of allowance. Although Sirrus had confidence that the technology would be patentable, it wanted to maintain the discovery as a trade secret if a patent could not be secured.

There was a key deadline with which Sirrus was concerned — the 18-month deadline, at which the application would publish. Sirrus wanted to determine patentability of its new technology *before* the 18-month publication date in the event the company decided to abandon the patent process in favor of trade secret protection.

On May 29, 2015, Sirrus filed a Track One Prioritized Examination non-provisional patent application directed to the technology. If Sirrus has started the process with a provisional application, it would not have been able to get clarity on the patentability of the claimed invention before the 12-month deadline, since provisional applications are not substantively examined. By filing a Track One non-provisional application as the first-filed application, Sirrus was able to aggressively speed up the patent process while the non-provisional application remained confidential. Notably, Sirrus did *not* check the non-publication request box at the time of filing, meaning that if it chose not to pursue patent protection it would need to take proactive efforts to abandon the application and avoid disclosure of the technology. This approach is a slight variant of the strategy outlined in the earlier play-by-play.

Rather than waiting years for a first USPTO response, Sirrus received a first action on November 5, 2015, less than six months from the original filing date. Fortunately for Sirrus, this first Office action from the USPTO indicated that some of the claims of the patent application were allowable. This confirmed the patentability of at least some of the claims in the pending and confidential, non-provisional application. Because Sirrus was more interested in securing a patent than maintaining the invention as a trade secret, it paid the issue fee after receiving a notice of allowance and a patent directed to the claimed technology issued as U.S. Pat. No. 9,334,430 on May 10, 2016. Because Sirrus was able to confirm the patentability of the technology before the 12-month international filing deadline, it also filed a PCT application on April 12, 2016 to preserve the company's ability to pursue patents in desirable foreign countries.

In this real-world example, Sirrus was able to secure its Plan A without having to rely on the Plan B option of a trade secret. What would have happened if Sirrus had been unable to secure allowable claims before the 12-month international filing deadline? If Sirrus was still working to secure a patent after the expiration of the 12-month deadline, it could have chosen not to file foreign patent applications and to prosecute the U.S. non-provisional application confidentially up until the 18-month pre-grant publication date. Prior to the pre-grant publication date, if desirable patentable subject matter could not be secured, Sirrus could have affirmatively abandoned the application such that it would never publish. Assuming Sirrus otherwise kept the information in the application confidential, the disclosure could still have been maintained as a trade secret.

CHAPTER 20

THE PATENT RELAY RACE STRATEGY—CREATING A PATENT DAISY-CHAIN

"IF YOU WANT TO GO QUICKLY, GO ALONE. IF YOU WANT TO GO FAR, GO TOGETHER."

– AFRICAN PROVERB

Why this strategy might be for you...

- You want to keep a patent application pending for all or a large portion of the available patent term

- Competitors may try to design around your issued patents

- You aren't sure which of the features or versions in your application will prove to have the most business value

- Issued patents combined with at least one pending application will help deter competitors

Relay races are a unique way for teams to compete against one another. In track and field, swimming, or any number of other sports, the relay is an event format that can be found in venues ranging from middle school sack races all the way to the Olympics. Why not just have four athletes simply run or swim the specified distance individually and then add up the scores? It's primarily because relays require an additional skill in the form of achieving a clean handoff.

Relay runners pass a baton and swimmers must touch a sensor pad before the next athlete is able to start his or her leg of the race. Individual athletes are still important, but it's the coordination between the athletes that makes for a gold medal-winning team. Dropping the baton or starting too early can result in a lost race or disqualification. The handoff in a relay race is like working the clutch on a manual transmission — both parts are moving together in a coordinated relationship and there is a sweet spot you find with practice. Miss this small window and you're liable to end up with problems.

Teams that have perfected the handoff can, together, become faster as a group than a competing team with individually faster athletes. Each individual in a relay race may have skills and attributes that make him or her well-suited for a particular role in the relay. The individual that struggles to accept the handoff may go first to minimize this weakness and a strong closer might be tapped to anchor the race. Whatever the strengths and limitations of each individual runner, the group as a whole can collectively go farther than any one individual.

Some relay teams are formed to accomplish something that an individual alone cannot. Ragnar® races were started in 2004 by Steve Hill, who had the dream of running an overnight, 24-hour relay across the mountains of Utah. That initial race, which spanned 188 miles from Logan to Park City, has blossomed into a nationwide movement of races throughout the United States. A Ragnar race team can include up to 12 people working together, without stopping, to complete a relay race of 200 miles or longer. For all but a few elite ultra-marathoners, a 200-mile race is impossible to complete as an individual. Splitting the race up between teammates allows the group as a whole to go farther. One of Ragnar's slogans is "doing things together that we could never do alone."

There is a patent equivalent to a relay race that can be effective for generating a series of patents with a daisy chain-like relationship. In the Patent Relay Race strategy, a series of applications are connected to one another in a serial arrangement such that when one application matures into a patent—or ends its race, so to speak—another application carries the "baton" forward. You will recall from Chapter 10, in the first section of this book, that patent applicants can spin off unlimited continuation or divisional patent applications from a parent application. Once *all* of the patent applications in a family have been issued or have become abandoned, the applicant loses the ability to file *any* new continuation or divisional patent applications. If this occurs, the applicant's issued patent claims are, for the most part, set in stone. There are worst-of-both-worlds scenarios where an applicant files a robust patent application with multiple embodiments, only protects one of those embodiments with a single issued patent, and then fails to file a continuation or divisional application to pursue additional subject matter. If this happens, the inventor has effectively dedicated *all* of the unclaimed subject matter to the public. It's a low IP IQ mistake to believe that a patent necessarily covers all of the subject matter disclosed and described in a patent application. In reality, it's very common for an issued patent to represent only a relatively small subset of the total disclosure.

The Patent Relay Race strategy is similar in many respects to the Bucket of Legos strategy described in Chapter 17, but with a different focus. The 20-year term for a patent family is like a 200-mile Ragnar race. Pending patent applications create flexibility for a patent applicant to target new claims, but it's impractical and generally undesirable to have a *single* application pending for the entire 20-year period. That would be like a single runner running a 200-mile ultramarathon on his or her own. Like a Ragnar race, the objective of the Patent Relay Race is to accomplish with multiple patent applications what a single application cannot. Scope in the Bucket of Legos strategy is focused on the broad coverage of technology elements whereas the Patent Relay Race is focused on retaining the flexibility to craft new claims and patent disclosed, but unclaimed versions, of the invention. To that end, this strategy keeps at least one patent application pending for as much of the available patent term as possible.

There is a co-pendency requirement for patent applications, where a spin-off continuation or divisional application *must* be filed before the priority application issues as a patent. This is the handoff in the patent game. If you receive a notice of allowance for a pending application, you must file a continuation before the allowed application issues or you will be barred from continuing the race. In most track and field relay races, the runners coordinating the handoff must complete the transfer during a specified distance or they will be disqualified. Similarly, if a notice of allowance is seen as entering this window in the patent game, then the issuance or abandonment of the application is when this window closes. Mastering a smooth handoff here will allow the prior runner to stop the race—either by issuing as a patent or becoming abandoned—while the newly filed application carries the baton forward.

Like a four-person relay race, the first leg—the initial patent application—will need to transition into the second leg—the continuation application—and this second into the third, and so on. Missing any of the handoffs during this race will disqualify you from filing future continuation or divisional applications. The characteristics of various patent applications may have a specific order in which they should be pursued. For example, an application with claims likely to be the fastest to allowance might be pursued first to establish a foundation, whereas slower runners with more endurance may be positioned in the middle stages. You can string together applications and patents for the entire available life of the patent family, and there are no limits to the number of applications that can be filed—you may need to manage a large number of runners and multiple handoffs.

Although not required, as shown in Figure 1, the Patent Relay Race frequently opens with the filing of a U.S. provisional application.

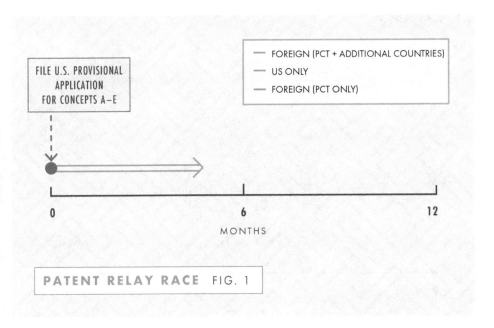

PATENT RELAY RACE   FIG. 1

This provisional application might be seen as the pacesetter for a group of runners. This individual rarely finishes first and, in some cases, doesn't finish the race at all. A provisional application, similarly, can start the process but by itself cannot become an issued patent and finish the race. The provisional application effectively drops out at some stage and lets the stronger non-provisional applications carry on.

The 12-month pendency of a provisional application sets a fixed period during which the handoff between the provisional and the non-provisional and/or foreign applications must take place. The Relay Race approach often maximizes most or all of this 12-month term, as shown in Figure 2, and pushes this handoff window to its very limit. The provisional patent application can include multiple embodiments or features in robust disclosure to support multiple continuation or divisional application filings in the near future. For a more detailed description on the benefits and drawbacks of including many versions, features, and methods in a single application, have a look at Chapter 17 discussing the Bucket of Legos strategy.

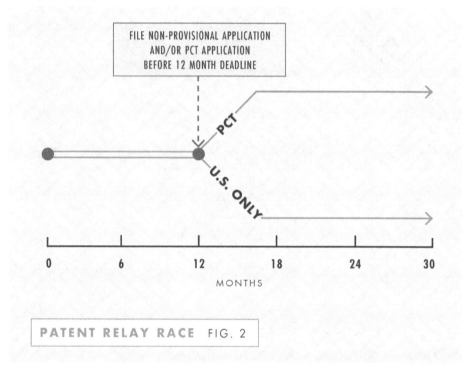

FILE NON-PROVISIONAL APPLICATION
AND/OR PCT APPLICATION
BEFORE 12 MONTH DEADLINE

PCT

U.S. ONLY

0   6   12   18   24   30

MONTHS

PATENT RELAY RACE   FIG. 2

The drawings and written specification of the first non-provisional application will contain the entire disclosure, but in accordance with USPTO practice, only one inventive concept can be claimed at a time.

As shown in Figure 3, when your first non-provisional application is deemed allowable by the USPTO, it will enter a second handoff period during which a new continuation can be filed to hand the baton forward. Before the issuance of this first patent, you must complete the handoff by filing a continuation or divisional application if you want to pursue any of the disclosed, but as yet unclaimed, features of your invention.

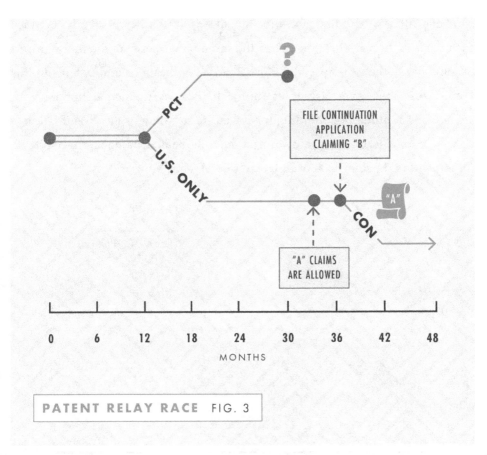

FILE CONTINUATION
APPLICATION
CLAIMING "B"

"A" CLAIMS
ARE ALLOWED

0   6   12   18   24   30   36   42   48

MONTHS

PATENT RELAY RACE   FIG. 3

This next leg in the relay, just like the prior non-provisional application, can be prosecuted before the USPTO until it becomes a second U.S. patent. As you may have guessed, before the issuance of that second patent, another continuation application must be filed during the handoff window for the patent relay race to continue.

As illustrated in Figure 4, these steps can repeat indefinitely while spinning off issued patents along the way. These connected patent applications form a daisy chain featuring several issued patents supported by the original application filing, each entitled to the priority date of the original.

The maximum term for the entire family in the illustrated example is 20 years from the filing of the first non-provisional application. Importantly, because each continuation application shares the same patent term as the first non-provisional filing, the expiration date for all of the applications and patents in this family will be the same. Using this approach, you can run the patent relay with at least one continuation pending for the entire duration of the patent family's 20-year patent term. Just be aware of the abbreviated patent term available for any granted patents achieved late in the relay race.

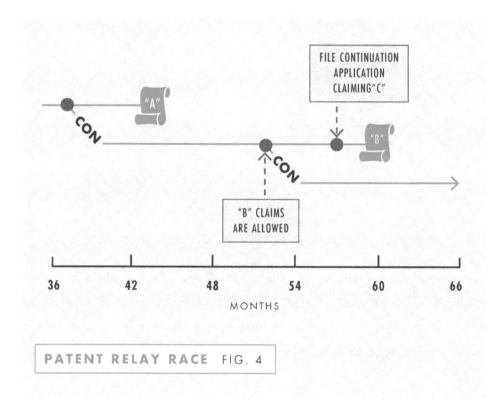

PATENT RELAY RACE   FIG. 4

BENEFITS OF THE PATENT RELAY RACE STRATEGY

- Maintains a pending application for all or a large portion of the life of a patent family

- Provides flexibility to pursue new claims in continuation or divisional applications

- Harder to design around because applicant has claim flexibility

- Ability to obtain multiple issued patents in series

- Can incorporate the benefits of a provisional application as a pacesetter

- Ability to discontinue the relay at the applicant's discretion

DRAWBACKS OF THE PATENT RELAY RACE STRATEGY

- Expense of maintaining a pending application, in addition to issued patents, for the life of a patent family can be high

- Initial disclosure should be robust, which can add to the application drafting expense

- For continuations, there will be shortened patent term because this is calculated from when the first non-provisional application is filed

- If your goal is to obtain maximum protection as quickly as possible, it may be better to file continuations at the same time rather than in series

- Not ideal for some technology fields, such as for discrete mechanical inventions or certain chemical compositions, where a single targeted or broad patent may provide sufficient protection

In 2017, Brainscope Company, Inc. was nominated for the 11th Annual Prix Galien USA Awards. The Galien Foundation hands out the award annually to examples of outstanding achievement in biomedical and technology products designed to improve the human condition.

Brainscope's nominated system, the Brainscope One, is an FDA-cleared, comprehensive head injury assessment device. The device enables urgent care physicians to objectively assess brain injuries, including concussions. It is handheld, easy-to-use, non-invasive, painless, and based on EEG technology. According to the company, it can be used on patients aged 18–85 years old within three days of a head injury. The device measures and interprets the brain's electrical activity and neurocognitive function for physicians to make clinical diagnoses.

Brainscope has been awarded more than 30 patents. One of its patent families provides a good illustration of the Patent Relay Race strategy in practical usage.

On March 8, 2013, Brainscope filed its first patent application directed to an "ELECTRODE ARRAY AND METHOD OF PLACEMENT" as U.S. patent application serial no. 13/790,149. The '149 application was filed "standard track" without accelerated examination and was granted a notice of allowance on December 12th, 2014. The applicant paid the issue fee on February 20th, 2015, and the patent ultimately issued as U.S. Patent 8,989,836, pictured here.

The '836 patent issued with 10 claims after very little prosecution or negotiation with the USPTO. It's very common for an applicant to have initially claimed only a portion of the subject matter contained in their as-filed application, which means that allowing the patent to issue without taking further action will result in all of that unclaimed material being dedicated to the public.

To avoid this potential loss of protection, Brainscope properly filed a continuation application, U.S. Serial No. 14/627,944, on the very same day (February 20th, 2015) that it paid the issue fee in the '149 parent application. By filing the continuation application before the parent application issued, Brainscope ensured that it maintained co-pendency between the new continuation and the soon-to-issue parent. Although it's only necessary to file the continuation before the actual issuance of the parent case, it is good practice to file the continuation at the same time the issue fee is paid in order to avoid a situation where the patent issues before the applicant has prepared and filed the continuation.

By retaining co-pendency with the now-issued '149 application, Brainscope was able to pursue new and different claims in its '944 continuation application. After additional prosecution, it was able to secure a second patent—U.S. 9,282,930—directed to subject matter disclosed in the parent application as filed, but not claimed in the first '836 patent. The '930 patent subsequently issued with 23 new claims based entirely on the disclosure of the original application.

A key benefit to the Patent Relay Race is that each subsequently issued patent is entitled to the priority date of the original filing, which in this case is March 8, 2013. Although the '944 application was a new filing, it was a continuation with a written description and figures substantively identical to the original parent filing and treated as though it was also filed on March 8, 2013.

Brainscope, still not content with the scope of the issued claims in two patents, again filed a continuation application, U.S. Serial No. 15/014,342, on the same day that it paid the issue fee in the '944 application. The newly filed '342 application has, as of the time this book was written, just received *another* notice of allowance for 31 claims different from the issued claims of both the '836 and '930 patents. It seems highly likely that Brainscope will continue its daisy chain patent strategy and pursue yet another continuation application before the issuance of the '342 application.

There are undoubtedly many reasons why Brainscope elected to use the Patent Relay Race strategy for this family of applications. As a developing technology, it's likely that at least some of the subject matter disclosed in the original application, but not initially claimed, had value to the company. If Brainscope had allowed its first application to issue without filing a continuation, it would have been unable to mine it to draft valuable new claims. By keeping a pending application alive at all times, Brainscope maintains its ability to craft new claims. According to Crunchbase, a website that discloses fundraising numbers for startups, Brainscope has raised over $50 million in venture capital, which speaks to the desirability of a patent portfolio with issued patents as well as flexible applications that can be molded by it or any acquiring party.

(12) **United States Patent**
Machon et al.

(10) Patent No.: **US 8,989,836 B2**
(45) Date of Patent: **Mar. 24, 2015**

(54) **ELECTRODE ARRAY AND METHOD OF PLACEMENT**

(71) Applicant: **Brainscope Company, Inc.**, Bethesda, MD (US)

(72) Inventors: **Lukasz W. Machon**, Darnestown, MD (US); **Neil S. Rothman**, Baltimore, MD (US)

(73) Assignee: **Brainscope Company, Inc.**, Bethesda, MD (US)

(*) Notice: Subject to any disclaimer, the term of this patent is extended or adjusted under 35 U.S.C. 154(b) by 152 days.

(21) Appl. No.: **13/790,149**

(22) Filed: **Mar. 8, 2013**

(65) **Prior Publication Data**
US 2014/0257073 A1   Sep. 11, 2014

(51) **Int. Cl.**
A61B 5/0478   (2006.01)
A61B 5/00   (2006.01)

(52) **U.S. Cl.**
CPC *A61B 5/6803* (2013.01); *A61B 5/0478* (2013.01); *A61B 5/6814* (2013.01); *A61B 5/684* (2013.01); *A61B 2562/164* (2013.01)
USPC **600/383**; 600/393; 600/544

(58) **Field of Classification Search**
CPC .. A61B 5/0478; A61B 5/6803; A61B 5/6814; A61B 5/6815
USPC 600/383, 393, 544, 545
See application file for complete search history.

(56) **References Cited**

U.S. PATENT DOCUMENTS

D560,809 S	1/2008	Causevic et al.	
D603,051 S	10/2009	Causevic et al.	
7,720,530 B2	5/2010	Causevic	
7,904,144 B2	3/2011	Causevic et al.	
D641,886 S	7/2011	Causevic et al.	
D647,208 S	10/2011	Rothman et al.	
8,364,254 B2	1/2013	Jacquin et al.	
8,391,948 B2 *	3/2013	Causevic et al.	600/383
8,473,024 B2 *	6/2013	Causevic et al.	600/383
8,821,397 B2 *	9/2014	Al-Ali et al.	600/301

(Continued)

FOREIGN PATENT DOCUMENTS

WO   WO 2009/100654 A1   8/2009

OTHER PUBLICATIONS

http://www.masimo.com/sedline/products.htm [Accessed Apr. 15. 2012].

(Continued)

Primary Examiner — Lee S Cohen
(74) *Attorney, Agent, or Firm* — Finnegan, Henderson, Farabow, Garrett & Dunner, LLP

(57)   **ABSTRACT**

A headset for detecting brain electrical activity may include a flexible substrate having first and second ends each configured to engage an ear of a subject and dimensioned to fit across the forehead of a subject. The headset may also include a plurality of electrodes disposed on the substrate and configured to contact the subject when the headset is positioned on the subject. First and second electrodes may contact top center and lower center regions of the forehead, respectively, third and fourth electrodes may contact front right and front left regions of the forehead, respectively, fifth and sixth electrodes may contact right side and left side regions of the forehead, respectively, and electrodes included within the securing devices may contact the ear regions. The third and fourth electrodes may be moveable in at least a vertical direction relative to the other electrodes.

10 Claims, 11 Drawing Sheets

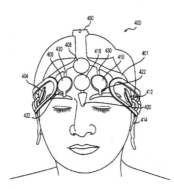

CHAPTER 21

THE SEE THE POKER FLOP STRATEGY—MINIMUM PROTECTION TO GET TO THE NEXT LEVEL

"MAY THE FLOP BE WITH YOU."

– DOYLE BRUNSON

Why this strategy might be for you...

- You want to see if there is commercial demand
  for your invention before investing heavily

- You have limited financial resources,
  but want to plant the flag on your invention

- You have a trade show, investor pitch, demo day,
  or other public event happening soon

- You want to be patent pending

- You would be willing to invest more in the patent process
  if the technology is a success or you can raise additional funds

If you've played poker recently, you probably played Texas Hold'em. The game hit its peak in the mid-2000s and turned math nerds, eccentrics, hustlers, and even one patent attorney into superstars. Many of the game's best players became household names via ESPN's reruns of the World Series of Poker events and every 20-something secretly dreamed of winning a coveted poker champion bracelet. Friday nights with my normally fun-loving friends turned into serious affairs with only water to drink and eventually — when the poker fad jumped the shark — sunglasses. I'm just saying, if you wear sunglasses at a poker table, you'd better be good.

For the unfamiliar, in Texas Hold'em players are initially dealt two down cards that are kept secret by the player for the duration of the hand. The object of the game is to make the best possible poker hand using those two down cards in combination with five community cards that are dealt face up in the center of the table. Players can use the best five of the seven cards available to them and, as they say, the best hand wins. There are multiple rounds of betting with an opportunity to fold during each round if you don't like your odds. The first round of betting begins 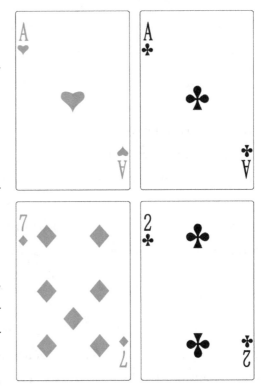 after the down cards are dealt, but before any community cards are shown. These community cards aren't laid down all at once: The first three are placed face up at the same time — referred to as the "flop" — followed by a single fourth "turn" card and a final fifth "river" card. There are rounds of betting before the flop, before the turn card, before the river, and then after all five community cards are placed.

You don't have to be a poker expert to understand that your two down cards, before any community cards are placed on the table, only give you a small amount of information on which to bet.

On many occasions I've seen a pair of "pocket" aces — the best starting hand — lose to a much weaker hand once the community cards are laid out on the table.

Even a 7 and 2 of different suits (called a 7-2 "unsuited" or "off-suit"), which is the statistically worst starting hand in poker, can beat a pair of pocket aces if the right community cards turn up.

You might find yourself sitting with the patent equivalent of a 7-2 off-suit. Or you might have something better than that, but not nearly as good as a pair of aces. Perhaps you have an invention that *might* be patentable, a business model that *might* work, or a startup that *might* be investable. To compound the problem, you could be low on chips and lack the cash to take a big loss on a poor investment. The temptation to fold a hand like this can be strong and sometimes that's the right choice. However, it may also be true that if you could just see the three cards of the flop, your poor hand might turn into a surefire winner. A *lot* can change in poker after the flop and it can be smart to stay in the game longer, if you can do so cost-effectively.

If you want to see the flop in a poker game, it's going to cost you something. Your decision to ante up and play is going to depend on how much it costs and how promising your hand is. If it's a "friendly" game and no one is betting aggressively, you might be able to see flop after flop with relatively poor hands for very little money. As Wayne Gretzky famously said, "You miss 100 percent of the shots you don't take." If you can stay in just long enough to get more information, to see the next three cards, then you might just end up taking the pot.

Many early stage businesses have inventions with strong patentable potential but lack the resources to invest heavily in patent protection at the outset. Many of these businesses have been told — or just assume — that the patent process is cost-prohibitive and, as a result, high-value developments are forsaken in favor of more immediate concerns. The See the Flop strategy can be an effective way for companies or inventors to establish an economical early filing date that can be followed by a more substantial investment once additional funds are raised, the product has demonstrated success, or the value of intellectual property has increased. This approach allows an inventor to plant a flag on the invention so that discussions can be conducted more freely with customers or investors without having to go "all in" until the odds of success have improved.

HOW THE SEE THE POKER FLOP STRATEGY WORKS

Unlike other strategies in this book, there may *not* be a substantial amount of work leading up to your opening move using this approach. Sometimes something is better than nothing and getting a basic and inexpensive provisional on file may be your best option. In an extreme example—and, mind you, this is not recommended—I've had companies approach me *one day* before they plan to attend a trade show, present at a demo day, publish an article on the technology, or make a sale. There are still options, albeit limited ones, in these scenarios to plant the flag and establish a filing date for your invention. Even when you are not in a rush, there may be reasons why getting a first basic provisional application on file makes sense. It's always better to have more time to prepare, but tight timing and budget constraints may limit your options.

The first step, as shown in Figure 1, is to file a first provisional patent application directed to as much of the inventive concept (in this case "A") as possible given time or budget constraints. Provisional applications can run the gamut in terms of quality and, in this approach, the first provisional filing may be on the low end of this spectrum. If you are playing a weak hand but can stay in the game and see the flop for a relatively low cost, it still might be worth it. A U.S. provisional application will expire 12 months from the initial filing date, which gives you some time to explore the market, raise capital, or establish product-market fit. During this 12-month period you will be patent pending, but you should not have any illusions about the quality of your provisional application or its ability to support strong claims in the future. Of course, your provisional may end up being of sufficient scope and quality to have substantive future value. Just keep in mind that cutting corners on timing and cost generally means there is increased risk that your technology isn't as protected as well as it could or should be. Still, something may be better than nothing.

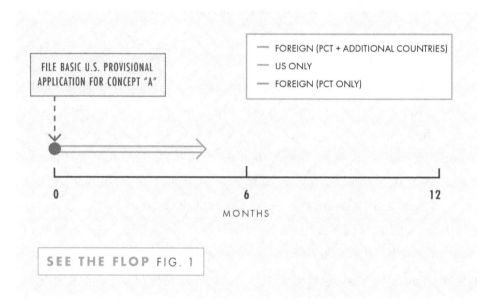

SEE THE FLOP FIG. 1

Your first U.S. provisional application is 100 percent confidential during the first year of pendency, just like your two down cards in poker. This provisional will *only* become visible to the public after a non-provisional application and/or PCT application, if pursued, has published. If you decide to fold your hand and do nothing by the 12-month deadline, your provisional application will become abandoned and will *never* become public—the patent equivalent of mucking your hand in poker.

Once the first provisional application is filed, you can try to monetize the invention, raise funds, test the technology, and so on. This additional information you'll work to collect is the patent equivalent of seeing the flop in poker. Once you gather this knowledge you might find your hand is terrible or you might be pleasantly surprised.

If your low-cost gamble pays off and it now makes sense to invest more substantially in the patent process, you should, as shown in Figure 2, file a *second* more robust provisional application as quickly as possible. You might have closed a funding round, started generating revenue, or otherwise established the value of patent protection. If you hit a straight after seeing the flop in poker, it's now time to seriously up the bet.

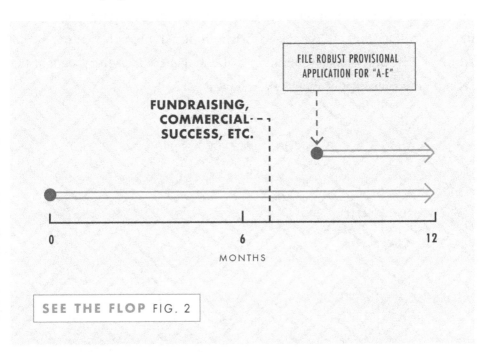

FILE ROBUST PROVISIONAL APPLICATION FOR "A-E"

FUNDRAISING, COMMERCIAL SUCCESS, ETC.

0   6   12

MONTHS

SEE THE FLOP FIG. 2

When you begin preparing your second provisional application, it may look quite different from that first provisional application filing. What differs between the first provisional application and the second is the content and scope of the applications. Where the first focused on simply planting the flag, the second provisional application might include a robust disclosure, multiple embodiments, high-quality images, improved formatting, and deeper technical details. This second provisional application should be filed *as soon as possible* after the decision to move forward is made. Newly introduced subject matter not included in the first provisional application will only get the later filing date of the second provisional application, so you'll need to hustle.

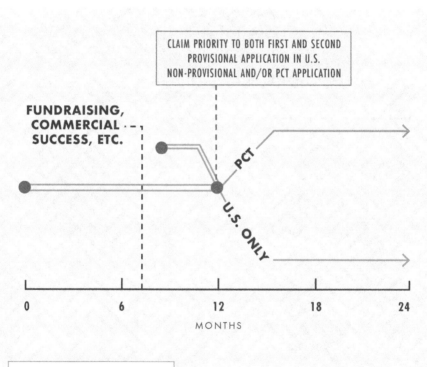

SEE THE FLOP FIG. 3

You can wait until the non-provisional application is filed at the one-year deadline to add the more robust disclosure, but it's not recommended. Holding off until the end of the 12-month window will lose you valuable months of priority that could have been secured by filing a second provisional application more quickly. Just because you have 12 months doesn't mean you should wait that long and just because you have a patent application on file doesn't mean you are fully protected.

As shown in Figure 3, at the end of 12 months from the filing date of the *first* provisional application, a U.S. non-provisional application, PCT application, or foreign national stage application must be filed if priority to the first application is still desirable. Your U.S. non-provisional should also claim priority to the second provisional application so as to integrate the newly-added subject matter. It's perfectly acceptable — and, at times, beneficial — to claim priority to *multiple* provisional applications in a single, subsequently-filed non-provisional application. For another example of the benefits of claiming priority to multiple provisional applications have a look at Chapter 16 on the Lean Patent Strategy.

The non-provisional application can eventually mature into a U.S. patent. The claims of the issued patent will be entitled to the priority date of the first application in which *all* of the subject matter of that claim was first disclosed. Some claims may be entitled to the filing date of the first provisional, whereas others may only be entitled to the filing date of the second provisional, and still others to the filing date of the non-provisional if you added more subject matter into that filing.

BENEFITS OF THE SEE THE FLOP STRATEGY

- Quickly and inexpensively establishes an early filing date for the disclosure

- Allows applicant to use patent pending to describe the technology to investors, customers, and partners

- Being patent pending may deter competitors

- First provisional application is 100% confidential

- A second, more robust provisional application can be filed once additional resources are secured or value can otherwise be demonstrated

- The non-provisional and/or PCT applications can claim priority to both provisional applications

DRAWBACKS OF THE SEE THE FLOP STRATEGY

- The first basic provisional application may not contain enough disclosure or be sufficiently enabled to provide much substantive value

- If the applicant chooses to reveal the first provisional application, the lower quality could reflect badly on the company

- If important technology is not entitled to the early filing date of the first provisional application, intervening prior art may block patentability

- 12 months may not be enough time to secure enough resources or get enough clarification on value to know if a more robust application should be pursued

- Applicants can have a false sense of security that they are adequately protected when they are not

Venture for America (VFA) is a prestigious two-year fellowship program for recent college grads to create jobs in non-Silicon Valley cities. VFA Fellows attend a five-week training camp, apply for jobs within VFA's vetted company network, and work for two years as full-time, salaried employees in one of 18 cities. When VFA Fellows are ready to start a company — be it two years after college or ten — VFA has resources like a crowdfunding competition, an accelerator, and a seed fund to help make that dream a reality. It's an incredible opportunity for those selected and I've had the privilege of working with and mentoring several of the companies, in addition to teaching intellectual property at the VFA accelerator.

I met Christine Schindler and Dutch Waanders during one of my VFA presentations on IP. As recent college bio-medical engineering graduates from Duke University, they were developing a sophisticated mobile pathogen-detection system. Christine and Dutch were both VFA fellows that had worked in-house with startups as part of the program before starting their own business with the support of VFA's accelerator. Their company, PathSpot Technologies, Inc., developed a mobile app that uses visible light fluorescent technology to determine contamination associated with pathogens. PathSpot's system can be used to improve employee sanitation in the workplace and as a part of a quality control system to evaluate health and safety regulation compliance for any establishment.

Although the VFA accelerator, like most, provided PathSpot with some initial capital, this funding was limited and was earmarked largely for the development and testing of its mobile technology. PathSpot recognized that its intellectual property position could become important for future investment or during acquisition, but spending its limited capital on a robust patent application would pull resources from development and testing. Many startups find themselves in this catch-22 where they recognize the value in securing intellectual property, but need to build a workable solution before they can attract the funding necessary to invest heavily and responsibly in patents. How can a promising company with smart founders secure intellectual property rights without jeopardizing key research and development milestones?

PathSpot's solution was to draft and file the best possible provisional it could given the limited budget and resources. Entrepreneurs and early stage companies tend to create a lot of content that can be repurposed for use in a provisional patent application—grant proposals, business plans, pitch materials, wireframes, user manuals, and the like can often be used to prepare a provisional application. Putting that together into a basic application will establish a filing date for key inventive concepts without breaking the bank. It might cut corners by not including formal drawings, for example, but a provisional application does not require formal drawings and the USPTO is lenient with the form and content for what it will accept in a provisional patent application. Of course, it's important that the invention be fully taught if the applicant wants to rely upon the early filing date of the provisional. But if intellectual property will later become important, then something is certainly better than nothing.

PathSpot helped improve the quality of its provisional patent application through a healthy amount of leg work in preparation. Too often, busy inventors want to send a few rough notes to their patent attorney with the expectation that their attorney will magically convert this into a robust and fully-enabled patent application. PathSpot was diligent in identifying existing documents, asking questions about what needed to be included in its patent application, and supplying information that had not already been created for some other purpose. By doing so, PathSpot gave itself a better chance at a quality patent application at a price they could afford.

In poker terms, PathSpot had a couple of solid down cards—in the form of a solid business idea and a strong academic pedigree — but it was still too early to go all-in on a heavy investment of capital in its intellectual property position. It recognized that intellectual property could become extremely valuable to its business if a few additional cards fell its way, so PathSpot spent enough money and did enough leg work to stay in the game and see the flop. Founders learn a great deal about product-market fit, whether they have the right team, and how viable their business model is in the first few years of their company's existence. If you can preserve your intellectual property position without cannibalizing other business needs, you have the chance to view the unseen cards and see if they fall your way. If they do, then hopefully you did enough to build upon that foundation. If they don't, then you haven't spent more money on your intellectual property position than you should have.

PathSpot is still waiting to see how the cards fall, but it has a seat at the table and is definitely in the game. As of this writing, they have been accepted into the prestigious TechStars Accelerator 2018 NYC cohort and continue to receive position attention in the startup and venture capital communities.

CHAPTER 22

"CALL MY BLUFF" STRATEGY— BASIC APPLICATIONS FOR PERCEPTION AND DETERRENCE

"THE WHOLE WORLD IS RUN ON BLUFF."

MARCUS GARVEY

Why this strategy might be for you…

- You want to be patent pending for perceptive or deterrence reasons

- You have limited financial resources

- Your invention has dubious patentability because
  of prior art or patent eligibility issues

Many games include some form of strategic bluffing. Games like Balderdash and Liar's Dice are built entirely around the concept of bluffing. The goal of the bluffer is to convince the other players that their hand, position, cards, or the like are better than what they are actually holding. Those who love bluffing tend to see it as an art form and an integral part of many games.

Although bluffing is a technique employed in numerous games, most people understandably associate bluffing with poker. We've used comparisons to Texas Hold'em in a number of our examples and, just like poker, there are elements of bluffing in the patent game. The value associated with any given patent strategy is part substantive and part perception, the latter of which can be measured by factors related to positive external perception and deterrence. Sometimes these perception-related factors are grounded in reality; sometimes they're not. In patent law, it's possible to play a weak hand well and effectively bluff your competitors into thinking your position is much stronger than it is.

The Call My Bluff strategy leverages the patent pending status accorded to provisional application filings to create the appearance of a strong patent portfolio that can serve to ward off competitors and attract customers. There can be meaningful benefits to having a pending patent application even if the application never ultimately issues as a patent.

There is an important distinction between this strategy and the See the Flop strategy described in the previous chapter. In the See the Flop strategy, a basic provisional application is filed as a placeholder until additional resources can be secured or knowledge gained that justify a more robust application filing. The objective with that approach is to try to capture as much substantive value as possible in the first provisional application filing, but quickly and on a budget. In the Call My Bluff strategy, discussed in this chapter, the applicant acknowledges (to themselves) that there is not and likely never will be much or any substantive value in having an issued patent. The objective is to be patent pending, to appear innovative, and to ward off competitors. If you can back down a competitor based upon a confidential and inexpensive provisional patent application, then there can be tremendous value in using this approach for relatively little cost.

HOW THE CALL MY BLUFF STRATEGY WORKS

Unlike other strategies in this book, there isn't a substantial amount of work leading up to the opening move. Because substantive protection is not a major concern with this approach and the application filings are primarily being used for perception and deterrent reasons, you might choose to put very little effort into each patent application.

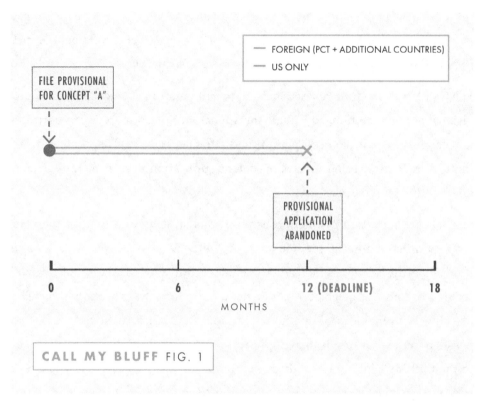

FILE PROVISIONAL
FOR CONCEPT "A"

FOREIGN (PCT + ADDITIONAL COUNTRIES)
US ONLY

PROVISIONAL
APPLICATION
ABANDONED

0   6   12 (DEADLINE)   18

MONTHS

CALL MY BLUFF FIG. 1

The first step is to file a first provisional patent application directed to a marginally inventive concept (in this case "A"), which may be a very basic or thin disclosure. The first provisional application might be a PowerPoint presentation, a grant proposal, a roughly completed template document, or something else in that vein. It may include hand drawings, photos, or other informalities allowed during the provisional filing process. You'll recall that a U.S. provisional patent application has a 12-month pendency and, once the provisional application expires, you will no longer be patent pending. The provisional application is 100 percent confidential and, once it goes abandoned, it will never become public.

One year of being patent pending may be helpful, but what if you want to continue bluffing? You could choose to file an expensive non-provisional application or PCT application before the end of the 12-month deadline, but this may be cost prohibitive if there is little or no substantive value in the invention.

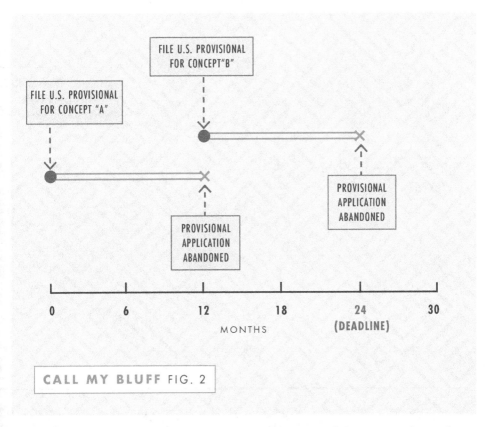

FILE U.S. PROVISIONAL FOR CONCEPT"B"

FILE U.S. PROVISIONAL FOR CONCEPT "A"

PROVISIONAL APPLICATION ABANDONED

PROVISIONAL APPLICATION ABANDONED

0   6   12   18   24   30

MONTHS   (DEADLINE)

CALL MY BLUFF FIG. 2

Another option to keep the game going, near the end of the 12-month pendency of the first provisional filing, is to file a second basic provisional application. If the second provisional application is filed during the pendency of the first provisional application — and it is directed to the commercial technology — then the applicant can continue to describe the technology as patent pending. One variation of this strategy is to file a low quality non-provisional application prior to the 12-month deadline, but the filing fees and preparation for even a basic non-provisional application may be too much to justify.

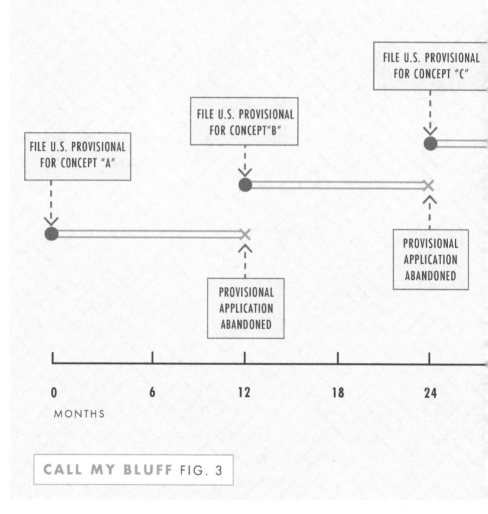

FILE U.S. PROVISIONAL FOR CONCEPT "C"

FILE U.S. PROVISIONAL FOR CONCEPT"B"

FILE U.S. PROVISIONAL FOR CONCEPT "A"

PROVISIONAL APPLICATION ABANDONED

PROVISIONAL APPLICATION ABANDONED

0   6   12   18   24

MONTHS

CALL MY BLUFF FIG. 3

When employing this strategy, you'll need to file provisional applications every 12 months if you want to maintain your patent pending status. In the illustrated example, each of the subsequently-filed provisional applications is directed to a new aspect of the technology (e.g., A, B, C, and D). Each subsequent filing may be only a minor variation of the prior filing, where something new is added in each that builds upon the original filing. As illustrated, this approach can last indefinitely with the applicant continuously filing low-cost provisional applica-

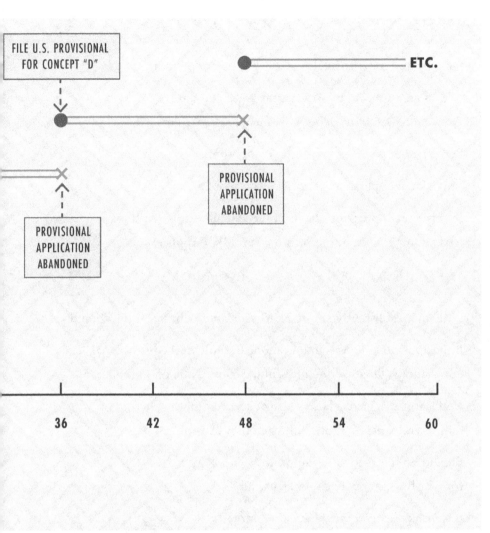

tions to create at least some positive perception and deterrent value. It is, of course, recommended that you discuss the specific risks of this approach with your patent attorney before proceeding.

BENEFITS OF THE CALL MY BLUFF STRATEGY

- Quickly and inexpensively establishes patent pending status

- Allows an applicant to use patent pending to describe
  the technology to investors, customers, and partners

- Being patent pending may deter competitors

- Provisional applications are 100% confidential

- Provisional applications have a much smaller USPTO filing
  fee as compared to non-provisional and PCT applications

DRAWBACKS OF THE CALL MY BLUFF STRATEGY

- Little to no substantive protection associated with the application filings

- If the applicant chooses to reveal one or more of the provisional
  applications, the lower quality could reflect badly on the company

- Applicants can have a false sense of security that
  they are adequately protected when they are not

- Should not be used with important technology
  for which a monopoly could be valuable

- It is unlikely a patent will ever be granted

REAL WORLD EXAMPLE #1—
STARTUP ACCELERATOR "DEMO DAY"

If your city doesn't currently have a startup accelerator (or several), it probably will soon. Accelerators act as a boot camp of sorts for startup companies. They generally last for only a few months and end with a "demo day" consisting of a public demonstration or pitch to an audience. There are now accelerators for a wide range of businesses, but most typically focus on tech-oriented growth businesses.

The most famous of these accelerators, Y Combinator, invests a "small" amount of money ($120,000) in a large number of startups twice a year. The startups move to Silicon Valley for three months, during which time mentors and inventors work intensively with the founders to get their company into the best possible shape and refine their pitch for demo day. Y Combinator companies have the opportunity to pitch to a carefully selected, invite-only audience made up largely of prospective investors.

In my practice, I have been fortunate to work with hundreds of startup companies. Many have been through one accelerator program when I work with them, some have been through several. Because these companies are usually at an early stage — often pre-revenue and pre-product — there is intense pressure during their accelerator time to accomplish a great deal and to check several boxes for investors. One of the boxes that's difficult for startups to check, but frequently asked for by investors, is the company's proprietary or intellectual property position.

Satisfying IP-related questions from investors can be particularly challenging for early stage companies. In many cases, the type of technology that accelerators are looking for also happens to fall in a category of technology that, presently, is very difficult to patent. This applies often to businesses making software-as-a-service products, mobile phone applications, or medical diagnostics, which I touched on when mentioning 101 rejections early in this book. Compounding this issue is that many startup companies do not yet have a workable solution to their problem and little or no cash to pay high-priced attorneys.

In some cases, it can be enough for the company's founders to explain a lack of intellectual property to prospective investors using some of the reasons mentioned above. However, there are still investors that fear a startup company without any form of intellectual property is simply too risky to justify investment. Or, given the fast-paced nature of demo days and early stage investing, a company may get a "no" from an investor before they have the chance to explain the rationale behind a lack of patent filings.

There are times when it's simply easier and more efficient for a startup company to file a basic provisional application and pursue the Call my Bluff approach in lieu of trying to explain in detail why a robust expenditure on patent applications is misguided. Many companies want to include "patent pending" in their pitch decks to appear innovative, to impress potential customers, and to deter competitors, but without spending scarce capital unnecessarily.

Pursuing the Call My Bluff strategy should not be construed as a license to misstate or overstate a company's intellectual property position. The use of patent pending can have a powerful impact on positive perception and as a deterrent, but there is certainly a line between gamesmanship and dishonesty that should never be crossed. Investors that aren't initially turned off by the lack of any patent filings may come to respect the founder's knowledge of intellectual property and the ability to create value without expending considerable amounts money once they have the opportunity to discuss a company's overarching IP strategy.

REAL WORLD EXAMPLE #2—AGING-IN-PLACE TECHNOLOGY BY CLEANCUT BATH, INC.

I have seen firsthand how impactful the use of this strategy can be from the other side of the table as well. I was approached several years ago by CleanCut Bath, Inc., which develops aging-in-place bathroom technology for the disabled and growing geriatric population. This company is able to make bathrooms more accessible for these individuals using their unique technology, allowing people to stay in their homes for as long as possible. Although this cutting-edge company is rarely interested in "me too" products, like all companies it sometimes finds inspiration or a business opportunity in product lines developed by others.

In one particular instance, the CEO of this company, Chris Stafford, was browsing competitors' websites to look at competitive offerings and he came across a purportedly patent pending product that would fit well in the CleanCut catalog. Understanding that patent pending is a caution, but not necessarily an impediment, the CEO asked that I find the company's intellectual property, evaluate its patents or patent application filings, and determine if CleanCut could consider making something similar without fear of infringing. This is a sophisticated request and something I wish all of my clients would do before diving headfirst into a product offering requiring a substantial commitment of resources.

During my patent search, I started with the company name of the competitor and found nothing. I identified the CEO of the company as well as a few seemingly key employees and searched various patent databases for their names as listed inventors. Still finding nothing, I started to explore keywords in various patent databases that might identify the specific technology, even if the application was not under the name of the company. I was striking out left and right.

Given the poor quality of the competitor's website, I started to suspect this company might be outright lying about having a patent application on file. It's circumstantial, but the company did not appear to have any patent filings and was a relatively small shop. That's not stone-cold proof, but it was enough to support my hunch that this competitor was improperly using the patent pending designation. Numerous other IP-related indicators such as trademarks and copyright notices were missing on its website and other materials. If I were a betting man — which I am — I would have bet heavily on this company having merely added "patent pending" to its website without filing even a basic provisional application. At best, I figured this competitor was probably using the Call My Bluff strategy of having something very thin on file to properly use the patent pending distinction, but even that was in serious doubt.

Unfortunately, the lack of any publicly available patent applications could not confirm that this company hadn't filed one or even many patent applications directed to the technology. The confidential nature of provisional applications means you will be unable to access this information unless it is given to you by the applicant, even if you know the serial number and title of the application. If the competitor had filed a non-provisional application it could still be impossible to identify, as these filings are typically not published until 18 months from the earliest filing date. Additionally, some applications won't publish at all until the patent application issues as a U.S. patent. There is effectively an 18-month blackout period for all patent application filings and this period can be even longer under certain circumstances.

Was this competitor bluffing? CleanCut's interest here wasn't particularly strong given this was a "nice to have" product. The company hadn't yet spent the resources to be pot committed to the extent that it would be hard not to move forward. I felt strongly this was a bluff, but CleanCut was understandably risk averse, had little to gain, and stood to lose a lot of time and money by potentially instigating a fight. Foregoing the new product line was the ultimate decision made by the company and was likely the right decision, albeit a frustrating one. As Kenny Rogers famously crooned, "you gotta know when to fold 'em."

Again, this is not to advocate that a company falsely claim their technology is patent pending or patented. But if this competitor had only a weak application on file, the outcome is still the same. This company effectively eliminated a competitor it will never know about without a fight for as low as the $70 fee it might take to file a provisional patent application. Looking at this from the opposite perspective, if you can create tremendous deterrent value by being patent pending with the proper use of this designation you may stifle competitors without you ever even knowing they were evaluating your technology.

CHAPTER 23
"FIND THE RIVER" STRATEGY—DELAYING TACTICS WHILE WAITING FOR VALUE

"LIFE! WHAT INSCRUTABLE CARD SHALL YE THROW NEXT UPON THE SOFT FELT OF OUR DAYS?"

– COLSON WHITEHEAD

Why this strategy might be for you...

- You need time to secure financial resources

- You are interested in both domestic and international patent protection

- You would be willing to invest more in the patent process once you raise additional funds

I discussed the See the Flop strategy in Chapter 21 as one approach that can buy you time to see how a particular technology, field, or business model will play out. This can be a powerful approach for a company or inventor needing time to evaluate the value of a given innovation. If this delay can be achieved at a relatively low cost, the company might ultimately still be able to exploit the invention later in the process.

In that Texas Hold'em-themed chapter, I laid out how just getting to see the poker flop in the patent game can provide value. Although the flop can dramatically improve your hand or give you a pretty good idea that your hand is garbage, the two remaining community cards to be flipped represent nearly a third of the total cards available. It can be expensive to see these last few cards, however, because players with good hands often try to push out weaker ones by placing big bets after the flop. But there are times when a player with a weak hand can hang around long enough to see four or even all five community cards. In poker, everyone who has played has a story about a bad beat where a surefire winning hand turned into a losing hand once the final card was shown. Sometimes, against all odds, that last river card, which is what the final card is called, saves what was a poor hand and miraculously turns it into a winner.

The Find the River approach is a great fit for companies desiring international patents — which are notoriously expensive — but have a limited initial budget and want to stall for as long as possible. Good candidates for benefiting from this approach include companies with technology that is yet unproven, startups that are fundraising, or companies that aren't sure which foreign markets will have commercial value. This strategy may also be a good fit for companies wanting to maintain the perception and deterrent value of being patent pending while preserving the ability to pursue foreign patent protection for as long as possible. In these circumstances, you want to see the patent-equivalent of the river card before fully committing.

As shown in Figure 1, the Find the River strategy begins, as many do, with the filing of a U.S. provisional application. As you will recall, a provisional application has a maximum 12-month pendency during which a U.S. non-provisional application, PCT application, and/or foreign national stage applications must be filed.

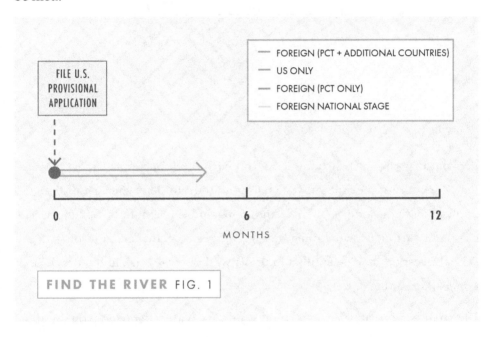

FIND THE RIVER FIG. 1

With reference to Figure 2, in this strategy, only a PCT application should be filed prior to the expiration of the 12-month period in order to preserve the priority date of the provisional application. If you have reviewed other strategies in this book, you'll recall that most of them include filing a U.S. non-provisional application in place of or in addition to a PCT application. The Find the River strategy relies upon the PCT application to delay substantive and costly patent prosecution, limit the number of application filing fees that are required, and to keep open the option of pursing patent protection in the approximately 150

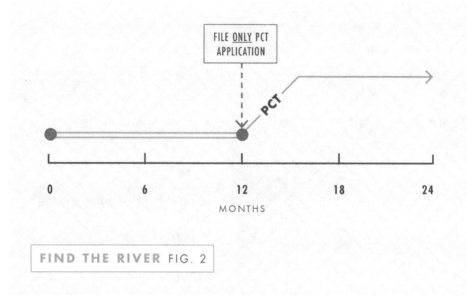

FILE <u>ONLY</u> PCT
APPLICATION

PCT

| 0 | 6 | 12 | 18 | 24 |

MONTHS

FIND THE RIVER FIG. 2

PCT-participating jurisdictions. This approach often maximizes most or all of the 12-month term of the provisional application to defer the cost of the PCT application for as long as possible and to maximize patent term. So long as this chain remains intact, subsequent foreign applications that claim priority to the PCT application may be entitled to priority all the way back to the provisional application's filing date.

The quality of initial provisional filings can vary widely depending on the applicant's goals and circumstances at the time. For this strategy, because substantive protection is important, the provisional application should be of a very high quality. You might also consider adding a robust disclosure, such as in the manner described for the Bucket of Legos strategy in Chapter 17, so that you preserve the ability to claim a large number of features, embodiments, and combinations domestically and internationally at a later date.

A PCT application is effectively a foreign placeholder application. It cannot itself mature into a patent, but it does buy the applicant additional time until foreign national stage applications must be filed. As shown in Figure 3, this ex-

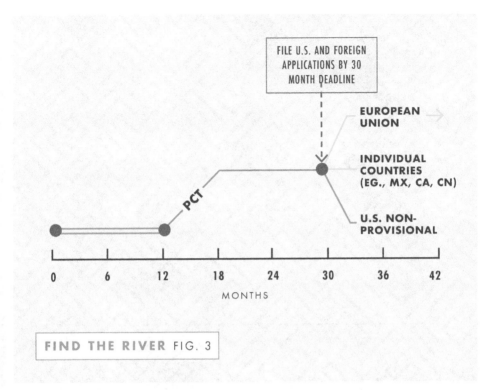

EUROPEAN
UNION

INDIVIDUAL
COUNTRIES
(EG., MX, CA, CN)

U.S. NON-
PROVISIONAL

PCT

| 0 | 6 | 12 | 18 | 24 | 30 | 36 | 42 |

MONTHS

FIND THE RIVER FIG. 3

tension of time, of course, is limited and the next significant date in the Find the River strategy is the 30-month deadline from the provisional application's filing date. In most countries, the extension afforded by the PCT application is exhausted by the 30-month deadline, so the applicant needs to be prepared to file direct national stage applications at that time. There is no such thing as a worldwide patent — patents are jurisdictional — so protection must be secured in each individual country where a patent is desirable. The 30-month deadline may be enough time for many applicants to secure funding or to establish the value of the patent portfolio, but if even more time is needed there are a few countries, as discussed in the Playing for the Last Shot strategy in Chapter 30, that extend this deadline even farther.

On or before the 30-month deadline, you must typically file your national stage patent applications in each country where protection is desired. As illustrated in

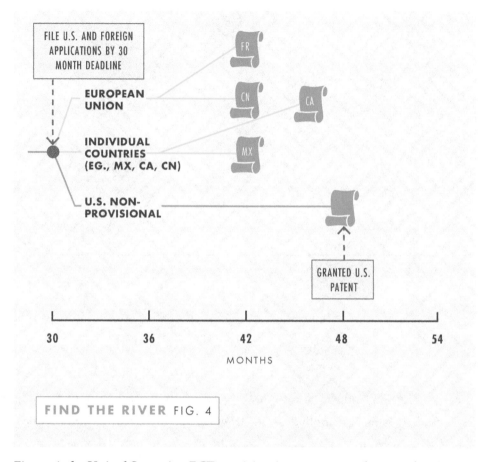

FILE U.S. AND FOREIGN
APPLICATIONS BY 30
MONTH DEADLINE

FR

EUROPEAN
UNION

CN

CA

INDIVIDUAL
COUNTRIES
(EG., MX, CA, CN)

MX

U.S. NON-
PROVISIONAL

GRANTED U.S.
PATENT

30   36   42   48   54

MONTHS

FIND THE RIVER FIG. 4

Figure 4, the United States is a PCT-participating country and entry of a non-provisional application which claims priority to the PCT application can be filed in
the U.S. This is in contrast to several of the other strategies in this book where a
non-provisional application is filed in parallel with the PCT application, a good
option for when the applicant wants to begin active prosecution in the United
States more quickly. However, when trying to be as cost-conscious as possible,
you might defer the filing of the U.S. non-provisional and use the PCT application as a priority vehicle for both domestic and international patent applications.
Using this approach, the U.S. non-provisional application can still benefit from
the priority date of the original provisional application.

As shown in Figure 4, the U.S. non-provisional and/or foreign national stage applications can eventually be granted by each respective patent office, securing a 20-year patent term starting from the filing date of the PCT application. If you are fortunate enough to get allowable subject matter in one country more quickly than the others, you might consider using the Patent Prosecution Highway (PPH) to aid in the process, as discussed in more detail with respect to the Checkers strategy in Chapter 27.

This strategy doesn't work particularly well for companies in a hurry to secure domestic or foreign patent protection. Lower cost options usually mean time and/or scope is sacrificed. In this case, the process is slowed down considerably and cuts into the applicant's available patent term. If the company has sufficient capital and the technology has strong patentable potential, it may be wiser to choose one of the more scope-centric strategies. Also, if the technology is going to be difficult to patent or enforce both domestically and abroad, then even this budget-conscious strategy could become a waste of money. The Find the River strategy is certainly a cost deferral option, but nothing involving international applications can accurately be portrayed as inexpensive.

BENEFITS OF THE FIND THE RIVER STRATEGY

- Cost effectively maintains an applicant's ability to pursue domestic and foreign patent protection for a long time

- Defers filing fees and response fees associated with later-filed patent applications

- The United States is a party to the PCT and can claim priority to a PCT application

- The patent term will not start running until the PCT application is filed

- The PCT application will publish 18 months from the earliest priority date such that it can then be used by patent offices to block later-filed third party patent applications

- Both the provisional application and PCT application allow the applicant to describe the technology as patent pending

- Slow nature of this approach may be beneficial

- By delaying a decision on which countries to pursue, the final selections may be more accurate and valuable

DRAWBACKS OF THE FIND THE RIVER STRATEGY

- The applicant will need to wait a long time to secure a patent because both the provisional application and PCT application are effectively placeholder applications

- The slow nature of the process can consume valuable patent term

- The initial provisional application may be costly because it should be robust and expertly prepared

- Should not be used when granted patents are desired quickly

- A very small number of countries are not available under the PCT system

REAL WORLD EXAMPLE: BARIATRIC STAPLERS BY STANDARD BARIATRICS, INC.

It can take a long time for startup companies to secure the vital funding needed to bring a product to market, particularly when the technology under development is a medical device. Standard Bariatrics, Inc. in Cincinnati, Ohio is a venture-backed medical device company that invented a novel bariatric stapling system for the treatment of obesity.

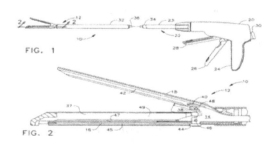

FIG. 1

FIG. 2

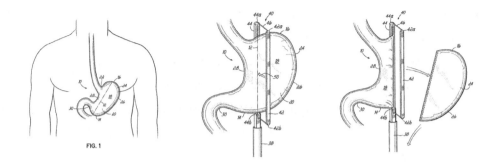

FIG. 1

Previous solutions used a stapling device—such as the one shown in the diagram above—to staple segments of a patient's stomach along a resection line and to remove all but a sleeve of stomach tissue.

This technique helps to reduce the appetite of the patient and can lead to life-saving weight loss and an improved quality of life. A downside to known technologies is that the stapler is much shorter than the length of the stomach, which means that the stapler needs to be removed, the cartridge changed, and then reintroduced as many as six times to complete a sleeve gastrectomy procedure. A more complex surgical method with the use of multiple cartridges can significantly increase the cost of the procedure for the patient.

In 2013, the founders of Standard Bariatrics began developing a novel solution to the multi-cartridge stapler problem. Its new bariatric stapling innovation uses a single cartridge that extends across the entire length of a patient's stomach such that the device only needs to be inserted once and there is no need to reload the staple cartridge.

After applying the staples and successfully forming the sleeve gastrectomy, the device can be removed through an access port placed in the patient.

The technology developed by Standard Bariatrics has enormous potential to improve the outcomes and cost-savings associated with bariatric procedures. However, to bring a new medical device to market is a long and expensive proposition requiring government approvals (such as FDA clearance) and trials to improve and validate the safety and efficacy of the device. Intellectual property is critically important to medical device startups, where protection in the U.S. and internationally may be desirable but can come with a hefty price tag. The cost of pursuing this intellectual property can be challenging because of competing costs associated with engineering, fundraising, and regulatory approvals. For this reason, early stage medical device companies are often good candidates for the Find the River strategy.

In 2013 and 2014 Standard Bariatrics began filing a number of provisional patent applications directed to its core stapling technology. These filings established an all-important filing date for the technology, especially in the highly competitive medical device space. A provisional patent application can serve as priority for both domestic and international pursuits, meaning Standard Bariatrics protected its ability to file in the U.S. as well as foreign countries with these U.S. applications. For early stage companies, the use of provisional applications can be a cost-effective way to establish a filing date while preserving both domestic and international filing rights.

Standard Bariatrics needed to file a U.S. non-provisional application, a PCT application, and/or direct national stage filings within the 12-month pendency of the provisional. Companies with deep pockets might choose to file all three types of applications before the 12-month deadline set by the provisional, but this can get *very* expensive and may not be an option for some. Standard Bariatrics had secured some angel funding by the 12-month expiration of its provisional applications, but it was not enough capital to support a robust application filing strategy without cannibalizing other important business needs. It needed the ability to buy time, while preserving its ability to file in the U.S. and internationally, at the lowest possible cost.

For this reason, Standard Bariatrics filed *only* PCT applications, claiming priority to its provisional applications on the very last day of 12-month deadline. Because a provisional application does not start the 20-year patent term, Standard Bariatrics chose to maximize the priority benefit of its provisionals without using up valuable patent term. Because the PCT applications were generally filed on the last day of pendency of the provisional application, Standard Bariatrics would have another 18 months (the 30-month window of the PCT minus the 12 months of provisional pendency) to determine if and where it wanted to file foreign and U.S. patent applications.

Despite Standard Bariatrics being based in the United States — one of the largest target markets for its device — it chose *not* to file U.S. non-provisional applications along with its PCT applications. Although getting a U.S. non-provisional application on file quickly can be beneficial because the application will enter the queue for review by the USPTO, it also means that USPTO actions may begin to arrive before the company has the budget to prosecute these applications.

Standard Bariatrics maximized the available 30-month pendency of the PCT application and filed U.S. national stage applications and foreign national stage applications, in some cases just days before the expiration of this 30-month period. By doing so, Standard Bariatrics was able to delay the expense of costly U.S. and international patent applications and the prosecution of those applications. Although maximizing the full 30-month pendency of the PCT application can use up valuable patent term, this can be an acceptable tradeoff for companies that are carefully managing cash flow.

In 2018, Standard Bariatrics was able to secure significant Series A funding from a major venture capital firm. This funding could now be used to more aggressively pursue its patent portfolio. Standard Bariatrics has now secured multiple patents, both in the U.S. and abroad, by staying in the game long enough to secure the necessary funding to bring its device to market and to build a powerful intellectual property portfolio. Standard Bariatrics was able to stay in the patent game long enough to secure a winning hand.

CHAPTER 24
SECURING A FIRST NARROWER PATENT AS A BEACHHEAD

"STRIKE FIRST. STRIKE HARD. NO MERCY."

—COBRA KAI MOTTO IN *THE KARATE KID*

Why this strategy might be for you…

- You want to secure an issued patent quickly
  for perceptive or deterrence reasons

- You want to dispel the notion that your technology is not patentable

- You will be able to more easily raise funds with an issued patent

- You are okay starting with a narrower first patent
  if you can later secure broader patent protection

In war—both in real life and in video games such as *Call of Duty*—success or failure can depend on your ability to establish an early beachhead. The need to establish a beachhead recognizes that, in many circumstances, it's more effective to concentrate your resources to establish an early win upon which you can build rather than dilute your resources by attacking and trying to hold too large an area all at once. Referring back to our Risk analogy, it can be much easier to take and hold the smaller territory of Australia than the much larger continent of Asia. If you can go in quickly and establish a position, you can expand from there to capture more valuable real estate. At that point, you may also have more resources, a better sense of what your competitors are doing, and know how to more effectively expand your empire.

In the patent game, securing an early beachhead can be critical to your long-term success. When starting the patent game, many applicants insist on pursuing the broadest possible claims because they want a broad patent. Intuitively, this can make sense; however, this may not be the best starting strategy. In Risk, it can seem attractive to try to conquer a huge territory such as Asia right from the start but, while there are times when this does work, it's easy to become spread too thin.

If you initially pursue an application with broad claims, you should expect to receive multiple rejections from the USPTO that will arrive in a series of Office actions spread out, in some cases, over several years. If you wind up in this type of protracted battle, you may begin to feel fatigue, your resources may run low, and the morale of your team might start to drop. It's at this point that frustrated inventors will quit the process, run out of capital, or perhaps incorrectly determine that the technology simply isn't patentable.

Instead of starting the process with extremely broad patent claims, or claims you might not have a reasonable expectation of getting allowed, you should consider establishing a *targeted* beachhead instead. As you will recall, there are no limits to the number of continuation applications you can file claiming priority to a single parent patent application. These spin-off applications can be used to go after broader versions of your invention in later-filed applications. A beachhead, in the patent game, is a quickly-issued patent that may be a bit narrower than you'd like but is one that gives you a position from which you can expand. By being more conservative with your claims and subsequent amendments, you can more quickly move your patent application to issuance.

Having an issued patent, even on patent claims that may not initially be as broad as you'd like, can be a powerful tool. Not only will being "Patented" have a positive perceptive and deterrent impact, but you'll also learn a lot about the prior art in your space, your USPTO examiner, and the reasons this first patent was allowed. Examiners generally include details about the features and/or rationale that led to a determination of patentability in a section called Reasons for Allowance. Used correctly, this information is patent gold. Once you're able to identify these key features — which I refer to as "the hook" — you'll know exactly what your examiner keyed in on when granting the allowance. Subsequently-filed continuation applications might strip back the claims to *only* this key subject matter and, with the odds being high you'll have the same examiner, a second notice of allowance for even broader claims may be within reach.

Some inventors are dismissive of this approach because they feel strongly that only broad claims have business value. The patent game is often a long one and, if a first narrower issued patent is merely a means to an end, it can still result in the desirable broad claims sought by the inventor. What you will learn about the prior art, your examiner, and the key points of novelty for your invention is in addition to any perception and deterrent benefits that come along with having patented technology.

- -

Our illustrated example opens, as do many of the strategies in this book, with a U.S. provisional application filing.

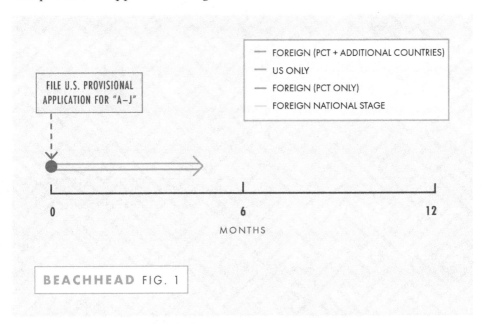

BEACHHEAD FIG. 1

As shown in Figure 2, at the 12-month deadline, you file a U.S. non-provisional application. Let's imagine your non-provisional application includes disclosure directed to features A-J, some of which are likely to be important and others that likely are not. Perhaps you would love to get a patent on just A or B individually at the outset. It can be very tempting to broadly claim only A or B in your initial claim set, but if establishing a beachhead has value, consider going narrower with at least some of your claims in this first application. In our beachhead non-provisional application example, one of the claims includes *all* of the elements A through J in the same claim. Your instinctive reaction may be that this claim is so narrow and includes so many elements that it'll be easy for a third party to design around. And you may be right. However, there can still be a huge benefit to being conservative with your claims to secure an early patent.

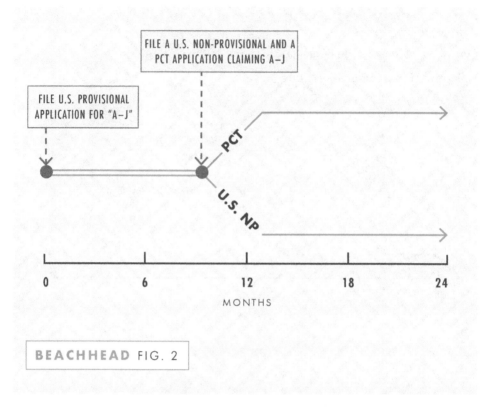

FILE A U.S. NON-PROVISIONAL AND A
PCT APPLICATION CLAIMING A–J

FILE U.S. PROVISIONAL
APPLICATION FOR "A–J"

PCT

U.S. NP

| 0 | 6 | 12 | 18 | 24 |

MONTHS

BEACHHEAD FIG. 2

Because of your conservative claim scope, the USPTO may have a very hard time finding prior art references that can be used to make novelty or obviousness rejections. Your claim may be overkill in terms of the features listed, but if that means you get an early notice of allowance and can secure a first patent, then that alone can be worth it.

Once this notice of allowance arrives, as shown in Figure 3, it may contain clues about which specific elements or key features the examiner felt were points of novelty. Let's imagine our notice of allowance for a claim including elements A through J is accompanied by a Reasons for Allowance statement suggesting features A and F are not taught or suggested by the prior art. In addition to an early-issued patent, you might be getting a wink-wink from your examiner that if you were to submit a new claim with *just* elements A and F, it might be quickly allowed. It's a bonus if the combination referenced by the examiner as a reason for the allowance is one of the combinations on your wish list.

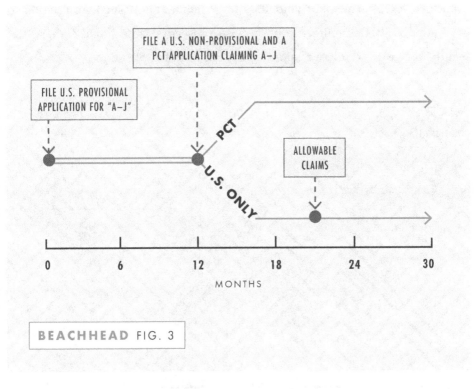

FILE A U.S. NON-PROVISIONAL AND A
PCT APPLICATION CLAIMING A–J

FILE U.S. PROVISIONAL
APPLICATION FOR "A–J"

PCT

U.S. ONLY

ALLOWABLE
CLAIMS

| 0 | 6 | 12 | 18 | 24 | 30 |

MONTHS

BEACHHEAD FIG. 3

As illustrated in Figure 4, you can file a continuation application now targeting this exact subject matter of just A and F with the rest of the elements stripped away. In many cases, continuation applications will be reviewed by the same examiner as the parent application, meaning your new set of claims is going to be reviewed by the same person who indicated that those features were the reason for allowance in the first application. Hopefully, your examiner will favorably review these new claims and send a first Office action notice of allowance on your new, broader claims.

What about those incredibly broad claims directed only to A or B that you still want to pursue? Consider filing these in new continuation applications claiming priority to your parent application. It's perfectly fine to pursue extremely broad claims once you've established a beachhead and you may have less pressure from investors, partners, or your boss to get something issued. You may also have good USPTO intelligence on how to prosecute these broad claims after seeing how your examiner responded to your initial application.

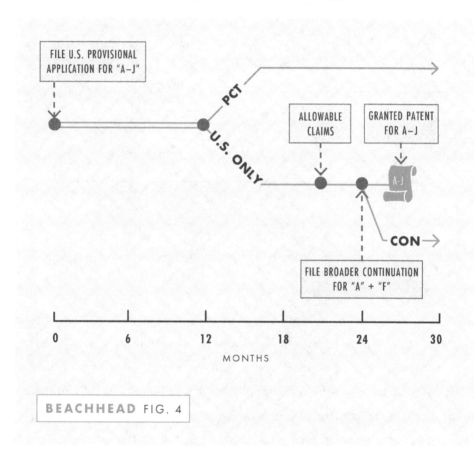

BEACHHEAD FIG. 4

BENEFITS OF THE BEACHHEAD STRATEGY

- An early issued patent, even if relatively narrow,
  can have perceptive and deterrence benefits

- Examiners will frequently include Reasons for Allowance when indicating that there is allowable subject matter. This information can be exploited in future filings.

- Allowable subject matter can be used with the Patent Prosecution Highway to secured issued patents in foreign countries

- Any number of continuation or divisional applications can be filed to later pursue broader claims

- Being patented can be more impactful than being patent pending

- Competitors with a low IP IQ might not realize patents can vary dramatically in scope of protection

DRAWBACKS OF THE BEACHEAD STRATEGY

- Beginning the process with narrower claims may delay the issuance of broader claims pursued in later-filed applications

- Savvy investors, partners, licensees, and competitors may not be impressed or threatened by a patent with narrow claims

- The applicant should be careful not to take positions with the USPTO to secure narrower claims that could limit the scope of later-filed broad claims

- This approach contemplates multiple application filings, which often increase the overall cost of the strategy

REAL WORLD EXAMPLE—MEDICATION DELIVERY SYRINGE BY TRUE CONCEPTS, LLC

Although being patent pending can be impressive, it's usually much more impactful to have secured at least one issued patent. Many investors—particularly those with a high IP IQ—realize that almost anything can be filed with the USPTO to establish patent pending status, particularly in a provisional patent application. It can be difficult to convince investors, prospective partners, and customers that you are ultimately going to secure valuable intellectual property with nothing but a pending application. Proving the novelty of your invention can be even more challenging if you are in a dense technology field, there are large and aggressive competitors, or if you don't have a strong track record of success. And establishing your technology as being truly innovative can be a make-or-break situation if you work in a field where patents play a critical role in establishing company valuation.

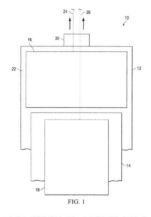

FIG. 1

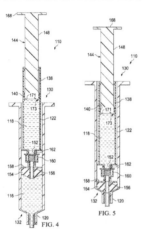

FIG. 4
FIG. 5

True Concepts, LLC was founded by Mick Hopkins, a registered nurse who developed a syringe-based system for the delivery of medication in cooperation with Cincinnati Children's Hospital Medical Center, one of the top three pediatric hospitals in the country. After securing the rights to his intellectual property from Cincinnati Children's, Mick began the process of building a patent portfolio and courting investors. True Concepts initially filed a number of robust U.S. non-provisional and PCT applications of more than 100 pages, covering a large number of embodiments related to Mick's newly-developed syringe technology. Many inventors, when working with an attorney to craft claims for the first non-provisional application, want the broadest possible claims and will intentionally try to strip out every non-essential element from the claims to get as much protection as possible. While broad claims can be incredibly valuable, it's also true that broad claims are much more likely to be rejected, require multiple rounds of prosecution before the USPTO, and take years to issue as a patent. If the broadest possible claims are the only ones with value, then this approach may be warranted.

But True Concepts' story provides an example of when it makes sense to secure a first patent on narrower claims before pursuing more aggressive claims in a continuation application.

One of the non-provisional applications filed by True Concepts included at least five distinct embodiments related to fluid-delivery syringes. These embodiments ranged in complexity, but each of the five versions had business value if an issued patent could be secured on claims covering that embodiment.

The broadest concept combines a first syringe with a second such that a first reservoir can be expelled, followed by a second reservoir in a single motion using a single device. Numerous medications require or benefit from providing a flush stage before delivering the medication, meaning a device integrating these two stages into a single device has tremendous value.

---

(12) **United States Patent**
Hopkins

(10) Patent No.: **US 9,962,489 B2**
(45) Date of Patent: **May 8, 2018**

(54) **SYRINGE SYSTEMS AND METHODS FOR MULTI-STAGE FLUID DELIVERY**

(71) Applicant: **Michael Hopkins**, Springboro, OH (US)

(72) Inventor: **Michael Hopkins**, Springboro, OH (US)

(73) Assignee: **TRUE CONCEPTS MEDICAL TECHNOLOGIES, LLC**, Springboro, OH (US)

(*) Notice: Subject to any disclaimer, the term of this patent is extended or adjusted under 35 U.S.C. 154(b) by 0 days. days.

(21) Appl. No.: **15/624,593**

(22) Filed: **Jun. 15, 2017**

(65) **Prior Publication Data**
US 2017/0361019 A1   Dec. 21, 2017

Related U.S. Application Data

(60) Provisional application No. 62/350,341, filed on Jun. 15, 2016.

(51) **Int. Cl.**
A61M 5/19	(2006.01)
A61M 5/315	(2006.01)
A61M 5/32	(2006.01)
A61M 5/178	(2006.01)
A61M 5/31	(2006.01)

(52) **U.S. Cl.**
CPC **A61M 5/19** (2013.01); **A61M 5/31513** (2013.01); **A61M 5/31596** (2013.01); **A61M 5/32** (2013.01); *A61M 2005/1787* (2013.01); *A61M 2005/3128* (2013.01); *A61M 2202/04* (2013.01)

(58) **Field of Classification Search**
CPC A61M 5/19; A61M 2005/1787; A61M 5/31596
USPC 604/191
See application file for complete search history.

(56) **References Cited**

U.S. PATENT DOCUMENTS

4,340,068 A	7/1982	Kaufman	
9,155,495 B2	10/2015	Bullington et al.	

(Continued)

OTHER PUBLICATIONS

Thomas, Shane; International Search Report and Written Opinion of the International Searching Authority, issued in International Application No. PCT/US2017/037789; dated Sep. 6, 2017; 9 pages.

(Continued)

Primary Examiner — Nathan R Price
Assistant Examiner — John Doubrava
(74) *Attorney, Agent, or Firm* — Ulmer & Berne LLP

(57) **ABSTRACT**

Embodiments of a syringe-based device for delivering fluid include a housing, a port, the port being positioned at about the distal end of the housing, a plunger assembly, the plunger assembly including, a plunger seal, a valve, and a cannula, a first fluid reservoir, where the first fluid reservoir retains a first type of fluid, a syringe including a syringe body, a syringe port, a plunger, and a second fluid reservoir, the second fluid retaining a second type of fluid, and where the syringe transitions from a first configuration in which a first portion of the first fluid type is delivered through the port, to a second configuration in which the second type of fluid in the second fluid reservoir is delivered through the port, to a third configuration in which a second portion of the first fluid type is delivered through the port.

20 Claims, 23 Drawing Sheets

Rather than selecting the very broadest concept, True Concepts opted to pursue a more sophisticated, but still-valuable embodiment, for its first set of non-provisional application claims.

This embodiment—which included a more complex syringe with additional features and functionality—would be useful to establish a monopoly in a niche but lucrative market for the delivery of a few particular medications. This embodiment used the same basic functionality as the very broadest embodiment, but claims directed to the much broader concept likely would have taken much more time to mature into an issued patent.

In the dense field of medical syringes, True Concepts was betting that a first set of claims directed to a more complex embodiment could be advanced quickly into a patent to establish an all-important beachhead. With this beachhead secured, True Concepts could then pursue additional and broader continuation applications.

A non-provisional application with claims directed to the more detailed embodiment was filed on June 15, 2017 and True Concepts received a first Office action—a notice of allowance—on the as-filed claims less than seven months later on January 31, 2018. After quickly paying the issue fee and filing multiple continuation applications directed to broader embodiments, True Concepts secured its first issued patent on May 8, 2018.

This first issued patent has been used aggressively by True Concepts to demonstrate the inventiveness of its portfolio to prospective investors and potential acquisition partners. True Concepts plans to aggressively pursue broad claim coverage, but by having an issued patent it can more credibly portray its innovations as truly novel by the USPTO's standards. Instead of waiting years to secure broader claims—at which point the funds to prosecute the application may have run out—True Concepts secured an early issued patent and is using that success to raise additional funds to build a robust and broad patent portfolio.

CHAPTER 25

THE 100 YARD DASH—
EXPEDITED PATENT
EXAMINATION

"I FEEL THE NEED—THE NEED FOR SPEED!"

– MAVERICK IN *TOP GUN*

Why this strategy might be for you...

- You want to secure an issued patent as quickly as possible

- You need an issued patent for perceptive or deterrence reasons

- You want to dispel the notion that your technology is not patentable

- You need an issued patent to sue an infringer

- You want to maximize all available patent term

- You want to determine if your technology is
  patentable before giving up the option of a trade secret

- You want to use allowable claims to expedite international patent prosecution via the Paten Prosecution Highway (PPH)

As I discussed in Chapter 13, there are a variety of tools patent applicants can pay for or qualify for that provide an added boost of speed. From *Mario Kart* to the aptly-named card game Speed, going faster is better in a lot of games. If you have the resources to secure a speed-boosting power up, your chances of winning are going to be higher.

There are a variety of reasons why securing an issued patent as quickly as possible can drive value. Patents are only enforceable once issued and issued patents carry significant weight in negotiations, license deals, and acquisitions. As such, reaching the finish line quickly can be worth an added cost. This approach can be used in combination with many other strategies outlined in this book to speed them up, such as when significant funding is secured or infringers are identified. A Track One accelerated application is available to anyone for a fee, but if you think you might qualify for free accelerated examination for health or age-related reasons, be sure to review Chapter 26 and the Playing from the Senior's Tees strategy.

HOW THE 100 YARD DASH STRATEGY WORKS

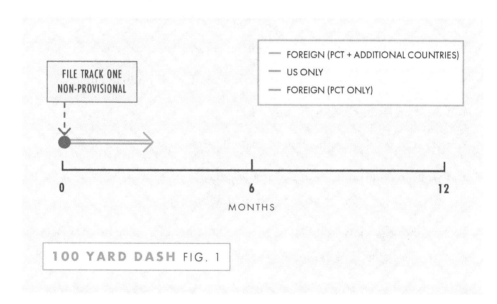

FILE TRACK ONE NON-PROVISIONAL

— FOREIGN (PCT + ADDITIONAL COUNTRIES)
— US ONLY
— FOREIGN (PCT ONLY)

0   6   12

MONTHS

100 YARD DASH FIG. 1

This strategy begins with the filing of a non-provisional application instead of the more common opening of a provisional application. If you are starting this strategy in the middle of the patent process, such as where you had initially picked a different slower-moving strategy that is now suboptimal, this opening non-provisional application can also be a continuation, divisional, or continuation-in-part application.

At the time of filing, the U.S. non-provisional application will include a request for Track One Prioritized Examination, a formidable power up. The non-provisional application must include the fee for the Track One program and must also comply with a number of administrative and formatting requirements. These additional requirements, which are not required in a standard non-provisional or provisional application, are necessary so the Track One non-provisional is ready for patent issuance as-filed. The Track One non-provisional application should be a complete application that includes a thoughtful claim set. You are allowed a maximum of 30 total claims, with a maximum of four of those being independent claims, when visiting this approach.

Once the Track One non-provisional application has been filed, it will enter the expedited queue at the USPTO to be picked up for substantive examination. The timing until a first action is mailed by the USPTO for a Track One application is usually four to six months. You must then respond promptly to any USPTO action or the application will be removed from the Track One program.

The Track One program is meant to give a final disposition on an applicant's case within 12 months. Essentially, the USPTO is trying to give the applicant two substantive rounds of examination within a 12-month period, a process that normally takes years with a standard track application. Expect, as always, for the USPTO's first response to include rejections of some or all the claims. If the examiner rules that some claims are allowable in this first action, you might choose to cancel the rejected claims and secure a patent quickly on the allowed claims.

After responding to the rejections in the USPTO's first action, you will soon thereafter receive a second Office action. This final disposition could be the notice of allowance that you're hoping for, especially if you made compelling arguments or thoughtful amendments in response to the first action's rejections.

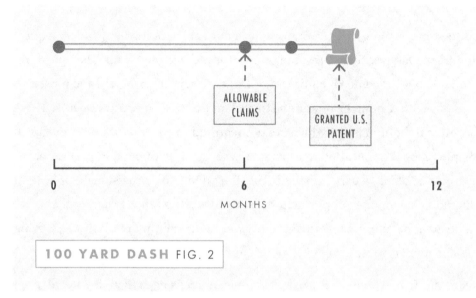

ALLOWABLE
CLAIMS

GRANTED U.S.
PATENT

0   6   12

MONTHS

100 YARD DASH FIG. 2

Within this 12-month timespan for Track One examination, you'll hopefully receive a notice of allowance or an indication of some allowable subject matter for the non-provisional application. As shown in Figure 2, if you get that notice of allowance, the application will issue as a U.S. patent after paying the issue fee.

As shown in Figure 3, this approach can also include the filing of multiple continuation applications to pursue subject matter disclosed, but not claimed, in the parent application. You may pursue claims in such a continuation as a Track One *continuation* application. It's perfectly acceptable to file Track One applications claiming priority to other Track One applications. There are no limits to the number of continuation applications—and subsequently issued patents—that can be filed and granted from a single parent application.

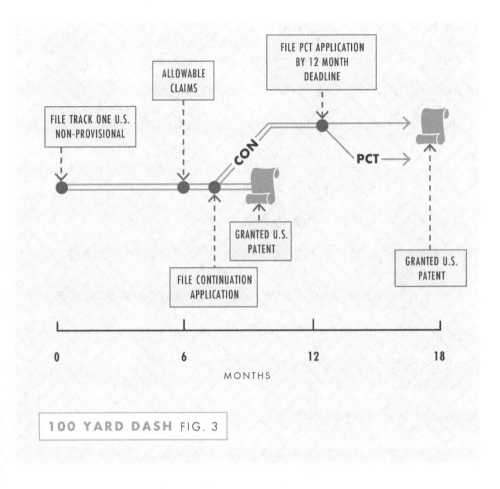

FILE PCT APPLICATION
BY 12 MONTH
DEADLINE

ALLOWABLE
CLAIMS

FILE TRACK ONE U.S.
NON-PROVISIONAL

CON

PCT →

GRANTED U.S.
PATENT

FILE CONTINUATION
APPLICATION

GRANTED U.S.
PATENT

0   6   12   18

MONTHS

100 YARD DASH FIG. 3

BENEFITS OF THE 100 YARD DASH STRATEGY

- An early issued patent can have substantive, perceptive, and deterrence benefits

- It's possible to secure an issued patent within 12 months from filing

- Allowable subject matter can be used with the Patent Prosecution Highway to secure issued patents in foreign countries

- Any number of continuation or divisional applications

can be filed to later pursue new claims

- Being patented can be more impactful than being patent pending

- Benefit from a long patent term because of fast issuance after filing

- Demonstrates your technology is truly innovative

- Great tool for targeting infringers

- Ability to file an infringement lawsuit more quickly

- Increased damages in infringement lawsuits

DRAWBACKS OF THE 100 YARD DASH STRATEGY

- Costs to prepare and file Track One applications can be relatively high

- Added USPTO fee to designate application as Track One

- Costs to prosecute Track One applications
can be relatively high because of the compressed time frame

- May not be an ideal approach for iterative or developing technology

- The speed of examination can lead to bad news arriving faster

REAL WORLD EXAMPLE: AGRICULTURAL TECHNOLOGY BY ARABLE LABS, INC.

The accurate measurement of rainfall is critical in agriculture when trying to maximize crop yield. Prior accumulation measurement methods are common due to low cost and simple operating procedures. But they have shortcomings: They can accumulate debris (including hail and snow) which requires routine maintenance, they can be poorly calibrated, they can suffer from wind-induced losses, and they frequently include moving parts that prevent them from being mounted in non-stationary environments.

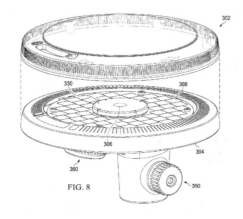

302

330

308

306

304

360

FIG. 8

350

Arable Labs, Inc., a venture-backed New Jersey corporation, recognized a market opportunity and developed an innovative disdrometer that overcomes the limitations associated with prior rainfall measurement devices.

Arable's novel disdrometer comprises an acoustic shell that, when struck by rain drops, generates sound waves. The frequency and amplitude of these rain-generated sound waves allow the device to identify various forms and rates of precipitation. The acoustic shell is transparent because, underneath the shell, the device includes a solar array to power the device. The acoustic disdrometer, which Arable calls the Mark®, is accurate, self-powered, and able to transmit the recorded information to a remote location for processing.

Arable is aggressively trying to capture market share and establish its technology as the gold standard in agriculture while also pursuing additional funding for its business. Arable closed a $4.25 million Series A funding round in 2017 and it sees tremendous value in securing a broad monopoly in the valuable and growing AgTech space.

On March 8, 2016, Arable filed a robust provisional patent application for its acoustic disdrometer to establish an early priority date for the technology. Having established early filing dates with a number of provisional applications, Arable was able to freely talk about its technology and intellectual property position without jeopardizing its U.S. or international patent rights with a premature disclosure. This also allowed it the freedom to focus on courting Series A investors. The strength of this intellectual property portfolio, in combination with a best-in-class team and workable prototypes, enabled Arable to secure substantial funding on favorable terms.

Arable recognized that its provisional application filings also benefited the company by not yet starting the 20-year patent term for the technology. For this reason, Arable chose to maximize the available 12-month provisional pendency and waited to file its non-provisional application and PCT application until March 7, 2017 and March 8, 2017, respectively. In doing so, Arable took advantage of every available day of priority afforded by its provisional application filing without sacrificing patent term. If the Arable technology does indeed become the gold standard in AgTech, maximizing the entire available patent term should boost its valuation.

After securing Series A funding, Arable made the decision to use its newly-acquired capital to move as quickly as possible to establish a patent portfolio. Arable properly petitioned for Track One Prioritized Examination in its non-provisional patent application and complied with the additional requirements — including executed declarations, paying the requisite fees, and including formal drawings — such that the as-filed application was in condition for early allowance and issuance.

Arable's non-provisional application was filed on March 7, 2017 and the petition for Track One status was granted only two weeks later on March 20, 2017. Things moved quickly from there, with a first Office action mailed by the USPTO on May 17, 2017. In this first Office action, claims 1 through 15 of the 23 claims filed were indicated as allowable by the examiner. Rather than disputing the rejected claims, Arable chose to take the allowable claims and cancel the rejected claims, resulting in an official notice of allowance on August 14, 2017.

Arable quickly paid the required issue fee and, on December 12, 2017, received U.S. Patent 9,841,533 directed to its acoustic disdrometer technology.

What about claims 16-23 that were rejected in Arable's first non-provisional

(12) **United States Patent**
Wolf et al.

(10) **Patent No.:** **US 9,841,533 B2**
(45) **Date of Patent:** **Dec. 12, 2017**

(54) **DISDROMETER HAVING ACOUSTIC TRANSDUCER AND METHODS THEREOF**

(71) Applicant: **Arable Labs, Inc.**, Princeton, NJ (US)

(72) Inventors: **Lawrence Adam Wolf**, Princeton, NJ (US); **Benjamin Joseph Siegfried**, Oakland, CA (US); **Adam Lee Smith**, Seattle, WA (US)

(73) Assignee: **Arable Labs, Inc.**, Princeton, NJ (US)

(*) Notice: Subject to any disclaimer, the term of this patent is extended or adjusted under 35 U.S.C. 154(b) by 0 days.

(21) Appl. No.: **15/452,457**

(22) Filed: **Mar. 7, 2017**

(65) **Prior Publication Data**

US 2017/0261647 A1   Sep. 14, 2017

Related U.S. Application Data

(60) Provisional application No. 62/305,211, filed on Mar. 8, 2016.

(51) **Int. Cl.**
G01W 1/00 (2006.01)
G01W 1/14 (2006.01)

(52) **U.S. Cl.**
CPC *G01W 1/14* (2013.01)

(58) **Field of Classification Search**
None
See application file for complete search history.

(56) **References Cited**

U.S. PATENT DOCUMENTS

5,125,268 A *	6/1992	Caron	G01W 1/14 340/602
5,528,224 A *	6/1996	Wang	G01W 1/14 250/573
6,856,273 B1 *	2/2005	Bognar	G01F 1/66 342/26 D
7,249,502 B2	7/2007	Luukkala et al.	
D686,929 S	7/2013	Rainer et al.	
8,714,007 B2	5/2014	Cullen et al.	
8,891,895 B2	11/2014	Garrett et al.	
9,037,521 B1	5/2015	Mewes et al.	
9,131,644 B2	9/2015	Osborne	
9,201,991 B1	12/2015	Mewes et al.	
D747,984 S	1/2016	Zhao et al.	
9,292,796 B1	3/2016	Mewes et al.	

(Continued)

FOREIGN PATENT DOCUMENTS

CN	202975367 U	6/2013		
GB	2412735 A *	10/2005		G01W 1/14
WO	WO2013001495 A1 *	1/2013		

(Continued)

OTHER PUBLICATIONS

Microarial Projects LLC, "Mapping without ground control points, does it work?", sUAS News 2015.

(Continued)

Primary Examiner — Andre Allen
(74) *Attorney, Agent, or Firm* — Ulmer & Berne LLP

(57) **ABSTRACT**

An acoustic disdrometer is provided for measuring precipitation. The acoustic disdrometer has an acoustic transducer positioned within an acoustic chamber defined by an acoustic shell. Precipitation impacting the acoustic shell generates sound waves that are collected by the acoustic transducer for processing.

15 Claims, 12 Drawing Sheets

filing? Arable disputed the USPTO examiner's rejection, but rather than fighting for these claims in the parent application it chose to file a continuation application on November 7, 2017 to target these claims. This was filed before the issuance of the '533 patent to maintain the required copendency. If Arable had not filed this continuation before the patent issuance on December 12, 2017 it would have been forever barred from doing so. This way, Arable kept open the option to file future continuation applications directed to anything disclosed in the original application filing, and these spin-off applications would be entitled to the original priority dates of the provisional application and parent non-provisional application.

Because Arable was aggressively trying to build its patent portfolio, it chose to again petition for Track One Prioritized Examination when filing its first continuation application. This continuation, like the parent application, met all of the requirements of the program and, on December 26, 2017, the Track One petition was granted. On May 11, 2018, Arable received another notice of allowance. For this well-funded technology company, the additional costs associated with the filing of a petition for Track One Expedited Examination were easily justified by the acquisition of multiple patents in a few short years. Had Arable chosen not to expedite its applications, it's possible that its parent application might have gotten caught in the USPTO's backlog and would still not have been substantively reviewed even today.

CHAPTER 26

PLAYING FROM THE SENIOR'S TEES—FREE ACCELERATED EXAMINATION FOR AGE OR HEALTH-RELATED REASONS

"SOME THINGS GET BETTER WITH AGE. LIKE ME."

– KEITH RICHARDS OF *THE ROLLING STONES*

Why this strategy might be for you...

- You are 65 or older or have a health condition that allows you to expedite the patent process

- You want an issued patent as quickly as possible

- You need an issued patent for perceptive or deterrence reasons

- You want to dispel the notion that your technology is not patentable

- You need an issued patent to sue an infringer

- You want to maximize all available patent term

- You want to use allowable claims to expedite international patent prosecution via the PPH

As I discussed in Chapter 12 at the beginning of this book, many games have a handicapping system to level the playing field. These classifications can be based upon age, gender, experience level, or any other metric. In golf, there are frequently three or more different tee box positions that help create parity among players of different skill levels. Blue tee markers are generally set the farthest back for expert or professional golfers. The next driving position up—the white tees—is frequently referred to as the men's tee, which is preceded by the green men's senior tee and then the red women's tee blocks. Of course, all generalizations are imperfect and there are plenty of women and seniors out-shooting guys younger than 55 (especially if that under-55 male happens to be me), but the sport tries to account for what differences might tend to exist be-tween these different classes of competitors.

If you're an over-55 man choosing to play from the senior's tee blocks you don't have to pay anything additional for the privilege. If you qualify, then you're free to drive that golf cart a little closer to the hole before teeing off. Of course, you aren't forced to. Some players may not even be aware of the option and others willfully choose not to play from these tees. But the short-ened distance to the hole will almost certainly improve your score and your chances of winning. If you're playing to win, you'll want to take every possible advantage you can.

There is an equivalent to the senior's tee in the patent game and, if you qualify, you can use this to great advantage. The USPTO recognizes that the patent pro-cess, like a Sunday golf game, can take a really long time to complete. This was particularly true before the pay-to-play Track One Prioritized Examination option came into effect some years ago. Because the process tends to wear on when using the standard track approach, there's a general concern that inventors of a certain age and those with serious health conditions may not live long enough to see the issuance of their patents or to see them commercialized. For this reason, the USPTO will allow inventors over 65 years old or anyone with a serious documented health condition to play from the patent equivalent of the senior's tees — you get free expedited examination in the USPTO for your applications.

In such cases, the USPTO is willing to advance prosecution of your patent application out of turn. There is an obvious benefit to an ill inventor (and his family) wishing to see his work come to fruition before he passes away, but inventors can still use this option if they're over 65 and in perfect health. Just because you qualify for a senior privilege doesn't mean you aren't a formidable competitor. An inventor that is 65 years of age is hardly old and may be in the prime of her or his inventing and innovating career.

If either of these two conditions applies to any one inventor associated with a patent application, then you can take advantage of this expedited examination without having to pay an additional fee. Companies with qualifying inventors may want to actively encourage them to make material contributions to a patent application so the process can be expedited at no charge. If just one of the inventors qualifies and the proper petition is filed, the application will be advanced at no additional cost.

HOW THE PLAYING FROM THE SENIOR'S TEE STRATEGY WORKS

As illustrated in Figure 1, the Playing from the Senior's Tee approach begins with the filing of a non-provisional application. At the time of filing, the U.S. non-provisional application can include a "petition to make special" for age and/or health related reasons. This is your power up card.

Unlike Track One Prioritized Examination applications discussed in Chapter 25 — in which the request *must* be filed when the non-provisional application is filed — a petition to make special for age or health can be filed at any point during the process. For example, if you're a 64-year-old inventor filing a non-provisional application, and you turn 65 a few months after the application is filed, you can file a petition to make special the very day of your 65th birthday. Because the standard patent process can easily take years, you should be cognizant as to whether you or any co-inventors may qualify even after the patent game has started. You may start the front nine from the white tees but play the back nine from the senior's tees.

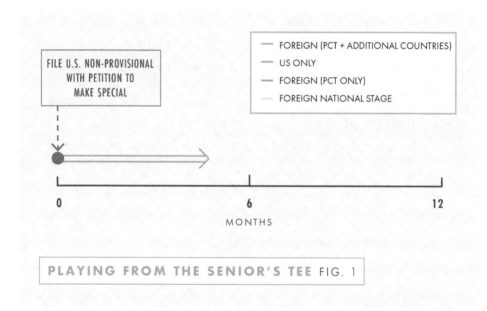

FILE U.S. NON-PROVISIONAL
WITH PETITION TO
MAKE SPECIAL

FOREIGN (PCT + ADDITIONAL COUNTRIES)
US ONLY
FOREIGN (PCT ONLY)
FOREIGN NATIONAL STAGE

0   6   12

MONTHS

PLAYING FROM THE SENIOR'S TEE FIG. 1

When petitioning based upon age, you can include any evidence showing you are 65 years of age or older. This can be as simple as a statement from your patent attorney that he or she has evidence you're north of 64 years old. In cases of health issues, the petition can include any evidence showing the state of health of at least one inventor is such that he or she may not be available to assist in the prosecution of the patent application if it were to run its normal course. Evidence of this type may include a doctor's certificate or other medical certificate. It's important to note that **personal and medical information submitted as evidence to support an age or health-related petition will be publicly visible if the patent application file and contents become available to the public** (such as when the patent application publishes or issues as a patent). If you do not wish to have this information become part of the application file record, there are some ways to keep this sensitive information confidential—be sure to consult with your patent attorney or agent before proceeding.

Once your non-provisional application has been filed with the appropriate petition, your application will enter the expedited queue at the USPTO for substantive examination. The timing until a first action is typically four to six months from when the petition is granted, which is much better than waiting a year or more to start the process.

Almost every aspect of the patent process will be expedited, which should help lead to a quickly issued patent, as shown in Figure 2.

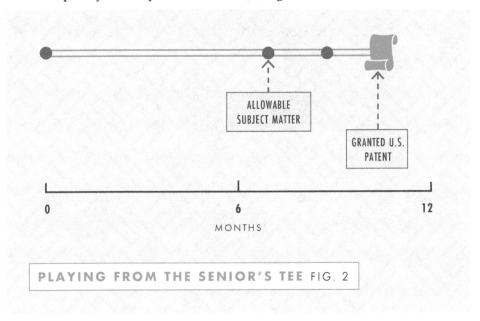

PLAYING FROM THE SENIOR'S TEE FIG. 2

This approach can also include the filing of one or more continuation or divisional applications to pursue additional subject matter disclosed, but not claimed, in the original non-provisional. It's perfectly acceptable to file continuation, divisional, and CIP applications with these same petitions for an expedited process if you qualify. You may also choose to pursue foreign protection, but be aware that many countries don't have these same age or health-related power ups. If you qualify in the United States, ask your patent attorney if there are similar benefits in foreign countries of interest.

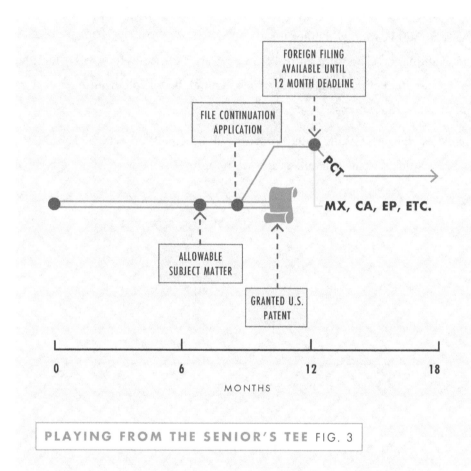

PLAYING FROM THE SENIOR'S TEE FIG. 3

BENEFITS OF THE PLAYING
FROM THE SENIOR'S TEES STRATEGY

- -

- An early issued patent can have substantive, perceptive, and deterrence benefits

- First substantive USPTO action in 4-6 months

- Possible to secure an issued patent within 12 months from filing

- No fee required if at least one inventor qualifies

- Petition to make special can be filed at any time during the patent process

- Specific age or health-related information can be redacted

- Allowable subject matter can be used with the Patent Prosecution Highway to secure issued patents in foreign countries

- Any number of continuation or divisional applications can be filed to later pursue new claims

- Long patent term because of fast issuance after filing

DRAWBACKS OF THE PLAYING
FROM THE SENIOR'S TEES STRATEGY

- -

- The speed of examination can lead to bad news, such as lack of patentability, arriving faster

- Due to the expedited process, costs of responding to Office Actions will be incurred sooner

REAL WORLD EXAMPLE—JOHN GOODENOUGH

In 1946, a 23-year-old U.S. Army veteran named John Goodenough headed to the University of Chicago with a dream of studying physics. When he arrived, a professor warned him that he was already too old to succeed in the field. Goodenough ignored the professor's advice and today, at 94, has set the tech industry abuzz with his blazing creativity. He and his team at the University of Texas at Austin filed a patent application on a new kind of battery that, if it works as promised, would be so cheap, lightweight, and safe it would revolutionize electric cars and kill off petroleum-fueled vehicles. His announcement has caused a stir, in part, because Dr. Goodenough has done it before. In 1980, at age 57, he coinvented the lithium-ion battery that shrank power into a tiny package.

WHEN INSPIRATION STRIKES

People granted international patents in information technology, materials science, and the life sciences by age, according to a survey of inventors. Those aged 46 to 60 received a majority of the patents.

26-30 31-35 36-40 41-45 46-50 51-55 56-60 61-65 66-70 71-75 76-80

Age Range of Patent Holders, 2011-2014

(12) **United States Patent**
Goodenough et al.

(10) **Patent No.:** **US 8,067,117 B2**
(45) **Date of Patent:** *Nov. 29, 2011

(54) **CATHODE MATERIALS FOR SECONDARY (RECHARGEABLE) LITHIUM BATTERIES**

(75) Inventors: **John B. Goodenough**, Austin, TX (US); **Akshaya K. Padhi**, LaSalle, IL (US); **Kirakodu S. Nanjundaswamy**, Ambler, PA (US); **Christian Masquelier**, Boulogne (FR)

(73) Assignee: **Hydro-Québec**, Montréal, Québec (CA)

(*) Notice: Subject to any disclaimer, the term of this patent is extended or adjusted under 35 U.S.C. 154(b) by 0 days.

This patent is subject to a terminal disclaimer.

(21) Appl. No.: **12/952,978**

(22) Filed: **Nov. 23, 2010**

(65) **Prior Publication Data**

US 2011/0068297 A1   Mar. 24, 2011

Related U.S. Application Data

(63) Continuation of application No. 11/179,617, filed on Jul. 13, 2005, now abandoned, which is a continuation of application No. 10/902,142, filed on Jul. 30, 2004, now abandoned, which is a continuation of application No. 10/307,346, filed on Dec. 2, 2002, now abandoned, which is a continuation of application No. 08/998,264, filed on Dec. 24, 1997, now Pat. No. 6,514,640, which is a continuation-in-part of application No. 08/840,523, filed on Apr. 21, 1997, now Pat. No. 5,910,382.

(51) **Int. Cl.**
H01M 4/58 (2010.01)
H01M 4/13 (2010.01)

(52) **U.S. Cl.** **429/218.1**; 429/221

(58) **Field of Classification Search** .... None
See application file for complete search history.

(56) **References Cited**

U.S. PATENT DOCUMENTS

2,736,708 A	2/1956	Crowley et al.	252/62.5
4,049,887 A	9/1977	Whittingham	429/112
4,197,366 A *	4/1980	Tamura et al.	429/333
4,233,375 A	11/1980	Whittingham	429/194
4,302,518 A	11/1981	Goodenough et al.	429/104
4,366,215 A	12/1982	Coetzer et al.	429/199
4,465,747 A	8/1984	Evans	429/194
4,512,905 A	4/1985	Clearfield et al.	252/62.2
4,526,844 A	7/1985	Yoldas et al.	429/30
4,587,172 A	5/1986	Roy et al.	428/450
4,844,995 A	7/1989	Noda et al.	429/189
4,925,751 A	5/1990	Shackle et al.	429/191
4,959,281 A	9/1990	Nishi et al.	429/194

(Continued)

FOREIGN PATENT DOCUMENTS

CA	2251709	10/1997

(Continued)

OTHER PUBLICATIONS

U.S. Appl. No. 12/877,811, filed Sep. 2010, Armand et al.*

(Continued)

Primary Examiner — Barbara Gilliam
Assistant Examiner — Adam A Arciero
(74) *Attorney, Agent, or Firm* — Baker Botts L.L.P.

(57) **ABSTRACT**

The invention relates to materials for use as electrodes in an alkali-ion secondary (rechargeable) battery, particularly a lithium-ion battery. The invention provides transition-metal compounds having the ordered-olivine or the rhombohedral NASICON structure and the polyanion $(PO_4)^3$ as at least one constituent for use as electrode material for alkali-ion rechargeable batteries.

22 Claims, 10 Drawing Sheets

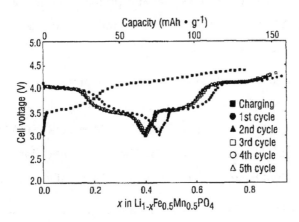

We tend to assume creativity wanes with age, but Dr. Goodenough's story suggests some people can become more creative as they grow older. According to a survey of inventors, international patents in information technology, materials science, and the life sciences were mostly awarded to inventors between the ages of 46 and 60.

There's plenty of evidence suggesting that late bloomers are no anomaly. A 2016 Information Technology and Innovation Foundation study found inventors peak in their late 40s and tend to be highly productive in the last half of their careers. Similarly, professors at the Georgia Institute of Technology and Hitotsubashi University in Japan conducted a joint study on data about patent holders and found that the average inventor in the United States sends in his or her application to the Patent Office at age 47 while the highest-value patents often come from the oldest inventors — those over the age of 55.

When asked about his late-life success, Goodenough said, "Some of us are turtles; we crawl and struggle along, and we haven't maybe figured it out by the time we're 30. But the turtles have to keep on walking." This crawl through life can be advantageous, he pointed out, particularly if you meander around through different fields, picking up clues as you go along. Dr. Goodenough started in physics and hopped sideways into chemistry and materials science, while also keeping his eye on the social and political trends that could drive a green economy. "You have to draw on a fair amount of experience in order to be able to put ideas together," he said.

On November 23, 2010, Goodenough and his team of inventors from the University of Texas at Austin filed a non-provisional patent application (U.S. Serial No. 12/952,978) directed to CATHODE MATERIALS FOR SECONDARY (RE-CHARGEABLE) LITHIUM BATTERIES. The '978 application ultimately matured into U.S. Patent 8,067,117 with four individuals listed as inventors.

What's particularly noteworthy about this issued patent is the date of issuance,

Title of Invention	Cathode Materials for Secondary (Rechargeable) Lithium Batteries

Attention: Office of Petitions
An application may be made special for advancement of examination upon filing of a petition showing that the applicant is 65 years of age, or more. No fee is required with such a petition. See 37 CFR 1.102(c)(1) and MPEP 708.02 (IV).

APPLICANT HEREBY PETITIONS TO MAKE SPECIAL FOR ADVANCEMENT OF EXAMINATION IN THIS APPLICATION UNDER 37 CFR 1.102(c)(1) and MPEP 708.02 (IV) ON THE BASIS OF THE APPLICANT'S AGE.

A grantable petition requires one of the following items:
(1) Statement by one named inventor in the application that he/she is 65 years of age, or more; or
(2) Certification by a registered attorney/agent having evidence such as a birth certificate, passport, driver's license, etc. showing one named inventor in the application is 65 years of age, or more.

Name of Inventor who is 65 years of age, or older

Given Name	Middle Name	Family Name	Suffix
John	Bannister	Goodenough	

A signature of the applicant or representative is required in accordance with 37 CFR 1.33 and 10.18.
Please see 37 CFR 1.4(d) for the format of the signature.

Select (1) or (2) :

○ (1) I am an inventor in this application and I am 65 years of age, or more.

◉ (2) I am an attorney or agent registered to practice before the Patent and Trademark Office, and I certify that I am in possession of evidence, and will retain such in the application file record, showing that the inventor listed above is 65 years of age, or more.

Signature	/Larissa A. Piccardo/	Date (YYYY-MM-DD)	2010-11-23
Name	Larissa A. Piccardo	Registration Number	60448

November 29, 2011. That's just a year and six days after Mr. Goodenough's filing date of November 23, 2010. And the process went even faster than it appears. A notice of allowance was actually sent by the USPTO on July 13, 2011, less than eight months after the initial filing date.

All of this patent prosecution before the USPTO took place before applicants were given the option to pay for Track One accelerated examination. So how did Goodenough get his patent so quickly? At the time the '978 application was filed, Goodenough's attorney properly submitted a petition to make special because he was over 65 years of age. As illustrated below the process is generally very efficient, particularly with age-related petitions. All that's now needed is for the applicant's attorney to sign off on the statement of age.

The only required proof was the submission of John Goodenough's driver's license or one of the other listed forms of identification, which can include *redact-*

ed sections to avoid disclosure of sensitive information. John's as-submitted driver's license is provided below for reference, where the redacted portions were removed in the original submission:

Importantly, only one of the inventors needs to satisfy the age or health requirement for the application to receive accelerated examination. Multiple inventors may qualify, but it's only necessary to list one for the purposes of filing a grantable petition.

Shortly after submission, the USPTO granted Mr. Goodenough's petition to make special.

How much of a difference does this make in the prosecution of a patent application? Instead of the years it can take some art units to pick up an application for initial examination, the '978 application — after the petition was granted — received a first Office action from the USPTO on January 21, 2011, less than two months after the initial filing date.

For individuals or teams with at least one qualified inventor, the ability to accelerate examination with a petition to make special can be of tremendous benefit. The applicants can enjoy the benefits of accelerated examination at no charge and with little administrative paperwork, then achieve a quickly issued patent that uses up very little of the valuable patent term. It's worth noting, the number of inventors over the age of 65 is increasing every year.

UNITED STATES PATENT AND TRADEMARK OFFICE

Commissioner for Patents
United States Patent and Trademark Office
P.O. Box 1450
Alexandria, VA 22313-1450
www.uspto.gov

Patent Department
Baker Botts, L.L.P.
One Shell Plaza
910 Louisiana
Houston TX 77002

MAILED

DEC 07 2010

OFFICE OF PETITIONS

In re Application of   :

Michel B. Armand   :
Application No. 12/952,978   :   DECISION ON PETITION
Filed: :   TO MAKE SPECIAL UNDER
Attorney Docket No. **078963.0138** :   37 CFR 1.102(c)(1)
                         :

This is a decision on the petition under 37 CFR 1.102(c)(1), filed November 23, 2010, to make the above-identified application special based on applicant's age as set forth in MPEP § 708.02, Section IV.

The petition is **GRANTED**.

A grantable petition to make an application special under 37 CFR 1.102(c)(1) and MPEP § 708.02, Section IV: Applicant's Age must be accompanied by evidence showing that at least one of the applicants is 65 years of age, or more, such as a birth certificate or a statement by applicant. No fee is required

The instant petition includes a statement by a registered attorney. Accordingly, the above-identified application has been accorded "special" status.

Telephone inquiries concerning this decision should be directed to JoAnne Burke at 571-272-4584.

All other inquiries concerning either the examination or status of the application should be directed to the Technology Center.

The application is being forwarded to the Office of Patent Application Processing (OPAP) for action on the merits commensurate with this decision.

/JoAnne Burke/
JoAnne Burke
Petitions Examiner
Office of Petitions

CHAPTER 27

THE PPH CHECKERS STRATEGY—USING THE PATENT PROSECUTION HIGHWAY (PPH)

"JUMP AROUND!
JUMP UP, JUMP UP, AND GET DOWN!"

– "JUMP AROUND" BY *HOUSE OF PAIN*

Why this strategy might be for you...

- You have allowable subject matter or an
  issued patent in at least one country or jurisdiction

- You want corresponding domestic or international patents
  to be cost effective and prosecuted as quickly as possible

- You need a domestic or international issued
  patent for perceptive or deterrence reasons

- You need an issued patent to sue an infringer domestically or abroad

- You want to maximize all available domestic and international patent term

I've made a few analogies to the board game Risk because, in many ways, the "board" the patent game is played on has many similarities. There are no world-wide patents—if you want to own a monopoly in a country like Irkutsk, you'll have to file and secure an issued patent in that jurisdiction. Although each country has its own laws—their own list of rules on the back of the box—there has been an effort over the last few decades to harmonize the world's patent laws. The patent process can be daunting for inventors, but it also presents a massive challenge to the countries themselves in terms of resources and infrastructure. You probably aren't going to feel too much pity for the government, but they are indeed looking for ways to create efficiency in the game much as you are for your own business.

As the requirements for patentability in different countries become more aligned with one another, it is easier for the patent office in one jurisdiction to trust the work done by another in a different part of the world. For example, the requirements for securing a patent in both the United States and Australia are similar and if a patent application has been allowed in the United States it could be efficiently and easily reviewed by the Australian patent office. Why should these countries do duplicate work when the standards for patentability are, for the most part, the same? The result of these similarities is a powerful international tool called the Patent Prosecution Highway (PPH). Like a game of checkers or the knight in chess, the PPH allows you to "jump" from one area to another so you can more efficiently accomplish your goals.

The PPH allows you to expedite the prosecution of claims allowed in one jurisdiction (e.g., the United States) to another PPH participating country (e.g., Australia). Countries in the PPH program want to improve the efficiency of the global patent process and quickly review allowed claims from another PPH country to advance those claims to an issued patent. Although not quite a rubber stamp, the allowance rates for PPH applications submitted in a participating country are generally high, often greater than 90 percent. Securing allowable claims in at least one jurisdiction can give you the ability to quickly jump that piece to other regions and improve your patent prospects in all PPH participating countries.

In one version of a strategy incorporating the Patent Prosecution Highway, you can open with the filing of a non-provisional application that can include a request for Track One Prioritized Examination at the time of filing. Track One applications are described in more detail in Chapter 25.

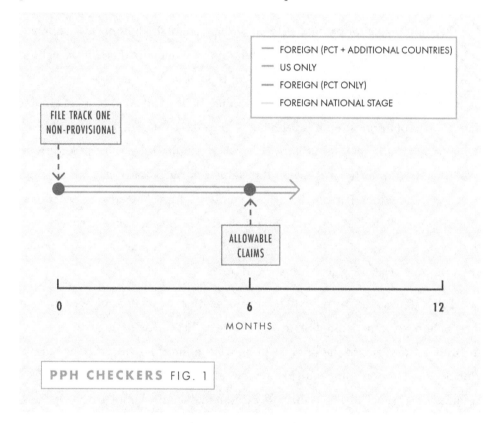

PPH CHECKERS FIG. 1

As shown in Figure 1, when your Track One petition for accelerated examination is granted, the non-provisional application will enter the expedited queue at the USPTO. Expect a first response in four to six months. With this process in motion, it's time to start looking at other countries to jump to.

The USPTO tries to perform two substantive rounds of examination for Track One applications within a 12-month period. The second action or final disposition will, hopefully, include at least one allowable patent claim. If not, you can continue to negotiate with the USPTO in a variety of different ways. For this example, let's assume all your claims were just found to be patentable and you've been mailed a notice of allowance. Nice work!

With your notice of allowable subject matter in hand, you can now file direct national stage applications in foreign countries of interest. You are not required to wait until you have allowable subject matter to do this, but you might feel more confident in investing in foreign applications if you do. Just be mindful of the 12-month deadline to pursue foreign patent protection. Although you have a lot of PPH choices, the example of Figure 2 uses Australia as an example of a PPH-participating country. This Australian application can be filed with a PPH request and, if the request is accepted, your allowable subject matter in the United States can jump to expedite prosecution of the same claims in Australia.

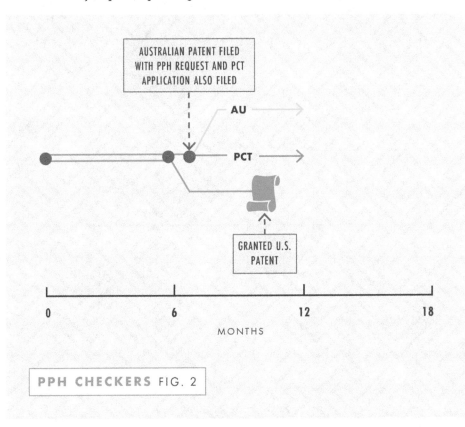

PPH CHECKERS FIG. 2

It's possible that you may be unsure which foreign countries you'd like to pursue within a year of your U.S. non-provisional application filing or you might not have the funds to aggressively pursue international protection. Instead of direct national stage filings — or in addition to one more national stage filings — you might choose to file a Patent Cooperation Treaty application. As discussed in Chapter 10, a PCT application is effectively a foreign placeholder that buys you time to decide which, if any, of the approximately 150 participating foreign jurisdictions to pursue. As shown in Figure 3 and 4, you can use the PPH to jump from one jurisdiction to another at a later date if slowing down the process becomes beneficial. It can take a long time to ascertain which foreign countries justify the cost of filing, annuity payments, and prosecution, even after you have secured allowable subject matter that could be leveraged via the PPH.

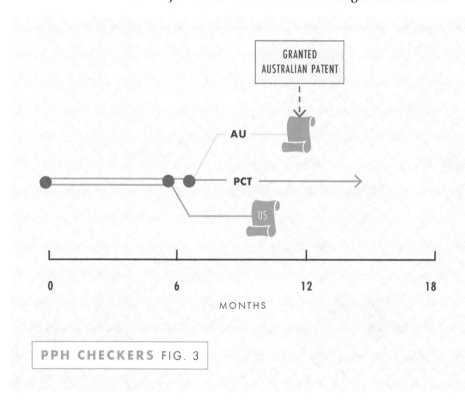

PPH CHECKERS FIG. 3

The PPH also goes in both directions. Allowable claims in Australia, for example, can be used to jump over to the United States to expedite the patent process. More advanced strategies will even use a form of forum shopping to try and secure allowable subject matter in foreign countries with the primary purpose of using that allowable material to expedite other domestic and international applications. If you receive an indication of allowable subject matter in any country you should check with your patent attorney to see what PPH options might be available.

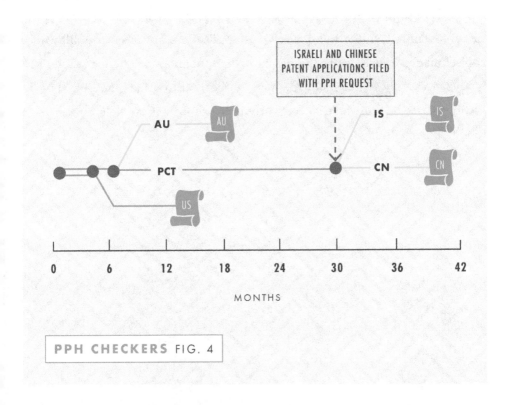

ISRAELI AND CHINESE PATENT APPLICATIONS FILED WITH PPH REQUEST

AU
PCT
US
IS
CN

MONTHS

0   6   12   18   24   30   36   42

PPH CHECKERS FIG. 4

Another important PPH option can arise from a favorable review of a PCT application. Although a PCT application is primarily a placeholder and this application type itself cannot issue as a patent, this application type is substantively examined. A PCT applicant will receive a Search Report and Written Opinion that evaluates the claimed invention for novelty, inventive step, and industrial applicability. These standards roughly translate into novelty, non-obviousness, and usefulness in the United States. If one or more claims are found to meet all three requirements, the PCT itself can be used to jump via the PPH into participating countries.

The illustrated example began with the filing of a Track One non-provisional application, but the option to use the PPH can arise in many scenarios where there is allowable subject matter in a domestic or foreign patent application or patent. For example, you might start the patent process with a provisional application, eventually file a non-provisional application, and then use allowable subject matter in that application to expedite foreign applications via the PPH. It's not necessary to have an expedited application to utilize the PPH, but by getting clarity on allowable subject early in the process it can help inform your foreign patent strategy.

GLOBAL NETWORK OF PPH ARRANGEMENTS

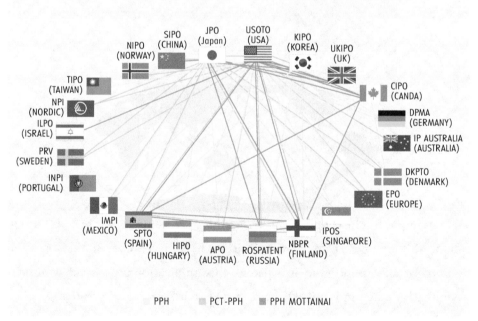

BENEFITS OF THE PLAYING PPH CHECKERS STRATEGY

- Faster prosecution and issuance of corresponding foreign or domestic patent applications

- Typically no additional fees to use the PPH

- Higher likelihood of early allowance and an issued patent

- The PPH request can sometimes be made after the patent process has already started

- Less expensive foreign patent prosecution

- Being patented internationally can be more impactful than being patent pending

- Longer patent term in PPH jurisdictions because of fast issuance after filing

- Ability to use a favorable PCT application Search Report for PPH purposes

REAL WORLD EXAMPLE: PPH INTO CANADA
FROM THE PCT AND THE UNITED STATES

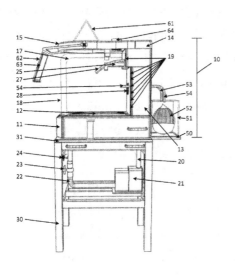

Just how fast and effective is the Patent Prosecution Highway? Canada has a reputation for being a particularly good PPH country, where the time from submitting a request to receiving a notice of allowance may only be *weeks*. If this jurisdiction is of interest and you have allowable subject matter in another PPH participating country, you should consider taking advantage of this useful tool.

As discussed earlier, you can take advantage of the PPH when you have allowable claims in a participating jurisdiction, but you can also use a favorable PCT written opinion and search report to qualify. Mauro Jaguan invented an Improved Portable Relaxation Therapy Massage Device for the Head, for which he filed a U.S. provisional patent application.

Mr. Jaguan went on to file a PCT application and he was fortunate enough to receive an indication of allowable subject matter in the PCT Written Opinion and Search Report. Mr. Jaguan was interested in protection in Canada and, on May 11, 2016, a PPH request was made in Canada based upon the positive PCT review. Just *seven weeks* later, on June 28, 2016, a notice of allowance was mailed that ultimately resulted in the grant of Canadian Patent No. 2,918,766.

It's also very common for patent applicants to leverage allowable subject matter in the United States to expedite prosecution and issuance in Canada. Robert J. Ditullio invented a Stormwater Chamber with Stackable Reinforcing Ribs, for which he initially filed a U.S. non-provisional patent application (U.S. App. No. 15/231,222).

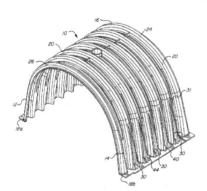

Mr. Ditullio received a notice of allowance for his U.S. application and was able to leverage this allowable subject matter to secure issued Canadian Patent No. 2,975,770. His PPH request in Canada was filed on August 23, 2017, which was followed by a notice of allowance in Canada on November 20, 2017, three months later.

In another instance, EasyDial, Inc. invented a Portable Hemodialysis Machine for which it initially filed a U.S. provisional patent application. EasyDial later filed a U.S. non-provisional (U.S. App. No. 14/753,982) for which it received a notice of allowance from the USPTO. Recognizing that this notice of allowance, even before the issuance of the U.S. patent, could be used to request expedited prosecution in Canada via the PPH, EasyDial submitted its PPH request in its corresponding Canadian patent application on March 30, 2017. Just two weeks later, on April 13, 2017, it received a notice of allowance that resulted in Canadian Patent No. 2,960,143.

CHAPTER 28

CORRESPONDENCE CHESS— MAKING YOUR PATENT MOVES AS SLOWLY AS POSSIBLE

"I AM A SLOW WALKER, BUT I NEVER WALK BACK."

– ABRAHAM LINCOLN

Why this strategy might be for you...

- You want to slow the patent process as much as possible

- You need to buy time to determine which version of the invention is commercially viable

- You have limited financial resources

- You need time to raise additional funds

- You want to be patent pending for as long as possible

Chess addicts these days are spoiled by websites that place them in a game against equally matched competitors from anywhere in the world within a matter of seconds. If you want to play a five-minute game against an expert, you can do so from the comfort of your iPhone and—if you don't mind the lack of human interaction—you'll never want for a game. Back in the dark ages before the internet, it was difficult to find an equally matched competitor with whom you enjoyed playing. And if a player was lucky enough to find a great adversary, he or she would frequently go to great lengths to keep a regular chess game going.

Correspondence chess, as it is commonly known, may date back to the 12th century and can incorporate any conceivable means of delivery for the players' moves. Notable methods of transmission include the post office, runners, and even homing pigeons. The International Correspondence Chess Federation was founded in 1951 and from its inception has organized more than 20 world championship events. The Guinness Book of World Records® credits Dr. Reinhart Straszacker and Dr. Hendrik Roelof van Huyssteen, both of South Africa, as having the longest ongoing correspondence chess relationship. The pair played their first game of correspondence chess in 1946 and, after 112 matches, the streak ended 53 years later with Straszacker's death in 1999. Doing the basic math, that's about six months per game. When you consider that many matches were played in parallel, the actual duration of each game was probably closer to a year. In an amazing testament to how well-suited these opponents were for one another, each man had won 56 games at the time Straszacker died.

In the patent game, you may consider playing the equivalent of correspondence chess with the USPTO if your goal is to play as slowly as possible. This approach is the exact opposite of the tactics used in the chapter covering the Blitz Chess strategy, where the goal was to respond as quickly as possible to the USPTO to move the process along expeditiously. If you instead want to drag your feet, there are a number of different strategies you can utilize to delay your moves for as long as possible. Remember to review the earlier chapter on Hitting the Pause Button for different options you can incorporate into your strategy.

HOW THE CORRESPONDENCE
CHESS STRATEGY WORKS

The opening in this strategy is generally a provisional patent application, which has a maximum 12-month pendency. Very near or at the end of the provisional's 12-month pendency, you should file a U.S. non-provisional application. Since this strategy is likely to eat up *a lot* of your 20-year patent term, it's important to protect it where you can. Using that 12 months can be key, not just for delaying the process, but also for keeping you in the game longer.

When it's time to file your non-provisional application, you may want to omit some of the USPTO's administrative requirements from your application filing. Before the USPTO examination takes place, your patent application must comply with formal requirements including payment of the basic filing and examination fees and inclusion of formal drawings. If you elect not to pay the fees at the time of filing, you'll still receive the all-important filing date for your application, but it will not enter the queue for substantive examination. Instead, at some point you'll be mailed a Notice of Missing Parts indicating the deficiencies of your application. You can take up to seven months from the mailing date of the notice to fix the deficiency. This helps you delay the game by a good bit if you're looking to really drag your feet.

If you want to delay even more, the USPTO currently offers an Extended Missing Parts Pilot Program. You can request a 12-month period to pay the search fee, examination fee, any excess claim fees, and the surcharge (for the late submission of the search fee and the examination fee) in your non-provisional application. The Extended Missing Parts Pilot Program can give you additional time to determine if patent protection should be sought—at a relatively low cost—by letting you focus your time, resources, and efforts on commercialization during this period. The Extended Missing Parts Pilot Program benefits the USPTO and the public by adding publications to the body of prior art and removing from the USPTO's workload those non-provisional applications for which applicants later decide not to pursue examination. If your non-provisional filing date is upon you, but you want to delay the timing of a first substantive USPTO action for as long as possible, consider filing the application without paying any of the fees and doing so under the Extended Missing Parts Pilot Program.

After submitting your response to the Notice of Missing Parts your application will, finally, get in line for review by the USPTO. If you are hoping for a slow process, you may get lucky and have years before the USPTO picks up your application for review. If you're curious as to how long this may be, the USPTO has a nice First Office Action Prediction application on its Patent Application Information Retrieval (PAIR) system. This will give you a fairly accurate approximation of how long it's likely to take the USPTO to get back to you.

When you do receive a first, non-final Office action from the USPTO, which in most cases will include one or more rejections or objections, you'll have a maximum of six months to respond to this action. If you fail to respond, your application will become abandoned. If you are playing the patent version of correspondence chess, you may consider waiting until the very end of this six-month period to file the required response.

Now that you've pushed the ball back into the USPTO's court, you'll have another waiting period while the USPTO prepares a response. This second Office action, assuming at least some of your claims are still rejected, will typically be a Final Office action. It's hardly as final as the name might imply, but your response to this type of action is more restricted than it was with respect to the first one. Again, you'll have another six months during which to respond to this Final Office action and it's prudent you maximize this period.

When you do respond to the Final Office action when playing the Correspondence Chess Strategy, your response may be different from the one you filed with respect to the initial Office action. One option to stall is to simply submit a single-page form called a Notice of Appeal. Filing a Notice of Appeal and paying the associated fee triggers another timer; you have seven months from sending the Notice to file a formal appeal brief. Are you actually planning to prepare and file an appeal brief? Probably not. The goal of this approach is to leverage the seven-month period available to you after submitting your Notice for more delay.

Now that you've stalled to the maximum extent possible and your seven-month period for response to the Notice of Appeal is coming to a close, how should you then proceed? At or near the end of the seven-month response period, you can file a new continuation application claiming priority back to your original non-provisional and provisional applications. Filing this continuation application — with or without the filing fees — **keeps your priority date while effectively restarting the entire process**. Once your fees have been paid, this new application enters the queue at the USPTO to be reviewed for substantive examination just like your first non-provisional, hopefully at some point well down the road.

Then rinse and repeat with the same stalling tactics for the continuation application. If you want the process to go slowly for an even longer period of time, look to the Avoiding the Blinds strategy discussed in Chapter 19 for tactics you can combine with the Correspondence Chess strategy.

BENEFITS OF THE PLAYING CORRESPONDENCE CHESS STRATEGY

- Slowing down the patent process can help spread costs out over a long period of time

- Delaying the patent process may give the applicant time to raise additional funds

- Delaying the patent process can be beneficial for technology fields where the law is presently in flux or where patentability is less likely

- If the invention has dubious patentable potential, there may be little incentive to rush getting a first Office action

- The all-important priority date of the first application filing is maintained

- Many delaying tactics are free and others, such as extensions of time, are relatively inexpensive

- Delaying the patent process can allow a commercial embodiment or business model to become more clear

DRAWBACKS OF THE PLAYING CORRESPONDENCE CHESS STRATEGY

- Delaying patent prosecution will correspondingly reduce patent term

- Some delaying tactics, such as the Notice of Appeal and continuation application filings, can be expensive and can increase the overall cost of the patent process

- Being patent pending for a long period of time might suggest the technology is not innovative or patentable

- An infringement suit cannot be brought until a patent has been granted

REAL WORLD EXAMPLE: DIGITAL WATCH CLASPS BY WEARATEC, INC.

Dilshan Modaragamage is a Canadian engineer who founded the digital watch clasp company Wearatec, Inc. Digital timepieces, like the Apple watch, are becoming more popular, but many consumers did not want to abandon their traditional Rolex, Cartier, or Movado watches for aesthetic or sentimental reasons. Traditional watches are, well, timeless and are frequently passed down from generation to generation. Recipients of such an heirloom, or those that prefer the aesthetic of an analog watch, had to choose between modern functionality and traditional styling. Mr. Modaragamage recognized that there was a market for a product that would allow consumers to wear their favorite watches without having to make this technological sacrifice.

FIG. 3

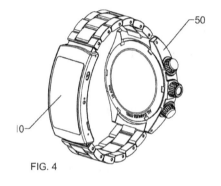

FIG. 4

Wearatec filed its first provisional application (U.S. Pat. App. 62/016,878) directed to a digital clasp—which could be retrofitted and used with any traditional watch—on June 15, 2014. Because of the potential market size and the need to establish a patent portfolio as quickly as possible, Wearatec chose not to wait the full 12-month pendency of the provisional before filing its non-provisional, U.S. Pat. App. 14/560,137, on December 4, 2014. Because Wearatec was a startup with limited financial resources, it waited the full 12-month period to file its PCT application in order to space apart costs without giving up patent term. It's perfectly acceptable and sometimes beneficial to file a U.S. non-provisional application and PCT application on different dates, but each must be filed within 12 months from the filing date of a provisional application to preserve that earlier filing's priority date.

Because Wearatec is a first mover in this space, it was able to secure a Notice of Allowance and a first issued patent relatively quickly, even without using Track One Accelerated Examination. Wearatec received a notice of allowance on August 12, 2015, a little over a year from when its non-provisional patent application was filed. This first allowance led to U.S. Patent 9,152,129. To keep the disclosure alive to pursue additional claims, continuation applications were filed prior to issuance that have led to additional granted patents.

Although Wearatec was able to secure patents in fairly short order, it was having a difficult time raising the capital needed to grow the business. Software start-ups can be appealing to investors because of the perceived low overhead costs when compared to physical product and hardware-centric companies. Wearatec recognized that, because digital watches and technology were on the rise, its prospects of securing funding would only increase as more time passed.

With multiple patents in hand and the desire to keep at least one application pending, such that the disclosure was flexible and could be used to target in-fringers, Wearatec needed a way to slow down the patent process. Significant funds had been expended to secure its first three patents, to pursue foreign pat-ent protection, and to file continuation applications on valuable technology. Continuing to be aggressive with this portfolio in hand would have a detrimen-tal impact on cash flow while adding only marginal value beyond what had al-ready been secured.

In July of 2018, Wearatec had three pending continuations directed to different combinations of elements dating back to its original application filings. Each of these applications, including U.S. Pat. App. 15/218,685, was slowly working its way through the USPTO. The '685 application received an Office action on Jan-uary 11, 2018, that included a rejection of all of the pending claims. Because an Office action response can be expensive, with costs often ranging from $3,000 to $5,000, Wearatec wanted to wait as long as possible before filing its response and kicking the ball back into the USPTO's court. There are response deadlines associated with nearly all USPTO actions and, from the mailing date of an Office action, an applicant is given a maximum of six months in which to respond. Wearatec choose not to file its response to this Office action until July 9, 2018, almost the full six months allowed from the mailing date of the Office action.

In a given strategy there may be times when an applicant wants to go as fast as possible and other times when it makes more sense to slow the process down as much as possible. Although responding slowly to the USPTO can negatively impact patent term, this can be a worthwhile tradeoff if the applicant needs additional time to secure funds, better define the market, or to ascertain which features of the invention have the most value. Slow rolling a continuation application, in combination with one or more issued patents, can be an effective way to establish a monopoly and demonstrate innovativeness, while keeping a flexible application pending for as low a cost as possible.

CHAPTER 29
AVOIDING THE POKER BLINDS—SERIAL CONTINUATION APPLICATION FILINGS

"SOMETIMES IF YOU HAVE A DIFFICULT DECISION TO MAKE, JUST STALL UNTIL THE ANSWER PRESENTS ITSELF."

– TINA FEY

Why this strategy might be for you...

- You want to slow roll the patent process

- You need to buy time to determine which version of the invention is commercially viable

- You have limited financial resources

- You want to be patent pending for as long as possible

- You recognize it might take years to demonstrate commercial value or to secure additional funding

There are many situations in a game of poker where stalling for time can be an effective strategy. In one scenario, you may be the chip leader in a large poker tournament that started with 5,000 players but where only the last 100 will be guaranteed to finish in the money. If you've outlasted over 4,000 players and are close to making it into the top 100, it behooves you to slow down your play, take your time, and wait for more desperate players to drop out.

In another relevant situation, in which you are most certainly not the chip leader and are running on fumes, you may want to stall as much as possible to get the absolute best starting hand before going "all in". If the strategy described in the prior chapter is like slow playing a single hand, the approach described in this chapter is more akin to slow playing a lot of hands to minimize cost while waiting for your best opportunity for success. If you have limited resources, both in poker and the patent game, you need to carefully determine when you are going to be aggressive.

Most Texas Hold'em tables start with nine players, but not every player is required to ante money into the pot on every single hand. Before the hand starts, only two players — the big blind and the small blind — are required to commit a predetermined amount of money to the pot before the two down cards to all players are dealt. Because these blinds rotate predictably around the table, this a fair way to make every pot worth at least some amount. At a table with nine players, seven of those players aren't required to bet anything after seeing the initial two down cards. Each would have to, at minimum, match the big blind to stay in the hand as betting progresses. If you aren't one of the blinds and you don't like your cards, you can throw them away without any cost, and live to fight another day.

When you are short stacked in poker, you're trying to tread water until you're dealt a hand you can win. If you only have a few chips remaining you may only get one shot so you're going to want the cards that'll give you the best chance at success. Why match the big blind on a 7-2 off-suit if you can throw those away for free and see a new set of cards? Players in dire straits often fold hand after hand if they're not the big or small blind, with the hope they'll get a more winnable hand later on.

There are times in the patent game where you may want to go as slow as possible, as introduced in the previous chapter's strategy. If the prior strategy from Chapter 30 is a micro-strategy, the strategy described in this section might be described as a long term or macro-strategy. Delaying the prosecution of a single application may buy you sufficient time, but there are scenarios where you might want to delay for a substantially longer period of time.

Like a poker player low on chips, and perhaps consistently getting bad cards, many entrepreneurs and inventors have limited resources that must be carefully conserved. Speeding up the patent process, submitting responses to USPTO rejections, and taking other actions are the patent equivalent of matching blind after blind. If your resources are limited and you're playing aggressively, then you may be forced to leave the table before you're ready. Slowing down the already-lengthy patent process can keep you in the game for longer.

Once you file your initial patent application — the equivalent of getting your first hand — you might not be satisfied with your cards or encouraged by the play of your competitors. In these circumstances, you might want to muck your hand to wait for something better. If you can fold that first hand at a relatively low cost, perhaps by not even matching the blind, you may be able to hold out long enough to get some great cards. At some point during this stalling process, your situation may change, other players may drop out, you may end up with a great hand, or your position otherwise materially improves. If you can survive and you're still at the table when this happens, then even the small stack in poker can come out on top.

So, you've found yourself short stacked and you need to buy time. You might be in a position where you, potentially, need a lot of time before your circumstances materially change. If you're in this unfortunate position, then this may be the strategy for you.

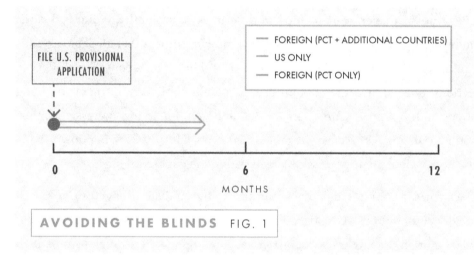

AVOIDING THE BLINDS FIG. 1

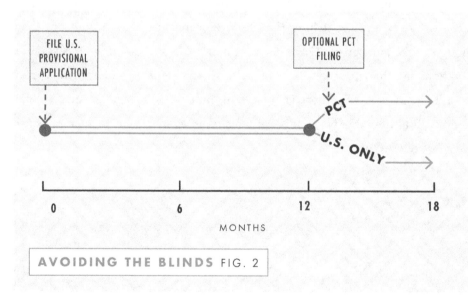

AVOIDING THE BLINDS FIG. 2

As shown in Figure 1, the opening in this strategy is generally a provisional patent application, which has a maximum 12-month pendency.

As shown in Figure 2, near or at the end of the 12-month pendency of the provisional application, you should file a U.S. non-provisional application. This approach should maximize most or all of that 12-month term, as well as any and all available delay periods for which an additional cash expenditure is not required. You're trying to stay at the table for as long as possible without wasting resources.

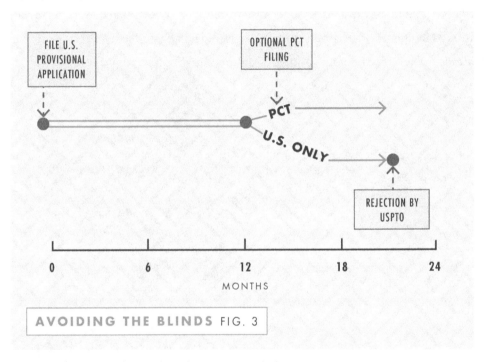

AVOIDING THE BLINDS FIG. 3

At some point during the pendency of your non-provisional application, you'll get your first USPTO Office action, likely containing a rejection of some or all your claims. This should not come as a surprise, although there are times when allowable subject matter is indicated in the first response. If you have limited resources, then this rejection, shown in Figure 3, puts you into the patent game equivalent of poker's short stack. Responding to Office actions can be expensive and, in poker terms, can be the equivalent of anteing up to match the big blind when you have just a few chips remaining. If only there were a way to fold your current hand and stay in the game more economically…

Assuming the first Office action from the USPTO was not favorable, you'll have a maximum of six months to file a complete response to this action at a cost of, perhaps, $3,000 to $5,000 or more in legal fees. The first three months of this six-month period won't generate additional fees, but each successive month will require the payment of an extension fee. Responding to Office actions can be costly depending upon the type and number of rejections you've received. You're facing an Office action that makes you feel like you have a 7-2 off-suit, the blinds are too big to match, and you're thinking about leaving the game.

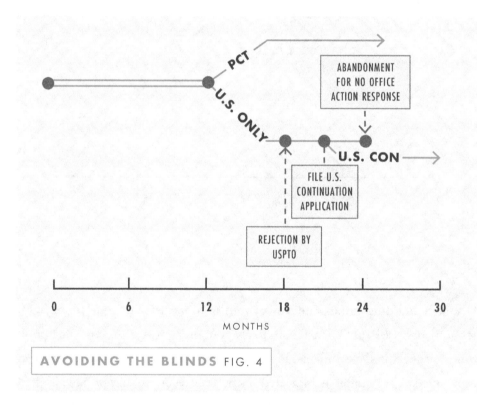

AVOIDING THE BLINDS FIG. 4

If you can't afford to respond to the Office action, current case law is not favorable, or you otherwise need to cheaply buy time, then you can file a first continuation application *just* before your non-provisional application goes abandoned. As shown in Figure 4, this first continuation application effectively "carries the ball forward" by retaining the priority date back to the provisional application, but you'll skip paying for that expensive Office action response.

You'll be responsible for government fees associated with the filing of your continuation application, so you aren't folding the hand for free. However, this may be much less expensive than the cost of a full response to the USPTO Office action. You could change the claims in your first continuation but, if you're really running on fumes, both the continuation application and claims can be *identical* to your prior-filed non-provisional application. This can help keep the associated attorney time and the costs that come with that at an absolute minimum.

The first continuation application will eventually enter the queue at the USPTO for substantive examination. It's difficult to predict how long it will take for the USPTO to issue another Office action; it may be a year or more before you get another response. During that time, your circumstances or financial resources may change materially. That change in luck can allow you to be more aggressive and shift to using some of the tactics described in Chapters 13 and 25.

Once the USPTO reviews your first continuation application, it issues another Office action for which you have six months to respond. If your circumstances improve and you want to more aggressively prosecute the application, that's great. However, you may still be waiting on a much better hand.

As shown in Figure 5, if you aren't ready to get aggressive, and you want to fold another hand, you can file a *second* continuation application before the expiration of the response period for the first continuation application. You can continue this continuation daisy-chain for the *entire* 20-year available patent term if you want to stay in the game, but go as slowly as possible. Just be mindful of how much term you're losing on an eventual patent if you were to get it granted at some point.

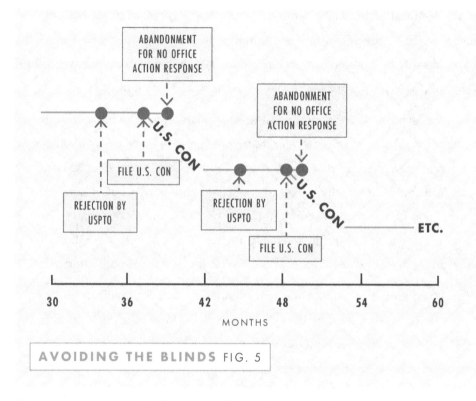

AVOIDING THE BLINDS FIG. 5

If you want to go as slowly as possible and you are also interested in maintaining your ability to file in foreign countries for as long as possible, turn to Chapter 30 on the Playing for the Last Shot strategy.

BENEFITS OF THE AVOIDING THE BLINDS STRATEGY

- Slowing down the patent process can
  help spread costs out over a long period of time

- Delaying the patent process may give
  the applicant time to raise additional funds

- Delaying the patent process can be beneficial for technology fields
  where the law is presently in flux or where patentability is less likely

- If the invention has dubious patentable potential there

may be little incentive to aggressively pursue patent protection

- The all-important priority date of the first application
  filing is maintained throughout the continuation daisy-chain

- Delaying the patent process can allow a commercial
  embodiment or business model to become more clear

DRAWBACKS OF THE AVOIDING THE BLINDS STRATEGY

- Delaying patent prosecution will correspondingly reduce patent term

- Some delaying tactics, continuation application filings, can be relatively
  expensive and can increase the overall cost of the patent process

- Being patent pending for a long period of time
  might suggest the technology is not innovative or patentable

- An infringement suit cannot be brought and damages
  generally do not begin until a patent has been granted

REAL WORLD EXAMPLE— COFFEE TECHNOLOGY BY SEVA TECHNOLOGIES, LLC

Keurig® coffee machines brew coffee contained within a sealed pod, but this coffee is pre-ground and pre-roasted which—for coffee connoisseurs, in particular—removes much of the freshness and quality from the coffee brewing process. Still, the speed and convenience of the Keurig technology has helped Green Mountain Coffee Roasters, the company that acquired Keurig, generate over $1 billion in sales annually.

In 2012, Dr. Deepak Boggavarapu began looking at ways to further revolutionize the coffee market. Dr. Boggavarapu, who has a Ph.D. in optical science from the University of Arizona, hypothesized that it was possible to create a Keurig-like machine that could roast, grind, *and* brew green coffee beans all within the same machine. By sealing unroasted and unground coffee beans within a pod similar to a K-cup, true coffee connoisseurs could make the freshest possible coffee within the comfort of their own homes. He realized that for the final device to be commercially viable, it would likely need to include this functionality in a device not much larger than the coffee machines customers were already accustomed to. Because the brewing step is the easiest of the three steps of roasting, grinding, and brewing, the Seva Coffee team knew that a great deal of time and money would need to be spent on engineering to make the system a reality.

Seva Coffee began filing provisional patent applications in 2012 to establish an early filing date for the technology. U.S. Prov. App. 61/743,946 was filed on September 15, 2012. Although the technology was still under development and early prototypes were not yet completed, Seva Coffee had enough information to disclose workable solutions to an integrated coffee system in its patent applications. Inventors are not required to have built their inventions before filing a patent application so long as the application teaches how to make and use the new innovation. To capture new improvements, Seva Coffee filed a second provisional application, U.S. Prov. App. 61/766,066 on February 18, 2013.

Seva Coffee wanted to maximize its future patent term and, for this reason, it chose to wait until September 16, 2013 to file its non-provisional patent application. A provisional patent application will establish a priority date for the invention, but it advantageously does not start the 20-year patent term clock. But Seva Coffee's first provisional application was filed on September 15, 2012; did this subsequently filed non-provisional application miss the 12-month deadline? The 12-month date from the original provisional filing happened to land on a Sunday in 2013, which means that an application filed on the next business day is still entitled to claim priority to the earlier-filed application. Because Seva Coffee's non-provisional application was filed on September 16th — the Monday following the weekend on which the 12-month deadline fell — the new application still retained co-pendency with the provisional application filing.

Seva Coffee's first non-provisional application, U.S. Pat. App. 14/028,459, advantageously claimed priority to *both* prior-filed provisional applications. By filing its non-provisional application within 12 months from the first provisional and by also claiming priority to its second provisional application in the same non-provisional application, Seva Coffee was effectively able to wrap up the disclosure of both provisional applications into a single non-provisional. Consolidating earlier-filed provisional applications can be a great way to capture the early filing dates of ever-improving technology without having the expense of multiple non-provisional applications.

As the deadline for filing a non-provisional approached, Seva Coffee did not have sufficient funding to support both its intellectual property and engineering efforts. A workable prototype was paramount and Seva Coffee opted to file the '459 non-provisional application with general placeholder claims. This robust application included a large number of different embodiments, features, and methods, but Seva Coffee did not want to incur the costs of preparing an expensive set of claims. Its goal was to keep the robust disclosure pending long enough to secure the necessary funding to complete engineering and, once those immediate needs were met, exploit the disclosure of the pending applications in an array of continuation application filings.

Because the '459 application filing was not expedited — such as with a petition for Track One Accelerated Examination — the USPTO finally mailed a first Office action on March 18, 2015, almost a year and a half after the application was filed. Seva Coffee was still using as much money for engineering as possible, so a fairly thin response was filed to maintain prosecution. This, in turn, resulted in a subsequent Office action on November 12, 2015. Responding to Office actions can become very expensive and the USPTO's responses tend to be mailed more quickly as its review of an application progresses.

Seva Coffee did not want to keep spending the capital to prosecute the place-holder claims of its applications at the expense of engineering improvements. While it could have let its '459 application go irrevocably abandoned, this might have killed the future prospects of the company given the potential value of a patent portfolio in the coffee hardware space. The company could also have filed response after response to USPTO Office actions, but each one required spending between $3,000 and $5,000, were required more frequently, and were based on sub-optimal claims. Seva Coffee needed to adopt a strategy that would keep its patents pending but at the absolute lowest possible cost.

Instead of filing an expensive Office action response, Seva Coffee chose to file a continuation application in the form of U.S. App. No. 15/058,934 on March 2, 2016, claiming priority back to the '459 application. This effectively carried the baton forward before the '459 application became abandoned. The specifications, drawings, and claims of the new continuation were almost identical to the parent filing, meaning Seva Coffee was able to kick the can down the road for a relatively low filing fee at micro-entity rates with very little legal time. The newly filed '934 continuation was eventually reviewed by the USPTO and a new Office action was mailed on July 5, 2016, having a six-month period for response. By filing a continuation application Seva Coffee was, for only the cost of a micro-entity filing fee, able to delay expensive prosecution of its patent application by almost a year.

You may know of Y Combinator, arguably the most well-known and prestigious of the startup accelerators in the United States. I've mentioned them and their model for funding early stage startups in this book. Y Combinator's three-month boot camp for young companies culminates in Demo Day, when the startups present their companies to a carefully selected, invite-only audience.

Seva Coffee was accepted into Y Combinator in 2015, due in large part to the progress it had made with its coffee system prototype. Maintaining its intellectual property created value for the company, but Seva Coffee made the business decision to invest more heavily in its technology while slow-rolling its patent applications until it was able to secure sufficient resources to build a proper patent portfolio. Having a workable product and being an alumnus of the prestigious Y Combinator opened doors for Dr. Boggavarapu, helping the company secure additional funding for the venture. Over the next several years, Seva Coffee was able to file additional patent applications directed to new developments, pursue expensive international patent applications, and more aggressively prosecute its U.S. patent applications.

For Seva Coffee, one of the biggest hurdles to overcome in fundraising was the disbelief many investors expressed that a workable coffee machine could roast, grind, and brew in a normally sized consumer product. Patents directed to such a system would have little value if potential backers of the project didn't believe the device could ever be commercialized. For this reason, Seva Coffee focused its efforts on development, but it also recognized that once the technology was proven there would be innumerable copycats. Using serially filed continuation applications to defer IP-related costs allowed Seva Coffee to focus on honing its technology while preserving critical intellectual property rights.

CHAPTER 30

PLAYING FOR THE LAST SHOT— STAGGERED FOREIGN FILINGS

"NEVER PUT OFF TILL TOMORROW WHAT MAY BE DONE THE DAY AFTER TOMORROW JUST AS WELL."

— MARK TWAIN

Why this strategy might be for you...

- You want to slow roll the patent process primarily for financial reasons

- You are interested in both domestic and international patent protection

- You get a better sense of the value of certain foreign markets as more time passes

- Spacing apart the cost of expensive foreign national stage applications is appealing

- You want to be patent pending

Plenty of folks have a buzzer-beater story where they successfully pulled victory from the jaws of defeat at the last possible moment, whether playing a sport, video game, or "friendly" board game. We've all sweated while watching those tiny, white grains of sand in the plastic hourglass. Although in most games it's better to finish long before the timer runs out, there are circumstances where waiting until the very last second is the best possible strategy. In the 1998 NBA Finals, Michael Jordan of the Chicago Bulls stole the ball from the Utah Jazz with just over 20 seconds on the game clock. Rather than rush his shot, Jordan methodically took the ball down the court, calmly broke poor Bryon Russell's ankles with a crossover dribble, and then hit the game-winning shot with only a few seconds left. There are risks associated with waiting until the very last moment to take action. But playing for the last shot in the patent game can make sense under certain circumstances when it comes to international filings.

Since there's no such thing as a worldwide patent, you may struggle with the filing, prosecution, and annuity costs associated with pursuing a robust international patent portfolio. Even large companies struggle with these fees and every applicant must evaluate these costs in view of the potential benefits of a particular monopoly. Although it's possible to file international applications early in the patent process, it's uncommon to do so. Most applicants delay this process for at least some period of time for a variety of reasons: As more time passes, countries of value may become clearer, allowed cases in a home jurisdiction may make the PPH available, or there's a strong interest in delaying the heavy costs associated with a robust foreign patent portfolio.

One of the most powerful pieces in the patent game is the PCT application, an incredibly versatile tool. A PCT is a foreign placeholder application that effectively buys you at least 30 months from your earliest priority date to finally file foreign applications. There are approximately 150 PCT-participating countries and most—but not all—of these require a national stage application to be filed by the 30-month deadline. However, it's possible in some cases to go beyond even this 30-month period. If you really want to play for the last shot and you want to file your foreign applications at the last possible moment, it's important to understand how this timing works.

HOW THE PLAYING FOR THE
LAST SHOT STRATEGY WORKS

Playing for the last shot can start by controlling the tempo of the patent game. You can begin with the filing of a U.S. provisional application as shown in Figure 1, which has a maximum 12-month pendency.

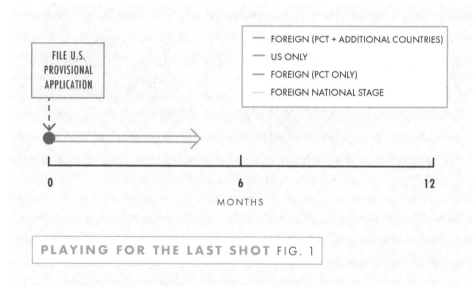

PLAYING FOR THE LAST SHOT FIG. 1

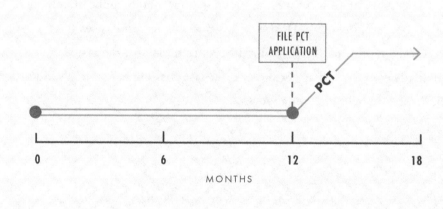

PLAYING FOR THE LAST SHOT FIG. 2

A provisional application is a useful delaying tactic because it preserves the priority date for the patent application, but does not negatively impact patent term.

Next, as shown in Figure 2, a PCT application should be filed near the end of the 12-month provisional term in order to stall as much as possible. The provisional application is important because the filing date of this application is treated as the priority date for subsequent foreign applications and patents.

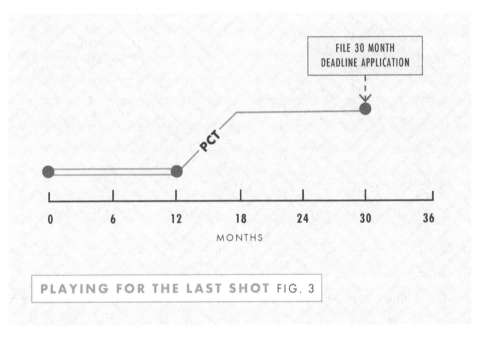

FILE 30 MONTH
DEADLINE APPLICATION

PCT

0   6   12   18   24   30   36

MONTHS

PLAYING FOR THE LAST SHOT FIG. 3

As shown in Figure 3, any countries that are party to the Patent Cooperation Treaty require a national stage application to be filed by this 30-month deadline. But importantly, not *all* jurisdictions require the national stage filings to be complete by this deadline.

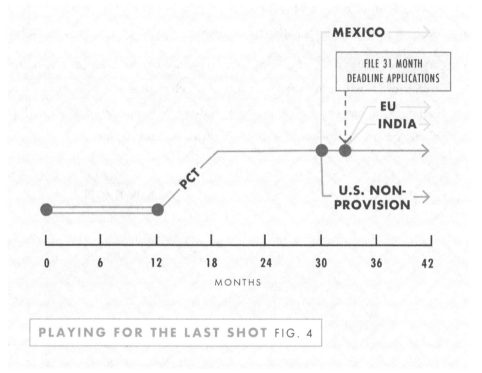

PLAYING FOR THE LAST SHOT FIG. 4

Quite a few regions — such as Europe (via the European Patent Office) and India, shown in Figure 4 — allow the applicant to file national stage applications 31 months from the earliest priority date. One additional month may not make a significant difference in terms of patent protection, but the ability to space apart these filings for budget reasons can have significant value to the business. Want more buzzer beating? Another commonly pursued country, China, has a national stage application deadline of 32-months, as seen in Figure 5.

Still not done? Canada, which may be of particular interest to United States applicants, has the longest available national stage application deadline at 42 months from the earliest priority date.

Once filed, these national stage patent applications will, hopefully, result in issued patents.

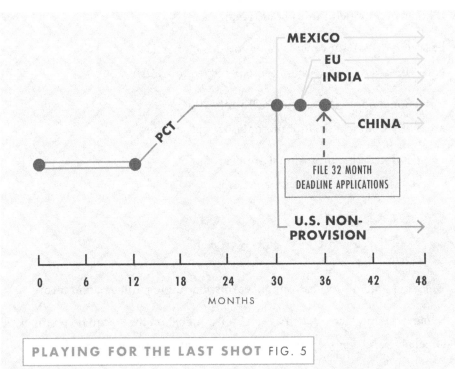

MEXICO →
EU →
INDIA →
CHINA →

PCT

FILE 32 MONTH
DEADLINE APPLICATIONS

U.S. NON-
PROVISION →

```
|    |    |    |    |    |    |    |    |    |
0    6    12   18   24   30   36   42   48
```

MONTHS

PLAYING FOR THE LAST SHOT FIG. 5

BENEFITS OF THE PLAYING
FOR THE LAST SHOT STRATEGY

- Slowing down the patent process can
  help spread costs out over a long period of time

- Delaying the patent process may give
  the applicant time to raise additional funds

- Delaying the patent process can help clarify
  which foreign jurisdictions have value

- Delaying the patent process can be beneficial for technology fields
  where the law is presently in flux or where patentability is less likely

- The all-important priority date of the first application

filing is maintained throughout the process

- Delaying the patent process can allow a commercial embodiment or business model to become more clear

- Provisional applications and PCT applications are effective domestic and international placeholders

- The pendency of a provisional application will not negatively impact patent term

DRAWBACKS OF THE PLAYING FOR THE LAST SHOT STRATEGY

- Delaying patent prosecution will correspondingly reduce patent term

- Some delaying tactics, such as the PCT application filing, can be relatively expensive and can increase the overall cost of the patent process

- Being patent pending for a long period of time might suggest the technology is not innovative or patentable

- An infringement suit cannot be brought and damages often do not begin until a patent has been granted

REAL WORLD EXAMPLE—MEDICATION DELIVERY SYRINGE BY TRUE CONCEPTS, LLC

Certain technologies, such as medical devices, can take a long time to bring to market because of regulatory requirements, clinical trials, and fundraising efforts. These delays in commercialization, combined with a plethora of non-intellectual property requirements, can leave med-tech companies looking for every opportunity to delay expensive patent fees. Foreign patent filings and prosecution can be a big ticket item when government fees, translation fees, and prosecution costs are factored into the equation. Although there are delaying tools, such as the use of a Patent Cooperation Treaty (PCT) application, some applicants may not be able to afford to pursue all of the foreign countries of interest by the 30-month deadline generally permitted by that application type. Sometimes the ability to space these fees out by even a month or two can make a big difference in cash flow and, ultimately, the company's success.

True Concepts, LLC, founded by Mick Hopkins in cooperation with Cincinnati Children's Hospital Medical Center, invented an impressive portfolio of syringe technology for both fluid collection and fluid delivery. True Concepts initially filed a number of robust U.S. non-provisional and PCT applications of more than 100 pages, covering a large number of embodiments related to the newly-developed syringe technology. Because medical devices often have strong international markets, True Concepts opted to file a Patent Cooperation Treaty prior to the 12-month expiration deadline of its provisional application filings. While True Concepts could have elected to file direct national stage applications in various foreign countries, it was far more attractive to this startup to buy 18 additional months to decide which of the approximately 150 PCT-participating countries was worth pursuing.

As the 30-month initial PCT deadline approached, True Concepts developed a spreadsheet of countries where foreign patents would add significant value to the company. After evaluating market size, ease of enforcement, and budget, True Concepts decided on Israel, Canada, Mexico, Japan, Europe and India. Because True Concepts had two PCT applications for which the 30-month deadline was the exact same day, it would have cost $42,640 to file twelve total foreign national stage applications for these two families by the initial 30-month PCT deadline. For a startup company managing cash flow and payroll, this is a sizable cash outlay for a single month, particularly when the 30-month deadline happen to fall in December before the end of 2018. If True Concepts could defer at least some of these fees until the next calendar year it would be highly advantageous for a number of cash management reasons.

Although a number of countries have PCT application deadlines beyond the initial 30-month window, Israel, Mexico, and Japan do not. For this reason, True Concepts was required to file national stage applications in these countries within the initial window if it wanted to maintain priority back to its earlier filed patent applications. Missing this deadline in these jurisdictions would almost certainly leave True Concepts without the ability to secure protection in these countries.

However, True Concepts was fortunate that several of the other countries on its list could be filed beyond the PCT application 30-month window. In particular, India and Europe both permit applicants to file national stage applications up to *31 months* from the initial priority date. While one month may not seem like a lot of time, spacing apart costly filings can give your company more time to budget and plan for these expenditures. Canada, the final country on the list, has the most favorable grace period of any country at *42 months* from the initial priority date. True Concepts elected to wait to file its national stage application in Canada to maximize the period of delay.

CHAPTER 31

THE "KING'S PAWN GAME" OR TRADITIONAL STRATEGY

"TRADITION BECOMES OUR SECURITY, AND WHEN THE MIND IS SECURE IT IS IN DECAY"

– JIDDU KRISHNAMURTI

Why this strategy might be for you...

- You have a discrete inventive concept that you want to protect

- You are concerned that adding unnecessary disclosure to your application could be used as prior art against your later-filed patent applications

- You file a lot of patent applications and you want each to be highly focused

- You have a strong sense as to what features or versions of the invention will have commercial value

- You don't anticipate needing a robust disclosure to support claim amendments to overcome prior art

- You have sufficient financial resources to file numerous patent applications directed to discrete and inventive concepts both domestically and abroad

Although combinations of chess moves are nearly endless in permutation, there are a few time-tested and popular openings favored by beginners and experts alike. But just because something is common or traditional does not mean that it's the best. The King's Pawn Game is arguably the most common opening in chess. Advancing the king's pawn two squares is useful because it occupies a center square, attacks the opposing center square at d5, and allows for the development of the white king's bishop and queen. Chess legend Bobby Fischer stated the King's Pawn Game is "best by test" and proclaimed that "With 1.e4! I win."

As is the case with the King's Pawn Game opening in chess, this next approach in the patent game is sometimes overused. There are certainly circumstances where this strategy is an excellent fit, but some practitioners will default to this opening, using it as a one-size-fits-all approach that might not be right for your invention or business. This strategy might be an excellent fit for some businesses, but it's certainly not the best fit for *all* businesses.

In chess, the King's Pawn Game opening has a *lower* win ratio than the next three most common opening moves of 1.d4 (55.95%), 1.Nf3 (55.8%), 1.c4 (56.3%), and 1.g3 (55.8%), despite being used the most frequently. Just because something is used the most *doesn't* mean it's the best option. If you want to win—and of course you do—it might be worth considering your other options before falling back on this old stand-by of a strategy.

This somewhat traditional approach focuses on the protection of a discrete inventive concept and any additional variations, if they exist, are pursued in separate and discrete patent applications. This strategy is in many ways the opposite of the Big Boggle strategy extra space—discussed in Chapter 17—which aims to include as *much* disclosure as possible in a single patent application. The King's Pawn Game strategy, by contrast, is much more narrowly focused. Businesses that can benefit from filing applications with a tightly defined scope are often those that are concerned with creating unnecessary prior art against their *own* future patent applications that can result by including half-baked ideas, the results of loose brainstorming sessions, or sub-optimal variations. By focusing on a defined inventive concept, companies can achieve laser-like precision in what they protect without creating unnecessary and potentially damaging additional disclosure. Most inventors and companies want to include as much information as possible in a patent application to take advantage of available permutations, but a company that files hundreds or thousands of patent applications a year instead may strive to limit the inclusion of extraneous information.

It should be noted that the King's Pawn Game strategy does not refer to the growing trend in which large companies file low-cost, commoditized, single-embodiment patent applications with little or no thought as to how these patents drive value for their business. Such an approach, which can't appropriately be considered a strategy, should be avoided.

HOW THE KINGS PAWN GAME STRATEGY WORKS

As shown in Figure 1, this patent strategy, like many in this book, often begins with a provisional patent application filing as illustrated.

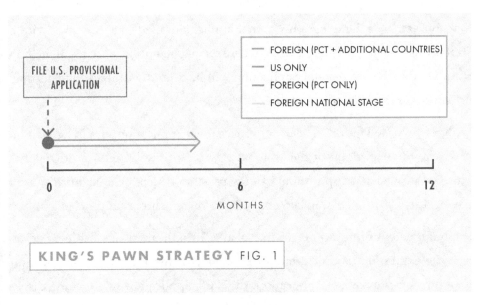

KING'S PAWN STRATEGY FIG. 1

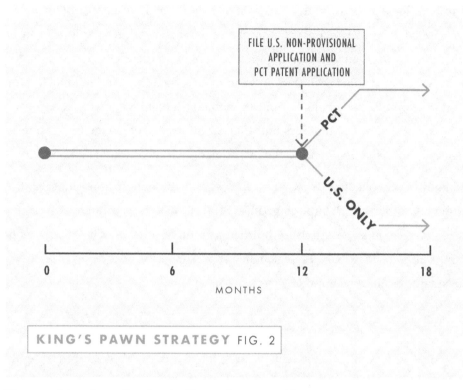

PCT

U.S. ONLY

0   6   12   18

MONTHS

KING'S PAWN STRATEGY FIG. 2

The provisional application is directed to a *specific* inventive concept (we'll call that concept "A"). Unlike a provisional application filed in accordance with a strategy like the Big Boggle strategy, where the patent application might include features A-Z, the provisional application will be carefully drafted to focus only on the single inventive concept of A.

With reference to Figure 2, a U.S. non-provisional application should be filed on or before the expiration of the 12-month period of the preceding provisional. This non-provisional application, like the pawn to which it claims priority, will have a disclosure and claims directed only to the inventive concept A.

If foreign patent protection is desirable, a PCT application can also be filed before the expiration of the 12-month pendency of the provisional application. Like the non-provisional application, this PCT application will include disclosure and claims directed only to the single inventive concept. Although not illustrated, one version of this strategy involves filing direct foreign national stage applications within the 12-month pendency of the provisional application in place of, or in addition to, the PCT application.

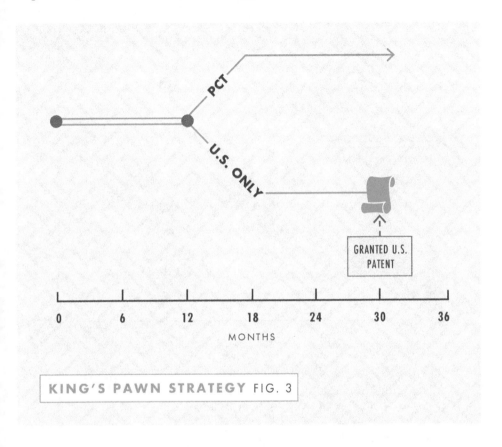

KING'S PAWN STRATEGY FIG. 3

As shown in Figure 3, the non-provisional application can mature into an issued U.S. patent that, you guessed it, is also directed only to the single inventive concept. Spinoff applications like continuation or divisional applications generally aren't used in this strategy because the limited scope of the application means that it can often be protected with a single issued patent. This focused issued patent will expire 20 years from the filing date of the non-provisional application.

With respect to the PCT application, the next significant date is the deadline for filing specific national stage patent applications in individual countries. The

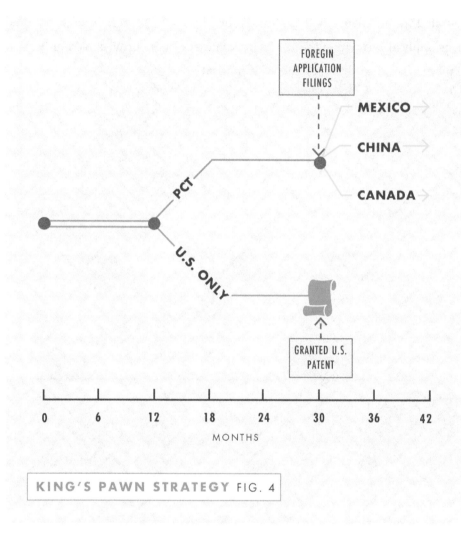

FOREGIN
APPLICATION
FILINGS

MEXICO →

CHINA →

CANADA →

PCT

U.S. ONLY

GRANTED U.S.
PATENT

0   6   12   18   24   30   36   42

MONTHS

KING'S PAWN STRATEGY FIG. 4

PCT application functions as an international placeholder to delay the filing deadline for these national stage filings until at least 30 months from the applicant's earliest priority date.

At or before this 30-month deadline, foreign national stage applications can be pursued in any or all of the approximately 150 countries that participate in the PCT. Each of these applications, like the rest of the patent applications associated with this strategy, will be laser focused on just the single inventive concept.

Like the U.S. non-provisional, these foreign national stage applications can mature into issued foreign patents as shown in Figures 4 and 5.

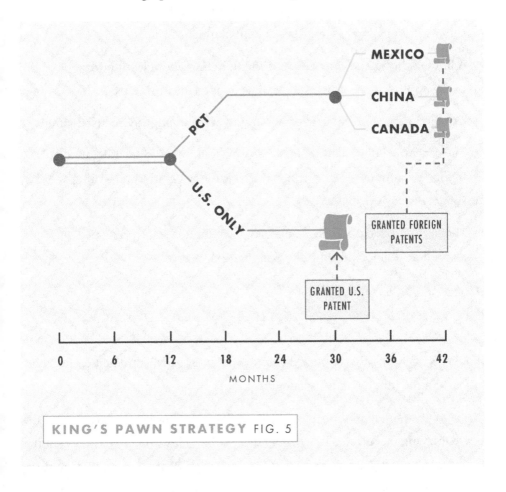

KING'S PAWN STRATEGY FIG. 5

BENEFITS OF THE KING'S PAWN STRATEGY

- Focused application filings can minimize the creation of prior art that could be used against the applicant's own future patent applications

- Focused patent applications can be less expensive to prepare and file because of this limited scope

- A good strategy for large companies that file a lot of patent applications

DRAWBACKS OF THE KING'S PAWN STRATEGY

- Disclosing and claiming a single inventive concept can result in narrow patent claims with marginal value

- A limited disclosure can make it difficult to find enough support in the application to amend the claims to overcome prior art

- Competitors may be able to easily design around a tightly-focused patent

- The concern about creating unnecessary prior art could be mitigated by filing continuation or divisional applications based upon a more robust disclosure

- The narrowly focused disclosure may have limited value in its use as prior art to block third party patent applications.

REAL WORLD EXAMPLE—
THE ORIGINAL MONOPOLY PATENT

It only seems fitting that we use the issued patent for the board game Monopoly as an example for one of our strategies.

Monopoly was patented on December 31, 1935 by Charles B. Darrow and the board, playing pieces, chance cards, and graphics today look remarkably similar to the as-patented game from nearly 100 years ago. Board games, like anything else, can be patentable if they are useful, novel, and non-obvious. I mentioned earlier in this book that it's not uncommon for patent applications to exceed 100 pages in the modern era. In contrast, U.S. Patent 2,026,082 directed to the Monopoly concept has a total of 14 pages, 7 of which are drawings. This style of highly-focused patent application used to be very common; you can sometimes find older patents directed to seminal technology that are only 2 or 3 pages in length. Thomas Edison's lightbulb patent, U.S. 223,898, is only five pages in length.

Although the size of a patent application does not necessarily correlate with the scope of the application, the two are often related. Typically, more drawings and pages of disclosure in an application means there is more subject matter the applicant can pick and choose from when crafting valuable claims, patenting variations, covering improvements, and targeting infringers. However, this older and traditional style of patent application drafting usually focused on a single embodiment with just a cursory mention that other versions of the invention are contemplated.

What are the potential drawbacks to including only a single embodiment in a patent application? If you were a Monopoly competitor, then it might be much easier for you to design around the issued claims of the '082 patent by making small changes (such as the board, pieces, or use of money) while staying true to the basic tenets of the game. A highly focused, single-embodiment patent application might have value, but what about different versions, features, improvements, and the like? It's more than a little ironic that the patent for Monopoly resulted in a much more limited real-life patent monopoly than could likely have been secured.

This type of limited-scope patent application is exactly in-line with the King's Pawn Game strategy. Although more contemporary applications might include additional disclosure in the application, the concept is still the same. It can be very tempting for you and your patent attorney to write up a description only disclosing the current, most promising version of your invention. As I've mentioned, doing so can have very serious negative consequences.

There are occasions where this limited-scope filing strategy still makes sense, but I've found that these circumstances have started to become more the exception than the rule. That said, you should always be careful not to include half-baked or non-enabled versions of your invention in your application because they can come back to haunt you. However, the relatively low risk of creating prior art that will damage future filings is often outweighed by the potential benefits of having more disclosure available for protection in spin-off applications, like continuation and divisional applications. The most frequent intentional users of the King's Pawn Game strategy are larger companies that generate a lot of patents in a niche technology field. If you or your company are trying to individually protect each marginally iterative improvement relating to an overall technology field, then the creation of any unnecessary prior art could be damaging. But, if you don't have these concerns and want the greatest amount of flexibility, you should be reluctant to heed suggestions to unduly limit the scope of the disclosure in your patent application.

CHAPTER 32

PROTECTING YOUR AVATAR— DESIGN PATENTS VS. UTILITY PATENTS

"GOOD DESIGN IS GOOD BUSINESS."

– THOMAS WATSON JR.

Why this strategy might be for you...

- You have an a physical product or user interface design that is distinctive and has business value

- You think there are perceptive or deterrent benefits to using the "patented" designation

- You want to secure a patent, but your technology field has patent eligibility issues

- You want to secure a patent, but your utility application is not patentable because of prior art

- Having both design and utility patents can make your portfolio appear more robust

A huge number of video games and mobile app games require players to create an avatar. This avatar, which is often a self-selected visual representation of the person playing, then interacts with the game and sometimes other avatars. Entire worlds, like Second Life, have been created around avatars and the virtual interactions between the participants. Sometimes an avatar closely matches the physical or personality characteristics of its creator; though in many cases, there is no resemblance at all. A game avatar is often selected to convey a certain message and to create a specific desirable perception of the player. Businesses, similarly, create brands with outward-facing personae intended to give customers an impression as to what the business values, what it offers, and why you should pay for its goods or services. A good product is important, but how that product is packaged or presented can be just as critical to its success. Most of the strategies in this book are focused on functional inventions and the utility patent applications that can be used to protect them. Design patents, however, when used alone or in combination with utility patents, can add meaningful value to a business or product.

Design patents, introduced and described earlier in Chapter 10 of this book, have experienced a significant uptick in filings over the past few years. Much of this explosion is attributed to their use by technology companies like Google, Microsoft, and Uber to protect valuable user interface designs. But consumer product companies, such as Coca Cola, have long seen the value in developing and protecting distinctive product and packaging designs.

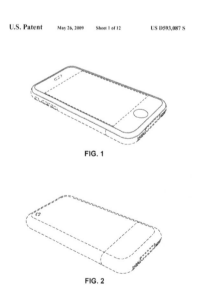

FIG. 1

FIG. 2

Apple has thousands of utility patents, but it also has a large number of design patents protecting its physical product designs and the digital user interfaces displayed on those products. In two separate lawsuits, Apple accused Samsung of infringing on three utility patents (United States Patent Nos. 7,469,381, 7,844,915, and 7,864,163) and four design patents (United States Patent Nos. D504,889, D593,087, D618,677, and D604,305). One of these design patents, D593,087, was found to be infringed upon by Samsung and contributed to the initial verdict of $1.049 billion in damages in Apple's favor. Over $1 billion in damages for infringement of a design patent!

A distinctive design — like the shape of an iPhone and the way the icons are presented on the home screen interface — might be worth protecting with one or more design patents. Having a portfolio of both utility and design patents can create a powerful picket fence that prevents competitors from copying the core technology as well as the unique look and feel of the products being offered.

Design patents can also be used effectively for perception-related reasons. Design patent applications are often relatively inexpensive to file and entitle the applicant to call the design patent pending, which can create a positive perception and may have some deterrent value as well. Design patents are often reviewed more quickly and issued more readily than their utility patent cousins. Pursuing design patents for a distinctive aesthetic innovation can create value, but even if you don't have a critically important design there can still be reasons to consider this type of protection. Having a "patented design", especially in certain technology fields, can create a positive perception about the innovative nature of a business.

PROTECTING YOUR AVATAR

There is no equivalent of a provisional application in design patent practice, so the first design patent application will need to have formal drawings, a claim, and meet the formal filing requirements set by the USPTO. Because design patents are directed to ornamental features only, these applications tend to include a lot of figures and very little written disclosure. The design patent will protect what the product or user interface looks like, not what it does or how it is used.

Once a design patent application has been filed it will typically be reviewed in less than a year and, just like a utility application, the USPTO will send you a first Office action based upon this substantive review. The examiner will conduct a search and, if your ornamental design is too close to another design, you will receive a rejection. A back-and-forth between the applicant and the USPTO can then ensue that, hopefully, will result in an issued design patent. Once issued, a design patent lasts for 15 years from its issue date, in contrast to the 20-year patent term from the filing date of a utility patent application.

BENEFITS OF PROTECTING YOUR AVATAR

- Design patents can provide protection and add business value for the distinctive look of products and user interfaces

- Design patents are generally examined more quickly than utility applications by the USPTO and sometimes are granted much faster than utility patents with less back-and-forth with the USPTO

- Design patents can be easier and less expensive to prepare because the bulk of the application is made up of drawings

- A design patent application allows an applicant to use the "patent pending" designation and an issued design patent allows the applicant to call the design "patented"

- Design patents can often be added to utility patents to make a patent portfolio more robust

- User interface design patents may be particularly inexpensive and relatively easy to prosecute to an issued patent

- Many products have the potential to be protected with both design patents and utility patents

DRAWBACKS OF PROTECTING YOUR AVATAR

- If a product or user interface design changes frequently,

then design patents may have little substantive value

- Design patents only provide protection for ornamental features, not functional aspects

- Design patents may be easier to work around by those interested in copying the underlying functionality

- If pursued for perception reasons, savvy investors, customers, partners, and competitors may not be impressed or threatened by a design patent

REAL WORLD EXAMPLE— EXERCISE EQUIPMENT BY INCLUDEHEALTH, INC.

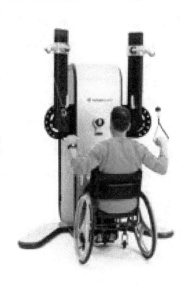

Ryan Eder, a graduate of the prestigious College of Design, Architecture, Art and Planning (DAAP) at the University of Cincinnati, perfectly married his design background and business acumen to solve a real problem for differently abled people. In his early 20s, Ryan watched as a man in a wheelchair tried, unsuccessfully, to use conventional equipment at a local gym. Nearly a decade ago the seed was planted that would eventually lead him to found IncludeHealth and to develop the Access Strength workout machine.

Ryan's vision was to create a workout machine and platform that could be used in regular gyms by anyone regardless of age or ability. The Access Strength machine can be operated, in combination with a mobile app, to set the position, weight, and other features of the device remotely such that it can be easily and readily accessed. No more having to awkwardly lift weights onto a bar, bending over to adjust pins, or needing assistance to adjust handles that are out of reach. Need to transition from one type of workout to another? Just open the user interface on the mobile app, push a few buttons, and the machine will transition to the desired position automatically. As an added benefit, the mobile app and Access Strength system can keep track of your workout, including exercise type, weight, and reps, and can send this data in real time to your trainer, physician, or physical therapist.

The Access Strength workout machine has novel functionality, and Include-Health understandably has a large number of utility patents, but the user interface and the machine itself are also aesthetically very appealing. So much so that Eder has won the People's Choice Award and Best of Show Award at the International Design and Excellence Awards for his designs. These distinctive designs, in combination with novel functionality, have allowed IncludeHealth to develop a robust portfolio of both design and utility patents.

As you will recall, there are many circumstances in which the same physical piece of technology can be protected by both utility and design patents. The function of the device can be protected with utility patents, but if that device also has a distinctive look then the non-functional appearance of the device can be protectable with a design patent as well.

On May 25, 2010, IncludeHealth was able to secure a utility patent directed to some of the functional aspects of the Access Strength system.

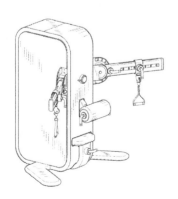

Issued patents on the underlying technology were then paired nicely with design patents covering the distinctive look of the commercial product. On July 1, 2014, IncludeHealth secured a design patent such that both the look and the functionality of its Access Strength product are protected.

Hardware plays a major role in the Access Strength device, but Eder also recognized that the software needed to make the system work was novel. To protect this, IncludeHealth filed a number of software-related patent applications and, on June 6, 2017, one of these issued as U.S. Patent 9,669,261.

In an effort to protect the Access Strength system as much as possible, and because of Eder's background in design, IncludeHealth also developed a novel interface for the mobile application and the machine itself. These user interface designs, being novel in their own right, were protectable with design patents such as US D760,285 issued on June 28, 2016.

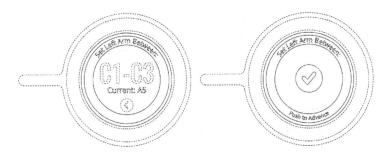

With a portfolio of more than 20 issued patents, IncludeHealth has raised more than $7 million in angel and venture funding. IncludeHealth's approach to intellectual property, and Eder's ability to recognize the value in both functional and non-functional elements of its Access Strength machine, has created enormous value for the company.

CHAPTER 33

GUESS WHO?®—USING TRADE SECRETS IN LIEU OF PATENTS

"IF YOU CHOOSE NOT TO DECIDE, YOU STILL HAVE MADE A CHOICE."

– RUSH, "FREEWILL"

Why this strategy might be for you...

- You see no value in any of the other patent-related strategies

- Your technology field has patent eligibility issues

- You feel confident that you can keep the
  trade secret confidential for 20 years or longer

The decision to *not* pursue patents is still a patent-related strategy. Pursuing a utility or design patent may not be right for you or your business, but before choosing a trade secret-only path, it's important to carefully evaluate the pros and cons of doing so. Too often, inventors or companies assume incorrectly that a patent strategy has to be expensive, can't add value to the business, or otherwise would be a waste of resources. These decisions are sometimes made based upon misinformation, poor coaching, or a lack of knowledge about the available options. Common misconceptions are that it's impossible to maintain a trade secret while pursuing patent protection (which can be done and is discussed in Chapter 21), trade secrets cost nothing or are less expensive than pursuing a patent strategy (there are many budget-oriented strategies such as those discussed in Chapter 4), or trade secrets can be easily maintained indefinitely. It's true that trade secrets do not have a formal registration process and can theoretically last forever, but there are risks associated with inadvertent disclosure, reverse engineering, transitory employees, and other events that can result in a loss of confidentiality.

If you are carefully weighing your options, and you are considering a trade secret-only approach, you should prepare yourself to play the intellectual property equivalent of the family game Guess Who?.

In this classic board game, each competitor sits opposite from the other and is given a secret picture of a character matching one of 24 different characters in the game. The winner is the first player to guess the secret character held by the other player after narrowing down the choices by asking questions and making guesses. To hone in on the correct answer, players ask questions that provide as much information as possible to eliminate incorrect options. Sometimes it takes a long time to reach the answer and, other times, players are able to guess the secret character rather quickly.

A trade secret is somewhat like the Guess Who? secret character you're hiding.

In the IP equivalent of this game, however, there are often more than 24 options from which to guess and your competitors, of course, aren't likely to openly ask you probing questions to try and determine what trade secrets you may be holding. Competitors may, however, gather intelligence in other ways such as by purchasing and disassembling your product, speaking with your salespeople and other employees, and reviewing all company disclosures, patent applications, and other publicly available information. To mitigate this risk, you'll probably be telling your competitors as little about your own trade secrets as you can. Although you won't generally see the kinds of direct questions you may see in a game of Guess Who?, your competitors are still going to be asking these questions and will be searching for ways to discover your secrets.

A trade secret can have an infinite duration, but only so long as it remains a secret. Despite best efforts, many companies still experience inadvertent disclosures of these key secrets because a salesperson is trying to close a deal, a new employee doesn't understand the importance of confidentiality, or a disgruntled employee takes a valuable trade secret to a competitor.

If you have physical products such as mechanical or electrical innovations, playing the intellectual property version of Guess Who? can be particularly challenging. Once your product is released, your competitors will buy it, dismantle it, test it, and look for ways to reverse engineer the technology. You may want to think twice about playing the trade secret game if you're in these fields, because it may not take your competitors long to get to the right answer. However, if your invention is more difficult to reverse engineer, is hard to ascertain because there are numerous available options, or is a process that only happens behind-the-scenes, then your chances of winning this game will be greatly improved.

So, how do you win our version of Guess Who? The math is relatively straightforward. A patent entitles you to a monopoly of 20 years, meaning a trade secret has more value than a patent if you can keep that secret for *longer* than 20 years.

As Dirty Harry said, "...you've gotta ask yourself one question: 'Do I feel lucky?' Well, do ya, punk?" Can you outlast your competitors trying to reverse engineer your technology, employees intentionally or inadvertently disclosing your technology, or even someone outright guessing your innovation? If so, then you may be a good candidate for this Guess Who? strategy, but play the game carefully and know it's possible you can lose everything at a moment's notice.

HOW THE GUESS WHO? STRATEGY WORKS

A trade secret, in layman's terms, can be anything that has business value, is not commonly known, and is treated as confidential. Once a technology is determined to be a candidate for a trade secret, you should move quickly to define the secret and to maintain its proprietary nature. You can and should take a number of precautions to ensure your trade secrets remain confidential. You need to make the game of Guess Who? as difficult as possible for your competitors.

Since there isn't a formal registration process, trade secrets can sometimes suffer because efforts are not made to clearly define them. If you're considering this strategy, you should extensively document the innovation and how you have protected it. The better defined the secret is that you're holding, and the better that you've protected it and documented those protections, the better position you'll be in to defend it. If you claim that something of value has been stolen, but you can't articulate clearly what was taken, or what steps you were taking to protect it, then it will be hard for you to win your case.

As for documenting the trade secret itself, you should make a concerted effort to clearly define the process, composition, technology, and other elements considered proprietary. A well-defined trade secret will pay dividends when considering licenses, raising capital, selling your business, or pursuing anyone who has misappropriated this information. If the metes and bounds of the proprietary information are not precise, courts may find you didn't have a protectable trade secret to begin with.

Your business might consider implementing a trade secret policy. This policy can be basic or comprehensive and can address critical considerations such as the definition of the trade secret, who has access to the trade secret, and protections and safeguards. Many trade secrets are inadvertently disclosed, so an internal policy can help mitigate the risks of employees revealing the proprietary technology accidentally. If you're playing Guess Who?, then everyone with knowledge of the trade secret needs to know that you're collectively playing this game.

Trade secrets can have a theoretically infinite life. If you've identified a good trade secret candidate with a long shelf life that's difficult to reverse engineer, then you could enjoy the benefits of holding that trade secret for a very long time with the proper safeguards in place. Unlike Guess Who?, our version of the game never has to end.

BENEFITS OF THE GUESS WHO? STRATEGY

- Trade secrets can theoretically last forever

- Trade secrets do not have a formal registration process and can be less expensive than pursuing patent protection

- Certain technology such as backend software, chemical formulations, and manufacturing methods may be particularly good trade secret candidates

- Trade secrets can be licensed and sold

- Use of proprietary designation may be just as valuable as being patented or patent pending

- Can be used to protect some technology, such as certain software business methods, which may not be patent eligible

DRAWBACKS OF THE GUESS WHO? STRATEGY

- Trade secrets can be lost if stolen, inadvertently disclosed, or reverse engineered

- Some technology may be too easily reverse engineered to be a good trade secret candidate

- The costs to maintain the confidentiality of a trade secret can be higher than you might expect

- Trade secrets may be harder to license and sell

- Trade secrets may not increase the valuation of a business as much as a patent portfolio

REAL WORLD EXAMPLE—SAAS COMPANIES

As I discussed in Chapter 8, it had long been uncommon for the claims in a patent application to be rejected as patent ineligible by the USPTO under 35 U.S.C 101. All of this changed some years ago when patent applications directed to software business methods and medical diagnostics started coming under fire. The timing couldn't have been worse for many technology companies, particularly Software-as-a-Service (SaaS) companies such as Salesforce, Slack, and Dropbox. Despite having novel and non-obvious innovations, many of these companies found it difficult or impossible to secure broad patents protecting the software and methods on which the businesses were built. If a patent could be secured it was often narrow and, because of this, the associated monopoly was in many cases not meaningful enough to justify the cost and expense of the patent process.

Many SaaS businesses rely upon complicated and ever-changing algorithms to interpret data and provide customers with valuable insights. These algorithms might analyze employee satisfaction to determine the risk of key employees leaving, help a salesperson quickly develop a new customer survey, or try to predict the stock market based upon a proprietary database of information. For most of these businesses, the underlying formulas driving the deliverables are impossible to discern from the outputs. This, combined with the oft-changing nature of the calculations, makes such algorithms a great candidate for trade secret protection. It's also relatively easy to keep this information confidential because many technology companies carefully restrict access to these formulas to a small and trusted group of computer programmers.

The relative ease with which many algorithms can be kept confidential — combined with a general perception by some that patents are of little value for software companies — has led many Silicon Valley businesses to choose a trade secret-only approach. If current case law suggests that a company's innovations are likely not patent eligible, and prospective investors see no value in patent applications, then choosing not to pursue patent protection can make sound business sense.

It's worth noting, however, that many leading software companies have surprisingly large patent portfolios, including those associated with Silicon Valley. Facebook, for example, has over 3,000 issued U.S. patents, Twitter has over 1,000, Salesforce over 1,200, and Microsoft has a massive 40,000 issued patents in the United States alone. Patent eligibility for software-related inventions is highly nuanced and company leadership should be careful not to throw out the baby with the proverbial bath water. The perception of value in having patents seems to fluctuate. So, before deciding to abandon the patent process altogether, it's worth consulting with experts in your field to make sure that a trade secret-only approach is the best option.